Fundamentals of Employee Benefit Programs

FOURTH EDITION

EBRI

EMPLOYEE BENEFIT RESEARCH INSTITUTE

© 1990 Employee Benefit Research Institute
Education and Research Fund
2121 K Street, NW, Suite 600
Washington, DC 20037-1896
(202) 659-0670

Library of Congress Cataloging-in-Publication Data

Fundamentals of employee benefit programs.—4th ed.
    p. cm.
Includes bibliographical references.
ISBN 0-86643-070-9.—ISBN 0-86643-069-5 (pbk.)
   1. Employee fringe benefits—United States.
I. Employee Benefit Research Institute (Washington, D.C.)
HD4928.N62U634   1990   90-31748
331.25'5'0973—dc20   CIP

Printed in the United States of America

Table of Contents

PART TWO
PUBLIC-SECTOR BENEFIT PROGRAMS

Foreword

Keeping pace with rapid and continuous change is a challenge each of us faces every day. Nowhere is this challenge more apparent than in the rapidly changing field of employee benefits. Every budget bill passed by Congress since the Tax Reform Act of 1986—including the Omnibus Budget Reconciliation Act of 1987, the Technical and Miscellaneous Revenue Act of 1988, and the Omnibus Budget Reconciliation Act of 1989—have included provisions affecting private employer-sponsored benefit programs. In addition, the federal regulatory agencies issue complicated regulations that spell out compliance requirements, but often not until months—or, in some instances, years—after the compliance deadline.

Dramatic as these changes are, they are by no means the only sources of change in the employee benefits field. The employers that sponsor these programs are continually reevaluating their benefit packages in an effort to keep them cost effective and responsive to employer and employee needs. As people live longer and continue to alter their life styles and their patterns of work, their expectations change about what they need to ensure their economic security.

Employee benefit programs are intended to provide assistance during our working years as well as in our retirement. During our working years, benefits may protect us against loss of family income because of ill health, disability, unemployment, and premature death. During retirement, they may protect us against poverty and low income and help assure that we have access to vital medical care that typically becomes more necessary, and more expensive, as we age.

The United States has a longstanding commitment to its citizens' economic security, based upon government-mandated programs, voluntary employer-sponsored programs, and individual efforts that are often encouraged by the government and by employers. This combination of public and private programs has been so successful, and so pervasive, that many individuals take it for granted. But it is one of the most important components of a worker's total compensation. It is also an area that is subject to great change.

I am proud to introduce the fourth edition of *Fundamentals of Employee Benefit Programs*, which has as its goal—as have its predecessors—education about the extent and the importance of employee benefits and the many changes being made by employers and by lawmakers.

In 1979, the Employee Benefit Research Institute (EBRI) began developing a series of educational pamphlets that provided basic information about the primary employer-sponsored benefit plans. The pamphlets were drafted by employee benefit experts, and they were used widely for employee training and consumer education. In 1983, the pamphlets were updated and compiled into one volume, used by more than 10,000 individuals, and widely acclaimed as a thorough, accurate, and readable primer on the whole range of employee benefits.

Tax and pension law changes in 1984 and new federal regulations caused EBRI staff, in cooperation with benefit experts, to issue an expanded and updated second edition in 1985. In 1987, the third edition was published, in which we incorporated the many changes wrought by the Tax Reform Act of 1986 and added several new chapters.

This fourth edition breaks ground in a number of areas. New chapters on pension coverage and participation and on cash balance pension plans have been added, and the scope of the book has been expanded to include an all-new 10 chapter section on public-sector benefit programs. For every chapter, the bibliographical references and other suggestions of sources for additional information have been expanded, while a comprehensive index makes this book an even quicker and more thorough reference guide—particularly when used in tandem with the *EBRI Databook on Employee Benefits*.

Fundamentals is, however, a primer. It does not provide legal, investment, or employee benefit plan design advice, and should not be used for such purposes without consultation with professional counsel. Due to constant economic, legal, and regulatory changes, individuals should always seek specific legal, financial planning, and employee benefit information from legal counsel, financial institutions, and employee benefit professionals. The applicability of the information in this book to a specific plan, plan sponsor, or plan participant must be determined by legal counsel.

An advance word about the organization of this book: Each chapter is designed to be read as a freestanding piece. Rather than to assume that the book is being read as a whole, which would require the reader to search for various definitions of terms, an editorial decision has been made to restate each term's meaning in each chapter as a convenience to the reader.

Appreciation is expressed to the members of the Employee Benefit Research Institute, who generously made their benefit experts available to oversee the technical information in this project. Particular gratitude is expressed to the following firms, organizations, and individuals, who served as reviewers and technical advisors: the American Federation of State, County, and Municipal Employees; Dwight K. Bartlett; the Blue Cross and Blue Shield Association; Buck Consultants, Inc.; C & B Consulting Group; the ESOP Association; A. Foster Higgins & Co., Inc.; Donald S. Grubbs Jr.; Hewitt Associates; the International Foundation of Employee Benefit Plans; Kwasha Lipton; Donna Lynn, director, New York City Employee Benefits Program; William M. Mercer, Inc.; Milliman & Robertson, Inc.; the National Resource Center for Consumers of Legal Services; the Prudential Insurance Company of America; Martin E. Segal Co.; Teachers Insurance and Annuity Association/College Retirement Equities Fund; Towers, Perrin, Forster, & Crosby, Inc.; the U.S. Department of Labor Women's Bureau; VALIC; and EBRI Fellows Jean Barber, Dalmer Hoskins, and Nancy C. Saltford.

Appreciation is especially expressed to the EBRI staff, in particular Charles Betley, Laura K. Bos, Shannon Braymen, Michelle Butler, Mary Catherine Calvert, William Custer, Deborah J. Chollet, Christine Dolan, Deborah Holmes, Karen Horkitz, Bonnie Newton, Cindy O'Connor, Joseph S. Piacentini, Stephanie L. Poe, Nora Super, and Jack L. VanDerhei, whose dedicated efforts made this fourth edition possible.

The views expressed in this book should not be ascribed to those whose assistance is acknowledged or to the officers, trustees, members, or other sponsors of EBRI, its Education and Research Fund, or their staffs.

DALLAS L. SALISBURY
President
September 1990

PART ONE
PRIVATE-SECTOR BENEFIT PROGRAMS

1. Employee Benefits in the United States: An Introduction

Employee benefits are intended to promote economic security by insuring against uncertain events and to raise living standards by providing targeted services. Employee benefit programs also add to economic stability by helping to secure the income and welfare of American families, which helps the economy as a whole.

The U.S. employee benefit system is a partnership among businesses, individuals, and the government. Most employment-based benefits, such as pensions and health insurance, are provided voluntarily by businesses. Other benefits, including Social Security, unemployment insurance, and workers' compensation, are mandatory. The government also supports individual programs of financial security through individual retirement accounts, favorable taxation of life insurance contracts, and tax-free death benefits. In addition, the government provides public assistance programs for needy persons who are not eligible for employment-based benefits.

A Brief History

Employee benefit programs have existed in the United States since colonial times. Early programs include the Plymouth Colony settlers' military retirement program in 1636; Gallatin Glassworks' profit-sharing plan in 1797; American Express Company's private employer pension plan in 1875; Montgomery Ward's group health, life, and accident insurance program in 1910; and Baylor University Hospital's formalized prepaid group hospitalization plan in 1929. The federal government's involvement in the provision of such benefits further expanded coverage. In 1935, Congress mandated basic retirement income protection under the Social Security program; in 1965, it added health insurance for the elderly and disabled under the Medicare program. Moreover, voluntary employer-provided benefit programs became more prevalent as (sometimes enhanced) federal tax preferences for employee benefits coincided with rising tax rates, strengthening incentives to provide private benefits.

The Role of Employee Benefits

Today's employment-based benefit programs represent a national commitment to provide some measure of income security and access to certain services (especially medical care) to active workers, displaced and disabled workers, retirees, and their families. This commitment is also reflected in government assistance programs, which are designed to provide income security and access to vital services for needy Americans.

Income Security—A family's income security can be threatened if a wage earner dies or becomes disabled. Group life insurance and long-term disability insurance, often provided voluntarily by employers, can help to alleviate such unexpected financial losses. Employer-sponsored pension and saving plans can also help to provide economic security for workers who look forward to a period of voluntary retirement in old age. Mandatory government programs also address the need for income security. The Social Security Old-Age, Survivors, and Disability Insurance program provides an income base, in the form of a lifetime annuity, to nearly all retired and disabled workers and their surviving spouses. Workers who become unemployed or disabled may qualify for temporary unemployment insurance or workers' compensation payments, respectively. Needy elderly, blind, and disabled Americans may qualify for Supplemental Security Income. Moreover, poor families with dependent children are protected under federal assistance programs.

Nearly all Americans will benefit from one or more private and public income security programs during their lifetimes. One-half of all civilian employees—more than 44 million workers—participated in employer-sponsored pension plans in 1988. In 1986, slightly more than one-half of all elderly married couples and almost one-third of all unmarried elderly individuals had income from employer-sponsored pensions. Among recent retirees, such benefits are more common. It is projected that nearly one-half of the workers who were aged 55–64 in 1979 and 7 out of 10 baby boom workers who were aged 25–34 in 1979 will eventually receive income from employer-sponsored retirement plans.

Mandatory government programs provide nearly universal coverage. In 1988, the Social Security system covered 128 million employees and self-employed persons, and as of the end of September 1988, 38.5 million persons, including the elderly, disabled, and their dependents and survivors, were receiving benefits. An estimated 92 percent of elderly married couples and 91 percent of elderly unmarried individuals received income from Social Security in 1986.

Access to Important Services—The U.S. employee benefit system also seeks to provide American workers and their families with lifelong access to certain vital services—especially medical care. Most

4

American workers participate in group health insurance programs sponsored voluntarily by their employers. These programs vary widely. Coverage may be limited to acute hospital care or may include such routine services as dental exams and physician visits. Often, an employee's dependents are covered. Sixty-six percent of the civilian population under age 65, or 134 million persons, were covered by employer-sponsored health insurance in 1986 (Chollet, 1988). Among full-time, full-year workers, 81 percent had coverage, and coverage often continues after retirement. In the same year, three-quarters of full-time health insurance participants in medium-sized and large private establishments were in plans that continued coverage after retirement.

Under the Medicare program, the federal government has assumed the role of primary provider of medical insurance to elderly Americans. In 1987, 32 million elderly and disabled persons were enrolled in the Medicare program, and 24 million received benefits. In addition, the federal/state Medicaid program helps finance medical care for some of America's most needy families and pays the cost of most nursing home care for elderly persons who lack sufficient financial resources.

Employee benefit programs are not limited to income security and health insurance. Specialized benefit programs help provide access to a wide range of important services, including ongoing education and training, child care, long-term care, and legal assistance. Other employee benefits, such as free parking, product discounts, and relocation expense reimbursement, can provide convenience and cost savings for employees. Employee benefits also include paid sick leave, holidays, vacations, and maternity or paternity leave.

A list of employment-based benefits is presented in chart 1.1. Although not exhaustive, the list shows the variety and range of the U.S. employee benefit system. Chart 1.1 also distinguishes between voluntary and mandated employee benefit programs and shows the wide variety of tax treatments that apply to these benefits.

Tax Treatment

Federal tax provisions for employee benefit programs are relatively new. The tax code has provided tax incentives since 1921 to employers sponsoring pension plans and since 1954 to those sponsoring health plans. The retirement income provisions of the Social Security program were enacted in 1935, and health insurance for elderly and disabled persons was added in 1965. The tax exclusion for compensation received for injuries or sickness was established in 1939.

CHART 1.1
Employment-Based Benefits in the United States

Types of Employee Benefits by Tax Treatment

Mandatory
- Social Security Retirement (OASI)
- Social Security Disability (DI)
- Medicare Part A (Social Security HI)
- Workers' compensation
- Unemployment insurance
- Medicaid[a]
- Supplemental Security Income[a]
- Public assistance[a]

Voluntary

Fully Taxable
- Vacations
- Paid lunch
- Rest periods
- Severance pay
- Cash bonuses and awards

Tax Exempt
- Employee and dependent health insurance
- Retiree health insurance
- Dental insurance
- Vision insurance
- Employer-paid Medicare Part B (Social Security SMI) premiums
- Medicare Part B (Social Security SMI)[b]
- Education assistance (up to limits)
- Legal assistance (up to limits)
- Dependent care (up to limits)
- Discounts
- Flexible spending accounts
- Parking
- Cafeteria facilities
- Meals

Tax Deferred
- Defined benefit pension plans
- Money-purchase plans
- Deferred profit-sharing
- 401(k) arrangements (pretax)
- Thrift savings plans
- Employee stock ownership plans
- Stock bonus plans
- Simplified employee pensions
- IRA and Keogh plans

Other Tax Preferred[c]
- Life insurance
- Long-term disability insurance
- Sick leave or sickness and accident insurance
- Other leave (maternity, funeral, jury, etc.)

(continued)

CHART 1.1 (continued)

Types of Employee Benefits by Function

Retirement Income Benefits
- Social Security Retirement (OASI)
- Defined benefit pension plans
- Money-purchase plans
- Deferred profit-sharing
- 401(k) arrangements
- Thrift savings plans
- Employee stock ownership plans
- Stock bonus plans
- Simplified employee pensions
- IRA and Keogh plans
- Supplemental Security Income

Health Care
- Employee and dependent health insurance
- Retiree health insurance
- Dental insurance
- Vision insurance
- Medicare (Social Security HI, SMI)
- Medicaid

Other Benefits
- Social Security Disability (DI)
- Long-term disability insurance
- Life insurance
- Workers' compensation
- Unemployment insurance
- Public assistance
- Severance pay
- Dependent care
- Vacations
- Sick leave or sickness and accident insurance
- Other leave (maternity, funeral, jury, etc.)
- Paid lunch
- Rest periods
- Legal assistance
- Education assistance
- Flexible spending accounts
- Bonuses and awards
- Parking
- Cafeteria facilities
- Meals
- Discounts

Source: Joseph S. Piacentini and Timothy J. Cerino, *EBRI Databook on Employee Benefits* (Washington, DC: Employee Benefit Research Institute, 1990).
[a]Financed from federal and state general revenues.
[b]Premiums may be includable in itemized deductions or may be paid from after-tax income. Financed largely from federal general revenues.
[c]Value of insurance and leave availability are not taxed; insurance benefits and leave pay generally are taxed when paid.

The general tax treatment of employee benefit programs has remained relatively consistent over the years. Employer contributions to health insurance remain tax exempt to employees, and taxes on most retirement programs are deferred until withdrawal. Other benefits, such as life insurance, dependent care, and education assistance, are tax exempt up to specified dollar limits. Vacations and other time-off benefits, bonuses and awards, and severance pay are fully taxable (chart 1.1).

Meeting Changing Needs

Given such a wide range of options, compensation packages can be tailored to achieve employer and employee goals and can change in response to workers' needs and preferences. Demographic changes in the American work force and general population are likely to influence the provision and design of employee benefit programs.

An Aging Population—One change in progress is the shift in the U.S. population's age distribution. Members of the large baby-boom cohort currently compose a disproportionately large part of the overall work force, especially in new and fast-growing industries. As this cohort ages, and the smaller baby-bust cohort enters the labor force, the age distribution of the work force will shift toward older workers, whose needs and preferences may differ from those of younger workers. As the baby-boom cohort begins to retire, an increasing proportion of Americans will be elderly and will depend on sources other than employment for income and vital services. These forces will affect both income security and health care insurance programs.

A shift in the type of pension plan most commonly offered may in part represent a response to work force changes. It has been well documented that in the private sector, participation in defined contribution plans (which promise a specified contribution to an employee's account) is growing faster than participation in traditional defined benefit pension plans (which promise a specified benefit at retirement). The number of participants in primary defined benefit plans grew an estimated 2 percent between 1975 and 1987 (from 33 million to 40 million), while the number in primary defined contribution plans grew more than 200 percent during those years (from 11.5 million to 37 million).

Defined contribution plans historically have offered faster vesting than defined benefit plans, and defined contribution lump-sum benefits are generally considered more portable than defined benefit plan deferred annuities. Thus, younger workers may anticipate future job

8

changes and therefore value faster vesting and benefit portability common to defined contribution plans. In addition, young families may be attracted to defined contribution plan provisions that allow access to money in the account prior to retirement in cases of financial hardship and on termination of employment (although preretirement lump-sum withdrawals are generally subject to a 10 percent excise tax and regular income tax). However, as the baby-boom cohort ages and the work force becomes weighted more toward older workers, preferences may shift again toward defined benefit plans, which are generally characterized as providing more secure retirement protection than defined contribution plans for long-tenure employees working at the same company until retirement.[1]

The effects of the aging population on retirement programs can already be seen in the Social Security Old-Age and Survivors Insurance (OASI) program. Partly as a result of increased life expectancies, past population shifts are reflected in a decrease in the ratio of OASI-covered workers to OASI beneficiaries from 16.5 in 1950 to 4.1 in 1970. In response, taxes imposed on employers and employees to finance the mostly pay-as-you-go OASI system were raised from 1.5 percent in 1950 to roughly 4.8 percent in 1983. The rates were revised again under the Social Security Amendments of 1983 and increased incrementally to 5.6 percent in 1990. Moreover, the retirement age will also rise incrementally by the year 2000 to age 67 in anticipation of the baby boom's retirement.

Health care benefit programs are also affected by the aging of the population. The elderly generally require more health care than the working age population. This trend is exacerbated by the rapid pace of health care price inflation. Between 1970 and 1986, the price level of medical services and commodities rose 259 percent, compared with a 182 percent increase in consumer prices overall. For hospital room services alone, the increase was 419 percent. Propelled by these factors, national health expenditures reached 11.5 percent of the U.S. Gross National Product by 1988, up from 7.4 percent in 1970. Between 1948 and 1988, employer spending for health insurance (excluding Medicare) increased an average of 15.3 percent per year, to $133 billion. In response to these developments, employers are taking steps to slow the growth of their health care costs. Increasingly, employers are requiring employees to share the cost of health insurance premiums and/or pay a larger portion of health costs out of pocket. It is

---

[1] For a detailed discussion of the merits of defined benefit and defined contribution plans, see Employee Benefit Research Institute, 1989b.

9

hoped that cost sharing and other cost management measures will discourage unnecessary utilization of health care services.

The Medicare program, like OASI, has already been affected by demographic shifts and rapid health care inflation. The employer/employee tax rate for Medicare Hospital Insurance (HI) increased from 0.6 percent in 1970 to 1.45 percent in 1990. In anticipation of further cost increases, Congress enacted limits on the prices Medicare would pay hospitals, based on diagnosis categories, that were phased in between October 1983 and October 1986. Nonetheless, it is projected that without further tax increases or benefit cuts, the HI trust fund will be depleted between the years 2005 and 2008, given intermediate economic and demographic assumptions.

As the population ages, the proportion requiring nursing home care or other long-term care will increase. Currently, private insurance for such health care needs is not widely available, and federal financing for nursing home care is generally available only under the Medicaid program, with eligibility subject to stringent means tests. Many find this situation unacceptable, and pressure is building to make other provisions for financing long-term care, either through expanded provision of voluntary private insurance (perhaps through employers), through a mandatory government program, or both.[2]

Working Parents—Family structure has changed radically from the days when it typically consisted of a father who was the sole wage earner, a mother who stayed at home, and two children. Today, both husband and wife often work, children are in day care, and there are many single-parent families. The increase in labor force participation by women—especially those with young children—has implications for employee benefits that cannot be overlooked. In 1950, 12 percent of women with children under age 6 were in the labor force, compared with 57 percent in 1987; in fact, in 1987 more than one-half of all women with children under age 1 worked. In total, nearly two-thirds of all mothers of children younger than age 14 were in the labor force in 1987. Examined differently, there are 12.8 million families with children in which both parents work; 3.5 million single mothers are in the labor force. These groups combined have 10.6 million children younger than age 6 and 15.7 million children aged 6–13. These parents and their children have employee benefit and work place policy needs that are different from those of families 30 years ago.

These trends have led to public and private responses that attempt to help workers better balance work and family needs. Legislation

---

[2]For more about long-term care, see Friedland, 1990.

has been considered that would require employers to provide a minimum period of parental leave and to promote federal and more state involvement in child care access, affordability, and quality.

Flexibility—Another response to a changing work force is the growing use of flexible benefit plans. Within such arrangements, employees are permitted choices among benefits and/or benefit levels. Employees thus may exchange benefits that they consider less valuable for others better suited to their needs.

Employee benefit programs, whether public or private, that address these and other needs can enhance the economic security of individual workers and their families and may strengthen the U.S. economy overall. The provision of benefits such as child care and parental leave can help smooth career progress, to the overall advantage of labor markets. Thus, these and other benefits can help families and employers reconcile the personal needs of the home with the economic needs of the work place.

Benefits and the Federal Budget

The expansion of federal tax incentives for new employee benefits that occurred in the 1970s has dramatically slowed and is unlikely to return during this decade unless the current federal budget situation eases.

Faced with billions of dollars in federal budget deficits, legislators are concerned with tax losses attributable to tax-favored employee benefit programs. Because some benefits are tax exempt (health) and others are not subject to taxes until some future time (pensions), the current tax revenue loss to the U.S. Treasury can be substantial. Thus, employee benefits are often targets in legislative revenue-raising efforts.

Employee benefit programs will remain an important piece of total compensation, but changes in employee benefit and tax policy appear to be continuing. Keeping up with and understanding the changes and their effects will be important not only for sponsors of benefit programs but for employees as well.

Bibliography

Chollet, Deborah J. *Uninsured in the United States: A Profile of the Nonelderly Population without Health Insurance, 1986.* Washington, DC: Employee Benefit Research Institute, 1988.

Employee Benefit Research Institute. *Business, Work, and Benefits: Adjusting to Change.* Washington, DC: Employee Benefit Research Institute, 1989a.

———. *What Is the Future for Defined Benefit Pension Plans?* Washington, DC: Employee Benefit Research Institute, 1989b.

Friedland, Robert B. *Facing the Costs of Long-Term Care.* Washington, DC: Employee Benefit Research Institute, 1990.

Piacentini, Joseph S., and Timothy J. Cerino. *EBRI Databook on Employee Benefits.* Washington, DC: Employee Benefit Research Institute, 1990.

U.S. Department of Labor. *Child Care: A Workforce Issue. Report of the Secretary's Task Force.* April 1988.

2. Social Security

Introduction

The U.S. Congress enacted the Social Security Act in 1935, and it became effective on January 1, 1937. The original legislation has been amended many times and has become a complex set of laws and regulations that affect the lives of almost all Americans. This chapter briefly discusses the current Social Security system, its benefits, and its costs.

What Is Social Security?

The *Social Security Handbook*, published by the Social Security Administration (an agency within the U.S. Department of Health and Human Services), provides a detailed explanation of the Social Security Act and its operation. In describing Social Security, the *Handbook* states:

> The Social Security Act and related laws established a number of programs which have the basic objectives of providing for the material needs of individuals and families, protecting aged and disabled persons against the expenses of illnesses that could otherwise exhaust their savings, keeping families together, and giving children the opportunity to grow up in health and security. These programs include:
>
> Retirement insurance
> Survivors insurance
> Disability insurance
> Hospital and medical insurance for the aged, the disabled, and
> those with end-stage renal disease
> Black lung benefits
> Supplemental Security Income
> Unemployment insurance
> Public assistance and welfare services
> —Aid to needy families with dependent children
> —Medical assistance
> —Maternal and child health services
> —Child support enforcement
> —Family support and welfare services
> —Food stamps
> —Energy assistance

The federal government operates the Old-Age, Survivors, and Disability Insurance (OASDI) programs; Medicare, which consists of the Hospital Insurance (HI) and Supplementary Medical Insurance (SMI) programs; the black lung benefit program; and the Supplemental Security Income (SSI) program. The remaining programs are operated by the states, with the federal government cooperating and contributing funds.

This chapter discusses OASDI and Medicare collectively as Social Security. These programs are financed primarily by the Social Security payroll taxes paid by employees, employers, and self-employed persons. An exception to this financing method is Medicare SMI, also known as Part B, which is financed by premiums paid by those electing to be covered by SMI and by general revenues.

Participation

Who is covered by Social Security and thereby eligible for OASDI and Medicare benefits? When Social Security became effective in 1937, it applied only to workers in industry and commerce—about 60 percent of all working persons. Since then, there has been a steady movement toward covering all workers.

The Social Security Act originally excluded all state and local government employees from coverage because of uncertainty concerning whether the federal government could legally tax state employers. Workers for certain nonprofit organizations that are traditionally exempt from income and other taxes were also excluded. Federal government employees were excluded because they were covered by the Civil Service Retirement System, which was established in 1920.

In the 1950s, coverage was extended to most self-employed persons, farm and household workers, and members of the armed forces.

Legislation enacted in 1950 (and thereafter) provided that employees of state and local governments and nonprofit organizations could be covered by Social Security on a voluntary basis under certain conditions. The Social Security Amendments of 1983 changed the law to *require* coverage of employees of all nonprofit organizations. This legislation also mandated that once state and local governments elected to become covered by Social Security, they could not later withdraw from the program. Additionally, beginning in 1984, new federal government employees became covered by Social Security.

Mandatory coverage now extends to private-sector workers, non-profit-sector workers, military personnel, 10 percent of all federal civilian employees who joined the government before 1984 (and who opted to become covered under Social Security), and federal civilian employees hired after December 31, 1983. Social Security currently covers approximately 95 percent of all employed workers, including the self-employed, in the United States (Bernstein and Bernstein, 1988).

Benefits

Because of the complexity of the Social Security program, this section gives a necessarily brief overview of its benefits. Consult the *Social Security Handbook* for more detailed information.

Social Security replaces a portion of covered earnings (discussed below in "How Social Security Is Funded") that are lost as a result of a person's old age, disability, or death, and it pays a portion of the medical expenses of aged and disabled persons. Social Security provides a much wider variety of benefits than is generally recognized. In fact, $79 billion of the $214 billion in benefits paid by Social Security in 1988 went to persons other than retired workers (U.S. Department of Health and Human Services, 1989).

Old-Age, Survivors, and Disability Insurance—The following benefits are provided under OASDI programs:

- monthly benefits to individuals who are at least 62 years old and are retired or partially retired, and to their eligible spouses and dependents;
- monthly benefits to disabled workers, their eligible spouses, and dependents; and
- a lump-sum death payment and monthly benefits to eligible survivors of deceased workers. (For more information on Social Security disability insurance and survivor benefits, see chapters 29 and 38, respectively.)

In general, today's workers will become fully insured (that is, eligible to receive full retirement benefits) after completing 40 quarters of coverage. A quarter of coverage is counted for every $520 of annual earnings reported (in 1990, indexed annually), up to four quarters per year.

A person aged 62 or older who has not acquired sufficient earnings to receive benefits on his or her own record can nevertheless receive a spouse's benefit, provided the spouse is retired or disabled and entitled to benefits. This benefit is equal to an extra 50 percent of the primary retiree's benefit if the recipient is aged 65 or over, but somewhat less if he or she is between the ages of 62 and 65.

An individual who is entitled to a benefit on the basis of lifetime earnings and also to a spousal benefit is entitled to receive whichever amount is greater.

A provision for divorced spouses became effective in 1985. In the past, a divorced woman, for example, could receive a spouse's benefit if she had been married at least 10 years to her former husband, but only if he had retired and started receiving his benefits. This created severe problems in cases where the former husband did not retire; the ex-spouse was thus ineligible for benefits. Now, if the husband is not retired, the ex-spouse can receive the benefit if they both are at least age 62, were married 10 years, were divorced at least two years, and the former husband worked under Social Security long enough to qualify for benefits.

Receipt of spouse's benefits by a former spouse does not reduce the amount available to a current spouse. Each can receive a spouse's benefit, although the current spouse must wait until the benefit earner retires.

The 1983 Social Security Amendments made significant changes in benefit eligibility. While reduced benefits will continue to be paid at age 62, the age for receiving full benefits—now age 65—will be increased in the future. The full benefit age will increase by two months a year for people reaching age 62 in the year 2000 through the year 2004. The age at which full benefits may be received will remain at 66 for people who reach age 62 in the year 2005 through the year 2016. The full benefit age will increase again by two months a year for people reaching age 62 in the year 2017 through the year 2022. It will remain at 67 for those who reach age 62 after the year 2022.

The early retirement benefit amount, which is payable at age 62, will be reduced over this period. The maximum reduction for early retirement benefits will increase from its present 20 percent to 30 percent for those who reach age 62 in the year 2022 or later.

Monthly benefit amounts are related to the average earnings on which a worker pays Social Security taxes throughout his or her career years. When computing benefits, a worker's average earnings are indexed to changes that have taken place in national average earnings over the worker's career years. To assist in achieving *social adequacy*, benefits are higher (relative to indexed preretirement earnings) for persons with low average indexed earnings than for persons with high average indexed earnings.

Social Security benefits are reduced or eliminated altogether if a participant under age 70 works after retiring and earns income that exceeds specified amounts in any given year. In 1990, retirees aged 65 through 69 can earn up to $9,360 without a reduction in Social Security benefits. Benefits are reduced by $1 for each $3 earned in excess of this amount. However, if 1990 is the initial year of entitlement, an alternative monthly test based on $780 of monthly earnings will apply, if more favorable. For those under age 65, the corresponding maximum amounts are $6,840 annually and $570 monthly. There is no limit on the amount an individual aged 70 or over may earn and still receive Social Security benefits.

Once monthly benefits begin, they generally are adjusted automatically each December to reflect changes in the cost of living. Prior to 1986, these adjustments generally occurred only if the consumer price index (CPI) increased by 3 percent or more since the last automatic adjustment. In 1986, Congress passed legislation that removed the 3 percent trigger for automatic adjustments, so that cost-of-living adjustments are tied to the rate of inflation.

Social Security benefits were not subject to federal, state, or local income taxes (or to Social Security tax) prior to the 1983 amendments. Beginning in 1984, however, up to one-half of Social Security benefits are included in taxable income for single taxpayers whose income (as will be defined) exceeds $25,000, married taxpayers filing jointly with a combined income of $32,000, and all married taxpayers who live with their spouses any time during the tax year and file separately. Income levels are calculated as follows: adjusted gross income, plus nontaxable interest income, plus one-half of Social Security benefits. (For more information, refer to Internal Revenue Service income tax form instructions.)

Social Security was not designed to meet all financial needs that arise from a person's old age, disability, or death. It is intended to serve as a supplement to private savings and employer-sponsored retirement plans. This applies particularly to persons who earn higher-than-average incomes during their working years because of the limit on covered earnings and the benefit formula tilt, which favors lower-paid workers.

During 1988, more than 38 million persons in the United States received a Social Security OASDI benefit payment. In the same year, total cash benefit payments reached about $217 billion.

Hospital Insurance and Supplementary Medical Insurance—The Medicare program has two parts: Part A, the Hospital Insurance program, pays part of the costs of inpatient hospital care and certain followup care after a patient leaves the hospital. HI provides benefits for individuals who are aged 65 or older, who receive Social Security disability benefits for more than 24 consecutive months, and/or who are disabled by chronic kidney disease that requires dialysis or a transplant. Part B, Supplementary Medical Insurance, pays for part of the costs of care provided by physicians and for other related health services.

Persons who are covered by Social Security or the Railroad Retirement plan are automatically covered under HI.

Additionally, beginning in 1983, all federal civilian employees became covered under HI, and state and local government employees hired after March 31, 1986, and whose jobs were not already covered under Social Security were covered by HI beginning April 1, 1986.

SMI is voluntary, and is offered to almost all persons aged 65 or older and to those under age 65 who are currently eligible for HI. Those who participate must pay a premium that is heavily subsidized by the government. Individuals not covered by Social Security or the Railroad Retirement program who elect HI must also pay for SMI. SMI coverage, however, can be elected independent of HI coverage. SMI helps to pay for physician services and outpatient hospital services, as well as many other medical items and services not covered by HI.

During 1987, approximately 28 million persons aged 65 or older, representing 95 percent of this group, were covered under HI and SMI. Another 3 million disabled persons under age 65 were also covered by these programs.

The Social Security Board of Trustees' 1989 annual report projects that total Medicare benefit payments in 1989 were $87 billion.

Social Security Benefit Estimates

Workers wishing to obtain a statement of their projected Social Security benefits can do so through a service recently initiated by the Social Security Administration. This free service—called the Personal Earnings and Benefit Estimate Statement (PEBES)—requires the completion of a request form that can be obtained by calling 1-800-234-5772, toll free.

Individuals requesting the PEBES are asked to submit information about their most recent earnings and anticipated future earnings and the age at which they plan to retire. In return, they will receive a year-by-year listing of past Social Security earnings from 1951 to the present; an estimate of their yearly FICA (Federal Insurance Contribution Act) taxes; and estimates of the Social Security benefits to which they will be entitled at ages 62, 65, and 70. The statement will also include information about the number of Social Security credits the individual will need for each type of benefit and how many of these credits he or she has already earned.

How Social Security Is Funded

Social Security is financed primarily by payroll taxes paid by employees, employers, and the self-employed. These taxes are held by special Social Security trust funds that are set up only to pay Social Security program benefits and administrative expenses. Any trust fund assets not needed to meet current costs are invested in U.S. government securities.

In 1988, payroll taxes accounted for about 95.1 percent of the total income for the Old-Age, Survivors, Disability, and Hospital Insurance programs. Approximately 3.6 percent of the income for these programs comes from interest earnings on the trust funds, 0.3 percent is from general revenues[1] and is used to finance special benefits, and 1.0 percent is derived from taxation of benefits. (Beginning in 1984, as a result of the 1983 amendments, OASDI began receiving income from the taxation of some Social Security benefits.)

General revenue contributions will increase in the future as a result of the 1983 amendments, which include a provision for shifting amounts equal to tax liabilities on Social Security benefits from the general fund to the Social Security trust funds. Also, general revenues will contribute amounts equal to the employer share of the Social Security tax with respect to coverage of federal employment.

The 1983 amendments also increased FICA tax rates for employers, employees, and the self-employed. To lessen the burden of the tax increases, tax credits (against Social Security tax liability) were provided to employees (in 1984 only) and to self-employed persons from 1984 through 1989 (2.7 percent in 1984, 2.3 percent in 1985, and 2.0 percent in 1986–1989).

In 1990, participating (non-self-employed) workers pay Social Security, or FICA, taxes of 7.65 percent on the first $51,300 of earnings. The employer pays an equal amount (6.2 percent of each is for OASDI and 1.45 percent of each is for HI). No taxes are withheld on earnings over $51,300 (adjusted annually). This limit is called the maximum taxable earnings base, or covered earnings. This base rises in future years at the same rate as the average earnings of all the nation's workers.

Self-employed persons have the same maximum taxable earnings base as other workers, but pay higher tax rates since they pay as an

---

[1]Includes income to the Hospital Insurance trust fund from transfers from the Railroad Retirement Account, reimbursements for uninsured persons, premiums from voluntary enrollees, and payments for military wage credits.

employer and an employee. The self-employed, or SECA (Self-Employed Contributions Act), tax rate for 1990 is 15.30 percent. The income tax credit for the self-employed was terminated beginning in 1990, but is replaced with an income tax deduction for one-half the SECA contribution. In addition, the self-employed may deduct 50 percent of their Social Security tax as a business expense.

Unlike the other Social Security programs, SMI is not financed by payroll taxes. The cost of SMI was originally financed through premiums imposed on participants and through matching payments from general revenues. At the present time, however, about 75 percent of SMI's total cost is paid from general revenues because, by law, premiums have not been permitted to rise as rapidly as program costs.

Outlook

Social Security's development is a continuing process. The program is a product of the decisions made by policymakers living in an ever-changing social and economic environment.

When men and women of the baby boom generation begin to reach retirement age in approximately 20 years, social and economic conditions are likely to be quite different than they are today or have been in the past. Accordingly, it is reasonable to expect society to begin now to make the changes necessary to assure that the Social Security program will be appropriate for the future social and economic environment.

We may, for example, anticipate that as we approach the next century there will be increased public debate regarding the appropriate retirement age, since some observers will criticize the higher retirement age of 67 as being unreasonably punitive to some, particularly those working in arduous occupations. Others will be in favor of raising the retirement age even further (for example, to age 70).

There will also be increased attention given to certain aspects of the Disability Insurance program, such as the high number of disability decisions that are appealed and subsequently overturned by the administrative judges and courts as well as the strikingly low number of beneficiaries who leave the disability rolls to return to work.

Finally, the continued growth in the number of married women in the labor force will focus attention on alleged inequities in the treatment by Social Security of married couples as compared with single workers. These and other issues, reflecting changing social and economic patterns, will influence the inevitable modifications to the Social Security program.

Public understanding or misunderstanding will play a more important role in determining the future shape of the program than it did in the past when Social Security taxes were relatively low and the average worker was less questioning. The fact is that, for the vast majority of American workers, the payroll tax burden for Social Security and Medicare exceeds their federal income tax liability (when both employer and employee rates are combined).

One problem confronting Social Security is a lack of public understanding about the program—its basic rationale, the type and level of benefits it provides, the tenuous relationship between individual taxes paid and individual benefits received, its method of financing, and the significance of its projected high future costs. The better we understand Social Security, the greater our chances that the program will be modified to coincide with our needs. Public acceptance will be necessary for a program that is scheduled to pay benefits and to require tax collections amounting to trillions of dollars during the next several years.

The Social Security Administration has expanded its efforts to educate the public. In addition, a number of advisory groups and commissions regularly study the various aspects of Social Security. This attention and scrutiny may result in a certain amount of turmoil; in the long-run, however, it should improve the Social Security program.

Conclusion

The changes in Social Security legislated in 1983 have resolved the immediate financial difficulties that plagued the system. The actuarial estimates made by the Social Security Board of Trustees in 1989 generally project that the OASDI program will continue to be financially sound, with the income rate generally exceeding the cost rate, resulting in substantial positive balances each year until about the year 2020. The funding of Social Security may well be the center of controversy and subject to change well before that date is reached, since the buildup of Social Security's reserves, resulting from the 1983 and previous amendments, has in itself set off a public debate.

As previously indicated, these reserves were intended by the legislators to provide a partial cushion for the higher numbers of retirees in the next century. However, the immediate result was for the enhanced reserves to be used to mask the real level of the federal budget deficit, since (at this writing) Social Security revenues are counted as assets for federal budget accounting. It has therefore become clear that Social Security financing is intricately related to the federal government's budgetary and fiscal policies. Some policymakers would like to make this relationship more clear and less interdependent by taking Social Security "off budget," meaning that Social Security revenues and outgoes would no longer appear in the federal budget. Some suggest repealing the scheduled payroll tax increases, thereby limiting the buildup in the Social Security funds.

The Medicare program could potentially be a much greater problem. Without changes, the program is projected to have insufficient funds by the beginning of the 21st century.

Social Security and Medicare are large, well established, and recognized as an integral part of the national socioeconomic structure. Nevertheless, important questions remain. Will the Social Security and Medicare programs continue to grow in a way that best reconciles beneficiaries' economic needs with taxpayers' financial abilities—or will they be curtailed because of heavy financial burdens? Will there be a more concerted effort in the future to formulate a more comprehensive national retirement policy that takes into account projected Social Security benefits as well as the retirement benefits that employees expect to receive from employer-sponsored plans and their individual savings initiatives (individual retirement accounts, thrift plans, etc.)? The answer depends largely on the dialogue and decisions of an informed citizenry.

Bibliography

Achenbaum, W. Andrew. *Social Security: Visions and Revisions.* New York: Cambridge University Press, 1986.

Bernstein, Merton C., and Joan Brodshaug Bernstein. *Social Security: The System That Works.* New York: Basic Books, 1988.

Boskin, Michael J. *Too Many Promises.* Homewood, IL: Dow Jones-Irwin, 1986.

Employee Benefit Research Institute/The Gallup Organization, Inc. *Public Attitudes on Social Security.* Washington, DC: Employee Benefit Research Institute, 1990.

Kingston, Eric R. *What You Must Know About Social Security and Medicare.* New York: Pharos Books, 1988.

Lubove, Roy. *The Struggle for Social Security, 1900–1935.* Pittsburgh, PA: University of Pittsburgh Press, 1986.

U.S. Department of Health and Human Services. Social Security Administration. *Social Security Handbook, 1988.* Washington, DC: U.S. Government Printing Office, 1988.

_____. *1989 Annual Report of the Board of Trustees of the Federal Old-Age and Survivors Insurance and Disability Insurance Trust Funds.* Washington, DC: Social Security Administration, 1989.

Additional Information

U.S. Department of Health and Human Services
Social Security Administration
Baltimore, MD 21235
(800) 234-577

3. Employee Retirement Income Security Act

Introduction and Overview

President Gerald Ford signed the Employee Retirement Income Security Act (ERISA) into law on Labor Day, September 2, 1974. It remains the most comprehensive employee benefits legislation enacted in the United States, affecting the millions of Americans who are covered by employee benefit programs.

ERISA has a long history. President John F. Kennedy appointed a cabinet-level committee in 1962 to study private pension plans. In releasing the report, the committee concluded "that private pension plans should continue as a major element in the nation's total retirement security program. Their strength rests on the supplementation they can provide to the basic public system." But the committee also noted that the pension system was inadequate in certain areas, such as participant rights, funding, benefit protection, and oversight. The report led to investigations by various congressional committees that spanned nearly 10 years.

During its investigations, Congress found that there were a substantial number of benefit plans, which were important to the well-being and security of millions of American workers and their dependents. Most plans were operated for the benefit of participants and beneficiaries, Congress found, but a small number were not. Congress determined that participants generally received insufficient information about their benefit plans, and that there was inadequate protection of their rights.

In designing ERISA, Congress wanted to address the problems mentioned above but at the same time promote "a renewed expansion of private retirement plans" and increase the number of participants receiving benefits. ERISA established standards that employee benefit plans must follow to obtain and maintain their tax-favored status. ERISA created standards for reporting and disclosure, funding, fiscal responsibility, and employee eligibility and vesting. ERISA set up a new government agency to insure most vested benefits against plan termination, and established contribution and benefit limits for retirement plans.

ERISA primarily applies to private retirement plans, but almost all employee benefit plans are subject to some provisions of the act. The legislation affects welfare plans, such as health insurance, group life insurance, sick pay, and long-term disability income; and retirement plans, such as pension and profit-sharing plans, thrift plans, stock bonus plans, and employee stock ownership plans.

ERISA supersedes all state law otherwise applicable to pension (and welfare) plans covered by the reporting, disclosure, fiduciary responsibility, eligibility, vesting, funding, and termination insurance provisions of ERISA. This is what is commonly called "ERISA preemption." It does not apply to state law regulating insurance, banking, or securities. ERISA does not apply to state and local government plans, church plans, or those covering only self-employed persons (except for certain rules dealing with qualified plans).

The U.S. departments of Labor and the Treasury have primary responsibility for administering ERISA. The Department of Labor (DOL) has primary jurisdiction over reporting, disclosure, and fiduciary matters, while the Treasury Department has primary jurisdiction over eligibility, vesting, and funding. The Pension Benefit Guaranty Corporation (PBGC), an agency of the federal government, administers the plan termination insurance program.

ERISA standards are set out in four titles to the act: Title I—Reporting, Disclosure, and Minimum Standards Administered by the Labor Department; Title II—Minimum Standards Administered by the Treasury Department (Internal Revenue Code provisions); Title III—Jurisdiction and Administration; and Title IV—Plan Termination Insurance.

As with all chapters in this book, this discussion is not intended to provide legal guidance or a guide to compliance. It provides a basic overview of the areas governed by ERISA. Further discussion of many areas is found in other chapters. Those who need more detailed information should consult additional sources.

Protection of Employee Benefit Rights

Reporting and Disclosure—ERISA's extensive reporting and disclosure requirements are rooted in a belief that availability of information serves two important needs. First, adequate communication about the plan to participants can lead to employees having more realistic expectations of their benefits. Second, periodic reporting to the government helps officials monitor legal compliance.

Employee benefit plan sponsors subject to ERISA are required to provide summary plan descriptions (SPDs) to plan participants and beneficiaries. The summary must be written so that the *average* participant can understand it and must be accurate and detailed enough to reasonably inform participants and beneficiaries of their rights and obligations.

The law does not dictate the exact form the SPD should take. It does, however, require inclusion of specific information. For example, among other things, an SPD must include:

- the name and address of the employer or employee organization maintaining the plan;
- the name and/or title and business address of each trustee;
- plan requirements for participation and benefit accrual eligibility;
- a description of provisions for nonforfeitable pension benefits;
- information regarding credited service and breaks in service; and
- a description of situations that may result in disqualification, denial, loss, or forfeiture of benefits.

In addition to the SPD, each participant and beneficiary must have access to financial information about the plan. This information is provided in summary form (summary annual report), drawn from a more extensive annual report (Form 5500 series) filed with the Internal Revenue Service (IRS), a division of the Treasury Department. Such information is intended to give participants and beneficiaries an awareness of the plan's financial status. (The full annual report, which IRS sends to DOL, includes detailed information on the number of plan participants; plan benefit obligations; distributions made to participants and beneficiaries; financial, actuarial, and insurance data; and the amount and nature of the plan's assets. The full report may be obtained from DOL.)

Participants are also entitled to see other documents relating to the plan (for example, complete annual report, insurance contracts, trustee reports, etc.). Once a year, participants and beneficiaries may request a written statement of accrued and vested benefits. A plan participant who terminates service with vested benefits that are not paid at that time must be given a statement showing the amount of accrued and vested benefits. A participant who requests such material and does not receive it within 30 days may file suit in a federal court. The court may require the plan administrator to furnish the materials, and it may impose a fine of up to $100 a day until the materials are received.

Other reports must be filed when certain events occur. DOL, for example, must be notified when a new plan is established (through the SPD) or when an existing plan is revised (through the Summary of Material Modifications). PBGC must be notified when private defined benefit plans are terminated. Other major reports required under ERISA include the Form 5500 series and the Summary Annual Report. (For a description of these forms, refer to Pension Benefit Guaranty Corporation, n.d.).

Fiduciary Requirements—Employers who sponsored retirement plans before ERISA were subject to one general fiduciary standard: plans had to be operated for the exclusive benefit of participants and beneficiaries. ERISA expanded this principle and applied it to almost all employee benefit plans. Fiduciaries are broadly defined as those who exercise control or discretion in managing plan assets; those who render investment advice to the plan for direct or indirect compensation or have authority to do so; or those who have discretionary authority in administering the plan. They include individual employers, officers, trustees, and plan administrators. But attorneys, actuaries, accountants, and consultants would generally not be considered fiduciaries when performing their normal professional services.

In fulfilling their responsibilities, fiduciaries must act in the exclusive interest of plan participants and plan beneficiaries, manage the plan's assets to minimize risk of large losses, and act in accordance with documents that govern the plan.

Fiduciaries must act "with the care, skill, prudence and diligence under the circumstances then prevailing that a prudent man acting in a like capacity and familiar with such matters would use in the conduct of an enterprise of a like character and with like aims." This standard is frequently referred to as ERISA's *prudent man rule*. Because the performance standard is so high, the prudent man rule is often referred to as the prudent *expert* rule.

Fiduciaries must meet this test in performing any aspects of plan operation for which they are responsible—from selecting the individual or institution that will handle plan asset investment to setting investment objectives. A fiduciary who violates ERISA's standards may be personally liable to cover any losses resulting from failure to meet responsibilities and may be required to return any personal profits realized from his or her actions. Additionally, fiduciaries may be liable for the misconduct of other fiduciaries, if they know about such misconduct.

DOL is responsible for enforcing these standards. In certain situations, DOL may bring suit on behalf of participants in plans that do not satisfy ERISA's fiduciary standards. DOL may also assess a monetary penalty for any breach of fiduciary responsibility even with respect to a person other than a fiduciary who knowingly participates in the wrongdoing.

Certain transactions between a pension plan and parties in interest are prohibited. Parties in interest include, but are not limited to, a fiduciary, a person providing services to the plan, an employer whose employees are covered in the plan, an owner of 50 percent or more of the business, a relative of any of the above parties, or a company at least 50 percent owned by any individual noted above. "Prohibited transactions" include: the sale, exchange, or leasing of property; lending money or extending credit; furnishing goods, services, or facilities; use of plan assets; and acquisition of qualifying employer securities and real property in excess of allowable limits. ERISA provides specific exemptions for certain circumstances as well as a process for applying for additional exemptions.

ERISA prohibits anyone, including the employer, from discriminating against a participant who has exercised his or her legal rights. If a participant is fired or otherwise discriminated against for exercising his or her rights, he or she may seek assistance from DOL or may file suit in federal court.

Assignment of Benefits—The assignment of benefits to another person (also called alienation) under a pension plan is prohibited, with certain exceptions, including: the assignment of up to 10 percent of a benefit that is in pay status; the use of an employee's vested benefit as collateral for a loan (if not a prohibited transaction); and payment pursuant to a qualified domestic relations order (QDRO). A QDRO assigns to an alternate payee (spouse, former spouse, or dependent) the right to receive all or a portion of the benefits payable to a participant (even though the participant is still employed).

Minimum Standards and Other Qualified Plan Rules

ERISA also sets specific standards for eligibility, coverage participation, vesting, benefit accrual, and funding of retirement plans. Most of these (funding standards excluded) represent minimum requirements (thus the term minimum standards); employers may adopt plans with more liberal standards.

General Eligibility—A pension plan may require that an employee meet an age and service requirement before becoming eligible for participation. However, the employer cannot require the employee to be over age 21 or have completed more than one year of service with the employer, defined as at least 1,000 hours of work in a 12 month period. An exception applies to plans with immediate vesting; such plans may require completion of up to two years of service.

Coverage and Participation—An employer has some flexibility in determining who will be covered under the pension plan(s). For example, employee groups may be defined on the basis of pay (hourly vs. salaried), job location, or unionization. An employer may have one plan covering all these types of groups (and others) or separate plans. However, tax-qualified plan(s) must generally satisfy a set of nondiscrimination rules (under IRS section 401(a)(4), 410(b), and, in some cases, 401(a)(26)) designed to ensure that the plan arrangement does not discriminate in favor of highly compensated employees in coverage, participation, and benefits provided. (For more information on coverage and participation, see chapter 17.)

Vesting—Participants generally attain nonforfeitable and nonrevocable—vested—rights to benefits after satisfying specific service (or years of participation) or age and service requirements. Once vested, an employee's rights generally cannot be revoked. ERISA requires a plan to adopt vesting standards for the employee's benefit (the account balance under a defined contribution plan or the accumulated benefit under a defined benefit plan) at least as liberal as one of the following two schedules: full vesting (100 percent) after five years of participation in the plan (with no vesting prior to that time, known as cliff vesting) or graded (gradual) vesting of 20 percent after three years of service and 20 percent after each subsequent year of service until 100 percent vesting is reached at the end of seven years of service. These rules apply to employer contributions to a single-employer pension plan. Employee contributions to either defined contribution or defined benefit plans and investment income earned on employee contributions to defined contribution plans are immediately vested.

Multiemployer plans may also use a 10 year cliff vesting schedule, which means that employees do not attain vested rights to employer contributions until they have completed 10 years of service, but become 100 percent vested at that time. Multiemployer plans may provide for cancellation of part of a vested benefit when the participant's employer "withdraws" (see "Plan Termination Insurance").

Full vesting must also occur when a participant reaches the plan's normal retirement age (commonly age 65, but sometimes earlier) or if the plan is terminated; some plans provide for it upon early re-

30

tirement, death, or disability. Loss or suspension of benefits can occur in some situations, however. If a participant and spouse have both waived the preretirement survivor option (discussed later in this chapter), the spouse will not be entitled to any benefit should the participant die before retirement. Additionally, benefits paid to retired participants may be suspended during reemployment with the same employer. Participants who take their own contributions out of the plan may—if they are not sufficiently vested—lose their rights to employer plan contributions but must be permitted to buy back the forfeited benefits upon repayment of contributions and interest.

In many cases, an employee who is not vested can have a break in service without losing credit for previous years of service. Revised *break-in-service* rules were legislated under the Retirement Equity Act of 1984 and require prior service to be reinstated unless the number of consecutive one year breaks in service is equal to, or exceeds, the greater of five years or the number of prebreak years of service. Benefit credit is further protected while an employee is on parental leave.

Form of Benefit Payment—ERISA requires retirement plans that offer an annuity as a payment option to provide a qualified joint and survivor (J&S) annuity for married participants as the normal method of benefit payment. This provides the surviving spouse with a lifetime monthly income equal to at least one-half the amount of the employee's benefit. In return for this protection, the employee's benefit usually is reduced. In order to select a pension paid over the duration of the *participant's* life only (or any other payment form), both the participant and the spouse must refuse the J&S option in writing. (The spouses' signatures must be notarized or made before a plan administrator.) The J&S need not be provided unless the participant has been married at least one year.

Plans may make additional death benefits available to vested participants in the form of a life insurance contract or a cash distribution as long as these benefits are "incidental" to the pension plan, which is defined explicitly by IRS.

Most plans must also provide *preretirement survivor* benefits to the spouse of a vested participant who dies *before* retirement. The benefit is payable in the form of an anuuity for the life of the surviving spouse beginning at what would have been the employee's normal retirement date or at the election of the surviving spouse, as early as the employee's earliest retirement date or death, whichever is later.[1] Unless

---

[1] Profit-sharing plans generally do not have to comply with spousal provisions.

both spouses waive this benefit option in writing, these benefits will be provided to the surviving spouse even if the participant had named someone else as his or her heir. The annuity must be equal to at least one-half of the participant's accrued benefit at the time of his or her death. To reflect the cost of providing survivor protection, employers are allowed to provide a lower benefit to the participant. Preretirement survivor benefits need not be provided unless the participant has been married at least one year.

Benefit Accrual—ERISA requires that plans use one of three alternative formulas to determine how defined benefit pension benefits accrue to participants. In general, benefit amounts accrue over the period of an employee's plan participation but they do not have to accrue evenly over that time. The law focuses only on the rate of benefit accrual; it does not mandate any specific benefit levels. However, benefit accruals may not be reduced or discontined because of age. Thus employees who work beyond normal retirement age will continue to receive credit for time worked and contributions made to their plan, but the employer is allowed to restrict the number of years of benefit accrual.

Funding—Assets in qualified pension plans must be kept separate from the employer's general assets. A plan may be funded through one of a number of vehicles. One method is to establish a trust agreement with a bank or similar institution. In this case, the trust holds the plan's money and invests it, and the employer does not have access to the funds. A plan may also be funded by an insurance company through allocated or unallocated accounts. If the allocated arrangement is used, separate accounts are established for each plan participant, and total contributions are divided among participants. Under an unallocated arrangement, a pool of funds is established and benefits are paid from it. Pension plans may also be funded through individual policies issued on each participant's life. Sometimes both arrangements are used.

To ensure that pension plans have sufficient assets to pay benefits when participants retire, ERISA established minimum funding standards for defined benefit and some defined contribution plans. Money purchase and target benefit plans are covered under these requirements, but not profit-sharing, stock bonus, or most employee stock ownership plans.[2] For money purchase and target benefit plans, the

---

[2]In a money purchase plan, employer contributions are mandatory and are usually based on each participant's compensation. A stock bonus plan is similar to a profit-sharing plan, but usually makes benefit payments in the form of company stock. A

minimum contribution is the amount set out in the plan formula. Single-employer defined benefit plans must make at least a minimum contribution equal to the normal cost of the plan plus amounts necessary to amortize in equal installments any unfunded past service liabilities, any experience gains or losses, any waived funding deficiencies, any changes in actuarial assumptions, an amount for certain unpredictable events, and other items.[3] The amortization period for past service liabilities is generally 30 years, and for experience gains or losses and funding deficiencies 5 years. For changes in actuarial assumptions, the amortization period is 10 years. For plan years beginning in 1992, the contribution must be made through quarterly payments, but for plan years beginning prior to that date, there are phase-in requirements. Employers and their corporate affiliates that do not make the necessary contribution are subject to an excise tax on the unpaid amount. The IRS can grant waivers of the minimum funding contribution in limited circumstances of employer business hardship. A company cannot obtain more than three waivers in any 15 consecutive years.

Accelerated contributions are required for certain underfunded plans (other than those with fewer than 100 participants and multiemployer plans).

The funding rules for multiemployer plans are somewhat different from those for single-employer plans. For example, multiemployer plans may amortize experience gains and losses over 15 years (rather than 5 years), and contributions to cover their required minimum funding do not have to be made in quarterly installments. Special funding rules for multiemployer plans that encounter financial difficulty were enacted in 1980 and, accordingly, are not subject to the special accelerated contribution rules noted above. (See chapter 6.)

There are also *maximum* funding limits on tax-deductible contributions. For defined contribution plans other than profit-sharing plans, the amount deductible may not exceed the limit on annual additions to the plan. (For further explanation, see chapter 4.) For profit-sharing

---

target benefit plan is a cross between a defined benefit plan and a money purchase plan, with a defined retirement benefit as in a defined benefit plan but with contributions allocated similarly to a money purchase plan. An employee stock ownership plan must be invested primarily in employer stock.

[3] The normal cost equals the cost of pension benefits earned that year and administrative costs. Past service liabilities occur when credit for an employee's past service prior to the inception of the plan is granted. Experience gains or losses result from changes in actuarial assumptions or methods.

plans, the maximum annual limit for deduction purposes is 15 percent of compensation.

For defined benefit plans, the maximum is normal cost plus 10-year amortization of unfunded past service liabilities, up to the "full-funding" limit. The full-funding limit is essentially the lesser of roughly 100 percent of projected benefits (100 percent of benefits based on projected salary increases) or 150 percent of the plan's current liability, which essentially is all existing liabilities to employees and beneficiaries, except for benefits contingent on certain unpredictable events. A deduction is always allowed for a single-employer plan to make a contribution up to the level of its unfunded current liabilities if it has at least 100 participants.

There is a 10 percent excise tax on nondeductible employer contributions. In practice, employers generally contribute no more than they can currently deduct.

Contributions and Benefits—ERISA also set maximum limits on annual contributions and benefits that qualified retirement plans may provide for each participant. The limits are known as "section 415" limits, referring to the Internal Revenue Code section that defines them. There are separate limits for defined benefit and defined contribution plans. (See chapter 4 for a description.)

Plan Termination Insurance

Title IV of ERISA established a federal agency, the Pension Benefit Guaranty Corporation, to insure payment of certain pension plan benefits in the event a covered (that is, private-sector defined benefit) plan terminates with insufficient funds to pay the benefits. Covered plans or their sponsors must pay annual premiums to PBGC to provide funds from which guaranteed benefits can be paid. Both single-employer and multiemployer plans are covered under Title IV, but under separate insurance programs. Coverage is mandatory if the employer is in interstate commerce or the plan is qualified for tax-favored status. Certain plans are exempt, including defined contribution plans, government and church plans, plans established by fraternal societies to which no employer contributions are made, and plans established and maintained by a professional service employer with 25 or fewer participants in the plan.

ERISA set the premium for single-employer plans at $1 per plan participant per year. The rate, which must be legislated by Congress, has subsequently been increased a number of times. The Omnibus Budget Reconciliation Act of 1987 (OBRA '87) not only increased the premium but significantly changed the premium structure for single-employer pension plans. Certain provisions of OBRA '87, also known as the Pension Protection Act, raised the base premium to $16 per participant. In addition, for plans with more than 100 participants, a variable-rate premium of $6 is imposed for each $1,000 of unfunded vested benefits, rising to a maximum total premium of $50 per participant per year.

Multiemployer premium rates, originally set at $.50 per plan participant per year, were raised by the 1980 Multiemployer Pension Plan Amendments Act (MPPAA) to $1.40 with scheduled increases reaching $2.60 in 1989. PBGC could have accelerated the move to $2.60 to protect the multiemployer program's financial soundness but found that was not needed and thus to date has not asked Congress for an increase beyond the $2.60 rate.

Termination Policy—Voluntary terminations of single-employer plans are restricted to two cases: a "standard" termination and a "distress" termination. (PBGC may, at its discretion, force a termination in certain situations. This is known as an involuntary termination.) A standard termination is permitted only if the plan has sufficient assets to pay all of the plan's benefit liabilities. These include all accrued basic benefits, including those that were not vested at the time of termination, and could include other benefits as well. The term "benefit liabilities" is to be defined by IRS, although it is a key element in PBGC's program.

Underfunded plans may only terminate in a distress situation, which is allowed only if the entire corporate (controlled) group would not be able to pay its debts pursuant to a plan of reorganization without the termination or would be unable to continue business outside the chapter 11 reorganization process. A distress termination is only possible with the approval of the bankruptcy court or PBGC.

For multiemployer plans, which cover the workers of two or more unrelated companies under a collective bargaining agreement, PBGC provided insurance coverage on a discretionary, plan-by-plan basis to participants of terminating plans until 1980, when MPPAA established an automatic benefit guarantee for all terminating covered multiemployer plans.[4]

---

[4]Under ERISA's 1974 provisions, certain plans that were maintained by "more than one employer" were treated as single-employer plans. MPPAA allowed these plans to irrevocably elect—within one year of MPPAA enactment—to remain classified as single-employer plans.

Covered Plans and Benefits—PBGC guarantees certain nonforfeitable retirement benefits, and any death, survivor, or disability benefit either owed or in payment status at plan termination, under defined benefit plans covered by Title IV should such a plan terminate. Benefit guarantees are expressed in terms of life annuities, which are regular payments beginning at age 65 and made over the life of the beneficiary.

There are certain restrictions on the monthly benefit amount PBGC will pay. In general, payment of guaranteed benefits is limited to a maximum dollar amount that is adjusted annually to reflect increases in workers' wages. The maximum monthly benefit in 1990 is $2,164.77. The limit applies to a participant's total guaranteed benefit under all plans in which he or she is covered; it is not possible to receive separate insurance protection under several plans and, thus, to increase the *total* guaranteed benefit.

Insurance on new benefit provisions (i.e., benefits resulting from newly established plans or recent plan amendments) is phased in at 20 percent per year (or $20 per month if higher). Therefore, *full* insurance coverage may not apply to some benefits until they have been in effect for five years prior to plan termination. The guarantee pertains exclusively to benefits earned while the plan is qualified for favorable tax treatment. Additionally, benefits are guaranteed up to the stipulated maximum.

For multiemployer plans, MPPAA established a level of guaranteed benefits that is much lower than single-employer plan benefit guarantees. *No* portion of a multiemployer plan benefit is guaranteed until it has been in effect for five years; the maximum amount guaranteed per year of service is 100 percent of the first $5 in monthly benefit rate plus 75 percent of the lesser of the next $15 of the accrual rate in excess of $5 (that is, a maximum of $20 per month for each year of service, or $600 per month for a 30 year employee). For a multiemployer plan the guarantee only applies at the point of plan insolvency.

Employer Liability to PBGC—If a plan terminates in a distress situation with insufficient assets to meet all benefit liabilities, the contributing plan sponsor and each member of the controlled group are jointly and severally liable to PBGC for the total amount of unfunded liabilities plus interest on such liabilities from the termination date.

Different rules apply for multiemployer plans. MPPAA imposes liability upon an employer for *withdrawal* from a multiemployer plan even if the plan is not terminated. *Withdrawal liability* is a legal obligation requiring an employer that discontinues or sharply reduces its contributions to a multiemployer plan to pay for its share of the plan's unfunded vested benefits. The employer must continue to make annual payments for 20 years or until the liability is satisfied, whichever occurs first.

Under MPPAA, *full withdrawal* occurs when an employer's contribution obligation to a plan permanently ceases, or if all of an employer's covered operations under a plan permanently cease. *Partial withdrawal* occurs when there is a gradual reduction in an employer's contribution base (i.e., if there is a 70 percent decline in the number of contribution units—for example, hours worked) continuing for three years. Partial withdrawal also results when an employer is no longer obligated to contribute under one of two or more collective bargaining agreements even though work continues that previously required contributions, or because one or more (but not all) of an employer's facilities withdraws from a plan even though work continues at the withdrawing facility. PBGC assumes liability only when the entire plan is in financial difficulty. Thus, for multiemployer plans, plan insolvency, rather than plan termination, is the insured event. Plan trustees are responsible for identifying withdrawing employers, calculating the amount of the withdrawal liability, and collecting this liability.

Multiemployer plan trustees can adopt one of four methods set forth by PBGC for computing the employer's share of the unfunded vested benefits or develop their own computation method subject to PBGC approval. If plans do not choose a method, MPPAA requires that they use a *presumptive rule*. This rule may be more complicated and more costly than some of the other calculation rules. Plan trustees, therefore, should carefully evaluate each of the withdrawal liability calculation methods to decide which is most practical for their individual circumstances.

Some limited exemptions from withdrawal liability apply to the building, construction, entertainment, trucking, moving, and warehousing industries. A *de minimis* rule also applies. Under this rule, withdrawal liability is waived for an employer whose share is less than $50,000 or 0.75 percent of the plan's total unfunded liability, whichever is smaller, and reduced if the allocated liability is larger (up to $150,000).

Conclusion

Since ERISA became law, thousands of plans have been amended to comply with its requirements. As areas that were initially overlooked or treated inadequately have been identified, the law has been amended. More changes can be anticipated.

Bibliography

Allen, Everett T., Joseph J. Melone, Jerry S. Rosenbloom, and Jack L. VanDerhei. *Pension Planning*. Homewood, IL: Richard D. Irwin, Inc., 1988.

Pension Benefit Guaranty Corporation. *A Legislative History of Public Law 45-214, 95th Congress*. Washington, DC: Pension Benefit Guaranty Corporation, Office of General Counsel Library, 1978.

_____. *Your Pension*. Washington, DC: Pension Benefit Guaranty Corporation, 1988.

_____. *Employer's Pension Guide*. Washington, DC: Pension Benefit Guaranty Corporation, n.d.

Pension Rights Center. National Pension Assistance Project. *A Guide to Understanding Your Pension Plan*. Washington, DC: American Association of Retired Persons, 1989.

Simone, Joseph R., and Fred R. Green. *The Pension Answer Book*. Greenvale, NY: Panel Publishers, 1990.

Additional Information

U.S. Department of Labor
Pension and Welfare Benefits Administration
Division of Technical Assistance and Inquiries
200 Constitution Avenue, NW
Washington, DC 20210
(202) 523-8776

4. Pension Plans

Introduction

The first pension plan in the United States was established in 1759 to benefit widows and children of Presbyterian ministers. But it was more than a century later, in 1875, before the American Express Company established a formal corporate plan (Allen et al., 1988). During the next century, some 400 plans were established, primarily in the railroad, banking, and public utility industries. The most significant growth has occurred since the mid 1940s. Today, private pension plans number more than 850,000 and cover more than 44 million workers (Piacentini and Cerino, 1990).

The statutory tax treatment of pensions was formally legislated through the Revenue Act of 1921, which exempted interest income of stock bonus and profit-sharing plans from current taxation and deferred tax to employees until distribution. Statutes enacted since 1921 have permitted employers to deduct a "reasonable" amount in excess of the amount necessary to fund current pension liabilities (1928); made pension trusts irrevocable (1938); and established non-discriminatory eligibility rules for pension coverage, contributions, and benefits (1942). These provisions were incorporated into the Internal Revenue Code (IRC) of 1954 and, along with major modifications made by the Tax Reform Act of 1986 (TRA '86), constitute the basic rules governing the tax qualification of pension plans.[1]

The tax treatment accorded *qualified* plans provides incentives both for employers to establish such plans and for employees to participate in them. In general, a contribution to a qualified plan is immediately deductible in computing the employer's taxes but only becomes taxable to the employee on subsequent distribution from the plan. In the interim, investment earnings on the contributions are not subject to tax. This preferential tax treatment is contingent on the employer's compliance with rules set out in the Employee Retirement Income Security Act of 1974 (ERISA) and administered by the departments of Treasury (under the IRC) and Labor (under ERISA).

---

[1]For a list and description of laws governing the tax treatment of pensions, see Piacentini and Cerino, 1990.

Plans not meeting ERISA qualification requirements may also be used to provide retirement income. "Nonqualified" plans are generally governed by trust law rather than the tax code.[2]

Types of Plans

Defined Benefit Plans—In a defined benefit plan, the employer agrees to provide the employee a nominal benefit amount at retirement based on a specified formula. The formula is usually one of three general types: a flat-benefit formula, a career-average formula, or a final-pay formula.

- *Flat-Benefit Formulas*—These formulas pay a flat dollar amount for each year of service recognized under the plan.

- *Career-Average Formulas*—There are two types of career-average formulas. Under the first type, participants earn a percentage of the pay recognized for plan purposes in each year they are plan participants. The second type of career-average formula averages the participant's yearly earnings over the period of plan participation. At retirement, the benefit equals a percentage of the career-average pay, multiplied by the participant's number of years of service.

- *Final-Pay Formulas*—These plans base benefits on average earnings during a specified number of years at the end of a participant's career; this is presumably the time when earnings are highest. The benefit equals a percentage of the participant's final average earnings, multiplied by number of years of service. This formula provides the greatest inflation protection to the participant but can represent a higher cost to the employer.

Flat-benefit formulas are common in collectively bargained plans or plans covering hourly paid employees. Career-average and final-pay formulas are most common in plans covering nonunion employees.

Under pay-related formulas, an employer has some discretion in defining *pay* for plan purposes provided the definition does not discriminate in favor of highly compensated employees, subject to the statutory and regulatory definition of compensation used in testing for nondiscrimination. Under ERISA's minimum standards, there is also some leeway in determining what employment period will be recognized in the benefit formula. The benefit may reflect only the plan participation period or may be based on the entire employment period.

---

[2]The discussion in this chapter focuses on qualified plan rules. For a good review of nonqualified plans, see Rosenbloom, 1988, chapter 33.

Defined Contribution Plans—In a defined contribution plan, the employer makes specified contributions to an account established for each participating employee. The final retirement benefit reflects the total of employer contributions, any employee contributions, and investment gains or losses. Sometimes the accumulated amount includes forfeitures resulting from employer contributions forfeited by employees who leave before becoming vested. As a result, the level of future retirement benefits cannot be calculated exactly in advance.

Employer contributions to defined contribution plans are based on a specific formula such as a percentage of participant salary or of company profits. The plans may be designed to include pretax or after-tax employee contributions, which may be voluntary or mandatory. There are several types of defined contribution plans. In a money purchase plan employer contributions are mandatory and are usually stated as a percentage of employee salary. In a profit-sharing plan total contributions to be distributed are derived from a portion of company profits. Stock bonus plans are similar to profit-sharing plans but usually make contributions and benefit payments in the form of company stock. A target benefit plan is a cross between a defined benefit plan and a money purchase plan—with a specified benefit, as in a defined benefit plan, but with contributions allocated to accounts, as in a money purchase plan. A thrift, or savings, plan is essentially an employee savings account, often with employer matching contributions. In a 401(k) arrangement, an employee can elect to contribute, on a pretax basis, a portion of current compensation to an individual account, thus deferring current income tax on the contribution. In an employee stock ownership plan, or ESOP, employer contributions to employee accounts must be primarily in company stock.

Contributions and Benefits

Individual Participant Limits—ERISA originally set limits on the contribution and/or benefit amounts that retirement plans could provide to individual participants on a tax-deductible basis under section 415 of the code. Under defined benefit plans, the original maximum annual benefit at age 65 was set at the lesser of $75,000 per year or 100 percent of the participant's average compensation over the three consecutive highest earning years. Under defined contribution plans, the maximum annual contribution (including a portion of employee contributions) was originally limited to the lesser of $25,000 or 25 percent of compensation.

Before 1983, the maximum limits were adjusted annually to reflect increases in the cost of living. The Tax Equity and Fiscal Responsibility Act of 1982 (TEFRA) imposed new benefit and contribution limits beginning in 1983 and froze them at these levels until 1985. The Deficit Reduction Act of 1984 extended the freeze on cost-of-living adjustments until 1988. TRA '86 made further changes, setting the dollar annual benefit limit under a defined benefit plan to $90,000, adjusted annually for changes in the consumer price index. (The 1990 limit is $102,582.) The annual dollar contribution limit for defined contribution plans was set at $30,000. This limit remains unchanged until the defined benefit limit reaches $120,000; the 4 to 1 ratio will thereafter be maintained. A special limit applies to participants covered by a defined benefit and a defined contribution plan maintained by the same employer.[3]

Employee Contributions—Both pretax and aftertax employee contributions are included in computing the above limits. Furthermore, each of these has its own separate limits. Employee pretax contributions are limited to $7,979 in 1990 (adjusted annually for inflation) for 401(k) arrangements and to $9,500 under a 403(b) tax-deferred annuity. After-tax contributions in practice may be limited by non-discrimination rules under section 401(m). (See chapter 9 for a description.)

There is an overall limit of $200,000 on annual compensation that can be considered for calculating benefit and contribution limits. This, too, is adjusted for changes in the cost of living beginning in 1990. The limit for 1990 is $209,200.

Top-Heavy Plans—TEFRA established a new category of plans known as "top-heavy" plans. A plan is top heavy if more than 60 percent of the accounts or accrued benefits under the plan are attributable to "key" employees. A key employee is defined as: an officer with annual compensation in excess of 50 percent of the annual defined benefit annual limit; 1 of the 10 employees owning the largest shares of the employer who have compensation in excess of the annual defined contribution limit; a 5 percent owner of the employer; or a 1 percent owner of the employer whose compensation exceeds $150,000.

A top-heavy plan must satisfy special requirements for vesting and for contributions and benefits. The required vesting schedules for a top-heavy plan are accelerated to three year cliff and six year graded (compared with five year cliff and seven year graded for non-top-heavy plans). Top-heavy plans must also provide a minimum benefit

---

[3]See Allen et al., 1988, for an explanation of the formula.

(for defined benefit plans) or a minimum contribution (for defined contribution plans) to nonkey employees.

Under a top-heavy defined benefit plan, the annual retirement benefit of a nonkey employee must not be less than his or her average compensation multiplied by the lesser of 2 percent × the number of years of service or 20 percent.

Under a top-heavy defined contribution plan, the employer's contribution for each nonkey employee must not be less than 3 percent of compensation. However, if the highest contribution percentage rate for a key employee is less than 3 percent of compensation, the 3 percent minimum contribution rate is reduced to the rate that applies to the key employee.

Plan Qualification Rules

Pension plans must satisfy a variety of rules to qualify for tax-favored treatment. These rules, created under ERISA and discussed in chapter 3, are designed to protect employee rights and to guarantee that pension benefits will be available for employees at retirement. The rules govern requirements for reporting and disclosure of plan information, fiduciary responsibilities, employee eligibility for plan participation, vesting of benefits, form of benefit payment, and funding. In addition, qualified plans must satisfy a set of nondiscrimination rules (under IRC sections 401(a)(4), 410(b), and in some cases 401(a)(26)) designed to insure that a plan does not discriminate in favor of "highly compensated" employees.

The nondiscrimination rules are satisfied through a series of complex rules that must be examined annually to ensure that the classification of employees who are eligible for participation (that is, covered) is nondiscriminatory and the proportion of eligible employees who actually participate in a plan is nondiscriminatory. In addition, the level of contributions and benefits under the plan(s) are tested to ensure that they do not disproportionately accrue to the highly compensated.

A highly compensated employee is defined as an employee who, during the current or preceding year: (1) owned more than 5 percent of the company; (2) earned more than $75,000 (indexed); (3) earned more than $50,000 (indexed) and was a member of the "top paid" group of employees; or (4) was an officer who earned more than one-half of the defined benefit limit for that year.

The 1990 dollar limits for the above are $85,485 for (2), $56,990 for (3), and $51,291 ($102,582/2) for (4). The top-paid group includes all employees whose compensation for the year is in the top 20 percent of the work force. Certain employees may be excluded in calculating the number in the top-paid group: employees who have not completed six months of service; employees who normally work less than 17½ hours per week; employees who normally work less than six months in a year; employees under age 21; nonresident aliens with no U.S. income; and union employees, if 90 percent or more of the employees are union and the plan being tested covers only nonunion employees. These tests are described in detail in chapter 17.

Types of Distributions and Tax Treatment

Pension plans generally offer retiring participants a choice between two payment options: an annuity, in which the benefit is paid out in a stream of regular payments, usually monthly and usually over the life of the participant (or lives of the participant and spouse), but sometimes over some other specified period; or in a lump sum. The type of distribution and when it is taken determines the tax treatment.

Distributions in the Form of an Annuity—Benefits from a qualified plan payable in the form of an annuity are only included in the employee's income as payments are received. A portion of any employee contribution to the plan is considered a return of the contribution and therefore is not taxable. This portion is derived using a formula that relates the amount of the participant's after-tax contribution, known as the "investment in the contract," or "basis," with the "expected return" to the participant (which is based on standard life expectancy tables). The ratio of the basis to the expected return is multiplied by the annual annuity payment provided under the plan to derive the nontaxable portion of the annuity. An employee may not exclude from taxation amounts exceeding his or her total contribution to the plan. Thus, once the total amounts excluded from taxation equal the employee's basis, any remaining payments are taxable.

Lump-Sum Distributions—A lump sum is commonly offered in defined contribution plans as an alternative payment option for distributions at retirement, death, or disability. For distributions for other reasons, a lump sum may be the only option. However, if the benefit amount exceeds $3,500, the employer may not "cash out" the benefit unilaterally.

A lump-sum distribution may be entitled to special tax treatment if it is a distribution of an employee's total accrued benefit from all plans paid within a single tax year and made on the occasion of the employee's death, attainment of age 59½, or separation from the employer's service (separate treatment applies to money purchase plans). Self-employed individuals may receive lump-sum distribution treatment only in the case of death, disability, or the attainment of age 59½. A distribution of an annuity contract from a trust or an annuity plan may be treated as a lump-sum distribution. The distribution must occur within one year of the qualified event.

TRA '86 substantially changed the tax treatment of lump-sum distributions. Under prior law, which is still applicable to certain individuals covered by a transition rule, favorable capital gains treatment and 10 year forward income averaging applied. Amounts distributed as lump sums from qualified plans were separated into pre-1974 amounts and post-1973 amounts. This computation was made by multiplying the amount distributed by a fraction: the numerator was the number of months of active participation in the plan before January 1, 1974, and the denominator was the total number of months of active participation. The resulting sum was deemed the pre-1974 portion and, in the absence of the election described below, was taxed as a long-term capital gain. Such treatment may have been favorable to the taxpayer because only 40 percent of such capital gain was subject to tax. The balance of the lump-sum distribution was deemed the post-1973 portion and was treated as ordinary income.

An employee participating in the plan for 5 or more years prior to distribution could elect to use a special 10 year forward income averaging method to compute the amount of tax on the post-1973 amount. Under this special income averaging rule, a separate tax was computed at ordinary income rates assuming single status on one-tenth of the post-1973 amount (less a minimum distribution allowance), and the resulting figure was multiplied by 10. Because of the progressive income tax rates and the fact that this tax was computed separately from the taxpayer's other income, the 10 year forward income averaging rule could result in substantial tax savings.

A separate election could be made to treat all pre-1974 amounts as ordinary income eligible for 10 year forward income averaging. Such an election could be advantageous since, depending on the amount of the distribution, 10 year forward income averaging might have produced a lower tax on the pre-1974 amount than would capital gains treatment. The election was irrevocable and applied to all subsequent lump-sum distributions received by the taxpayer.

TRA '86 phases out capital gains treatment for lump-sum distributions over 6 years beginning January 1, 1987, and eliminates 10 year forward averaging for taxable years beginning after December

31, 1986. Instead, it permits a one-time election of 5 year forward averaging for a lump-sum distribution received after age 59½. Under a transition rule, a participant who attained age 50 by January 1, 1986, is permitted to make one election of 5 year forward averaging or 10 year forward averaging (at 1986 tax rates) with respect to a single lump-sum distribution without regard to attainment of age 59½ and to retain the capital gains character of the pre-1974 portion of such a distribution. Under the transition rule, the pre-1974 capital gains portion would be taxed at a rate of 20 percent.

Distributions from some tax-favored retirement plans are not eligible for lump-sum treatment. Consult the chapters on other types of pension plans for more information.

Distributions for Special Events—Most pension plans pay benefits when events other than normal retirement or separation from service occur. Most of the benefit distributions are not mandatory. The amount of such benefits is usually based on the participant's accrued benefit at the time of the event.

- *Early Retirement*—Early retirement benefits are generally payable when a participant satisfies certain age and/or age and service requirements. The early retirement benefit is usually the accrued benefit reduced to reflect a participant's increased duration of benefit receipt. Sometimes, to encourage early retirement, subsidized early retirement benefits are paid until the participant is eligible for Social Security retirement benefits. This type of benefit may be limited to participants with long service or to those who are retiring because of a plant shutdown or staff reduction.

  The maximum benefit payable from a defined benefit plan under section 415 must be actuarially reduced for retirees who claim benefits before the Social Security normal retirement age, which is currently 65 but scheduled to rise gradually to age 67 beginning in the year 2000.

- *Disability Benefits*—Plans generally pay full benefits upon disability. Disability benefits may be tied to age and/or age and service requirements and are usually contingent on satisfying the plan's definition of disability. The definition of disability for plan purposes may be linked to the definition of disability under Social Security (see chapter 2).

  The benefit may be a flat-dollar amount that continues until the participant's normal retirement date (assuming he or she remains disabled); then, at the normal retirement date, the normal retirement benefit would become payable. Or, the plan may pay the participant the unreduced, accrued benefit during the period before he or she reaches normal retirement age. Under yet a different method, the plan may reduce the participant's accrued benefit to reflect that benefits are paid before normal retirement. In some plans, disabled participants continue to accrue benefits from the time they become disabled through their normal retirement age. Where an employer also provides a long-term disability

(LTD) plan, the pension plan benefit is usually postponed until the LTD benefit stops to avoid duplicate payments (see chapter 29).

- *Late Retirement Benefits*—Most pension plans specify age 65 as the normal retirement age for plan participants, but employers may not force employees to retire because of age. These plans must reflect how benefits will be calculated for participants who remain employed beyond age 65. As a result of recent statutory and legal decisions, a plan must now recognize earnings and/or service after age 65 for pension contribution and benefit purposes.

- *Death Benefits before Retirement*—Most plans must provide a preretirement survivor benefit to the spouse of a vested participant who dies before retirement The benefit is payable in the form of an annuity for the life of the surviving spouse, beginning at what would have been the employee's earliest retirement date, or death, whichever is later. The annuity must be equal to at least one-half of the participant's accrued benefit at the time of his or her death. To reflect the cost of providing survivor protection, the law permits employers to provide a lower benefit to the participant. Written spousal consent is needed to elect out of the coverage. A preretirement survivor annuity need not be provided unless the participant has been married at least one year and is at least 35 years of age.

- *Death Benefits after Retirement*—Retirement benefits must be paid to married persons as a joint and survivor (J&S) annuity (if an annuity is a payment option). This provides the surviving spouse with monthly income equal to at least one-half the amount of the participant's benefit. To reflect the cost of the survivor protection, the participant's benefit is usually reduced. Both the participant and the spouse must give written consent to waive the J&S annuity, either to select a pension paid over the duration of the participant's life only or to elect that pension payments be paid to a nonspouse or be paid over a specified period. The J&S need not be provided unless the participant has been married at least one year and is at least 35 years of age.

  Typically, any participant contributions (exceeding employer contributions) are refunded to a beneficiary if a participant dies before receiving his or her benefits.

- *Estate Benefits*—At one time, all but the portion of pension benefit attributable to employer money was free of estate tax, subject to certain limits on contributions and other rules. Under current law, however, pension plan payments are included in a decedent's gross estate and taxed accordingly, subject to regular estate tax deductions (including one for the spouse).

- *Premature (Early) Distributions*—A 10 percent penalty tax is imposed on most pension plan distributions paid to individuals prior to age 59½. (Before TRA '86, it only applied to distributions from individual retirement accounts and simplified employee pensions.) The penalty is designed to discourage the use of these funds prior to retirement. Distributions under certain conditions are exempt from the tax, including amounts rolled over to an IRA or other qualified plan, as are most distributions in the form of an annuity. Payments made upon the participant's death or disability, made after the participant has separated from service on or after age 55, used for medical expenses to the extent deductible for federal income tax purposes (section 213), or made to or on behalf of an alternate payee pursuant to a qualified domestic relations order are also exempt from the penalty tax.

- *Loans*—The availability of loans to participants is an exception to ERISA's general principle that transactions between a plan and parties in interest—such as participants—are prohibited because of potential abuse of funds earmarked for retirement. Plan loans are generally not treated as taxable distributions and are restricted to limited circumstances defined under IRC section 72 and section 408(b)(1) of ERISA. (The regulations promulgated on the latter were released in July 1989 and include some provisions that involve subjective determinations. Readers should consult the actual regulations for complete guidance.)

  A plan loan must be described in writing. The amount of a new loan plus the outstanding balance of any other plan loans cannot exceed the lesser of (a) $50,000 or (b) the greater of one-half of the present value of the employee's nonforfeitable accrued benefit under the plan or $10,000. The $50,000 limit is reduced by the excess of the highest outstanding loan balance during the one year period ending on the day before the new loan is made, over the outstanding balance on the date of the loan. A plan is permitted to impose a minimum loan amount as high as $1,000.

  Loans must be repaid within five years. A longer term is available only for loans used to acquire the participant's principal residence. The loan must require substantially level amortization payments, payable at least quarterly. The interest rate must reasonably reflect rates charged on comparable loans made on a commercial basis. The deductibility of interest on plan loans follows general income tax rules, except that interest on loans made to a key employee or attributable to elective deferrals under a 401(k) arrangement or tax-deferred annuity is not deductible. Interest paid to the plan also does not increase the individual's basis in the plan or tax-deferred annuity. Loans to owner-employees from Keogh plans continue to be prohibited transactions.

  The loan must be "adequately secured," so that in the event of a default, the participant's retirement income is preserved and loss to the plan is prevented. Up to 50 percent of a participant's vested accrued benefit may be loaned without additional security being required.

- *Rollovers*—In general, lump-sum distributions from a qualified pension plan may be rolled over tax free into an individual retirement account (IRA) or another retirement plan. The transfer must be made within 60 days of the participant's receipt of the distribution from the first plan. A partial distribution from a qualified plan may be rolled over to an IRA if the distribution is at least 50 percent of the participant's account balance or accrued benefit and only if the distribution is made because of separation from service or the death or disability of the covered employee. If an amount otherwise eligible for the special lump-sum tax treatment discussed above is rolled over into an IRA, the special tax treatment is not available on subsequent distribution from the IRA.

Timing of Distributions—Distributions of qualified plan balances must begin by April 1 of the year following the year in which the individual attains age 70½. A minimum distribution is required to be paid out each year, loosely equal to the value of the individual's account divided by the individual's life expectancy, if the form of benefit payment is a lump sum. If the form of benefit is an annuity, the required distribution is the amount of annual annuity payment. A 50 percent nondeductible excise tax is imposed on the individual in any taxable year on the difference between the amount required to be distributed and the amount actually distributed.

There is also a limit on the total annual amount that an individual may receive in retirement plan distributions. If total withdrawals in one year from all retirement plans (including IRAs) exceed the greater of 125 percent of the defined benefit plan limit for that year or $150,000, a 15 percent excise tax is imposed on the excess. (The defined benefit limit in 1990 is $102,582.)

A separate limit is used for any distribution that includes a lump-sum distribution in which forward averaging or capital gains treatment is elected. In this case, the lump-sum distribution is treated separately from the other distributions and is subject to a limit that is five times greater than the applicable limit for the year. Thus, in 1990, the limit is equal to the greater of $750,000 or $641,140. A special rule allows a portion of an individual's benefit accrued before August 1, 1986, to be "grandfathered"—that is, exempt from the tax.

Integration

Social Security benefits replace a greater proportion of preretirement earnings for lower-paid employees than for higher-paid employees. This is caused by two factors. Social Security taxes and benefits are based on earnings up to the taxable wage base, rather than on all earnings. In addition, the Social Security benefit formula produces higher benefits—relative to earnings—for lower-paid employees. Pension plan benefits can be coordinated with Social Security benefits to reflect the tilt in Social Security's benefit formula. Thus, to help compensate for Social Security's benefit tilt, employers are permitted to provide proportionately higher pension benefits to higher-paid employees than to lower-paid employees. This benefit coordination is known as integration. See chapter 16 for a full discussion.

Plan Termination

Although pension plans must be established with the intent that they will be permanent, employers are permitted to terminate their plans. If a defined benefit plan terminates with assets greater than the amount necessary to pay required benefits, the employer may "recover" the excess assets and use them for business or other purposes. A 15 percent excise tax is imposed on the amount recovered.

ERISA established plan termination insurance to protect participants' benefits in the event a plan terminates with insufficient assets to pay benefits. Consult chapter 3 for a detailed discussion.

Bibliography

Allen, Everett T., Joseph J. Melone, Jerry S. Rosenbloom, and Jack L. VanDerhei. *Pension Planning*. Homewood, IL: Richard D. Irwin, Inc., 1988.

Pension Rights Center. National Pension Assistance Project. *A Guide to Understanding Your Pension Plan*. Washington, DC: American Association of Retired Persons, 1989.

Piacentini, Joseph S., and Timothy J. Cerino. *EBRI Databook on Employee Benefits*. Washington, DC: Employee Benefit Research Institute, 1990.

Rosenbloom, Jerry S. *The Handbook of Employee Benefits*, 2nd ed. Homewood, IL: Dow Jones-Irwin, 1988.

Simone, Joseph R., and Fred R. Greene. *The Pension Answer Book*, 5th ed. Greenvale, NY: Panel Publishers, Inc., 1990.

Additional Information

U.S. Department of Labor
Pension and Welfare Benefits Administration
Division of Technical Assistance
200 Constitution Avenue, NW
Washington, DC 20210-0999
(202) 523-8776
(For information on fiduciary, reporting, and disclosure requirements. Can provide free publication, *What You Should Know About the Pension Law*.)

U.S. Department of the Treasury
Internal Revenue Service
Employee Plans and Technical and Actuarial Division
1111 Constitution Avenue, NW
Washington, DC 20224
Taxpayers' Assistance Service: (202) 566-6783, 566-6784

(1:30–4 p.m. Monday–Friday)
(For information on pension plan funding, vesting requirements, and compliance with federal tax laws. Can provide free publication, *Filing Requirements for Employee Benefit Plans* (IRS/DOL/PBGC Pub. 1048).)

Pension Benefit Guaranty Corporation
Coverage and Inquiries Branch (25440)
2020 K Street, NW
Washington, DC 20006-1860
(202) 778-8800
TTY/TDD for the hearing disabled: (202) 778-8859
(For additional information on the single-employer defined benefit pension plan insurance program or defined benefit plan termination. Can provide free publications, *Your Guaranteed Pension* and *Your Pension: Things You Should Know About Your Pension Plan*.)

5. Defined Benefit and Defined Contribution Plans: Understanding the Differences

Introduction

Both defined benefit and defined contribution pension plans offer various advantages to employers and employees. The features of each are generally distinct and quite different. This chapter describes the basics of each plan type, then looks at the specific factors that make each approach different.

Defined Benefit Plans

In a defined benefit plan, each employee's future *benefit* is determined by a specific formula, and the plan provides a guaranteed level of benefits upon retirement. Usually, the promised benefit is tied to the employee's earnings, length of service, or both. For example, an employer may promise to pay each participant a benefit equal to a percentage of the employee's final five year average salary times number of years of service at retirement, or the employer may pay a flat dollar amount per year of service. A defined benefit plan is typically *not* contributory—that is, there are usually no *employee* contributions. And there are no individual accounts maintained for each employee. The employer makes regular contributions to the entire plan to fund the future benefits of each participant. The *employer* bears the risk of providing the guaranteed level of retirement benefits. In 1989, 63 percent of full-time employees of medium-sized and large establishments were covered by defined benefit plans (U.S. Department of Labor, 1990).

Defined benefit plans use several formulas for determining final retirement benefits. These include:

- *Flat-Benefit Formulas*—These formulas pay a flat-dollar amount for every year of service recognized under the plan.

- *Career-Average Formulas*—There are two types of career-average formulas. Under the first type, participants earn a percentage of the pay recognized for plan purposes in each year they are plan participants. The second type of career-average formula averages the participant's

53

yearly earnings over the period of plan participation. At retirement, the benefit equals a percentage of the career-average pay, multiplied by the participant's number of years of service.

- *Final-Pay Formulas*—These plans base benefits on average earnings during a specified number of years at the end of a participant's career (usually five years); this is presumably the time when earnings are highest. The benefit equals a percentage of the participant's final average earnings, multiplied by the number of years of service. This formula provides the greatest inflation protection to the participant but can represent a higher cost to the employer.

Defined Contribution Plans

In a defined contribution plan, employers generally promise to make annual or periodic contributions to accounts set up for each employee. (Sometimes defined contribution plans are referred to as "individual account" plans.) The *current contribution* is guaranteed but not a level of benefits at retirement, as in a defined benefit plan. In 1989, 48 percent of full-time employees in medium-sized and large establishments participated in one or more defined contribution plans, up from 45 percent in 1988 (U.S. Department of Labor, 1990).

The contribution to a defined contribution plan may be stated as a percentage of the employee's salary and/or may be related to years of service. Sometimes there are only employer contributions, sometimes only employee contributions, and sometimes both. The benefit payable at retirement is based on money accumulated in each employee's account. The accumulated money will reflect employer contributions, employee contributions (if any), and investment gains or losses. The accumulated amount may also include employer contributions forfeited by employees who leave before they become fully vested, to the extent such contributions are reallocated to the accounts of employees who remain. These are called forfeitures.

There are several types of defined contribution plans, including money purchase plans, profit-sharing plans, 401(k) arrangements, savings plans, and employee stock ownership plans. These are described briefly below. For more detail, consult individual chapters.

Savings, or Thrift, Plan—A savings, or thrift, plan is essentially an employee-funded savings plan. An employee generally makes regular contributions on an after-tax basis to an account set up in his or her name. The contributions are stated as a percentage of pay. The contributions may be matched (in full or in part) by the employer, but there is no statutory obligation for employer contributions.

Profit-Sharing Plan—A profit-sharing plan usually provides for contributions to the plan based on annual profits for the previous year.

However, profits are not required for contributions, and a company is under no obligation to make contributions on a regular basis. Contributions are typically divided among participants in proportion to their respective earnings.

Money Purchase Pension Plan—Employer contributions are mandatory in a money purchase plan. They are usually stated as a percentage of employee salary. Retirement benefits are equal to the amount in the individual account at retirement.

Employee Stock Ownership Plan—An employee stock ownership plan, or ESOP, is a tax-qualified employee benefit plan that provides shares of stock in the sponsoring company to participating employees. An ESOP is required to invest primarily in employer stock and is permitted to borrow money on a tax-favored basis to purchase this stock.

401(k) Arrangement—A qualified cash or deferred arrangement, under section 401(k) of the Internal Revenue Code (IRC), allows an employee to elect to have a portion of his or her compensation (otherwise payable in cash) contributed to a qualified profit-sharing, stock bonus, or pre-ERISA money purchase pension plan. The employee contribution is most commonly treated as a pretax reduction in salary.

An employer may adopt a defined contribution plan:

- as a step toward achieving employees' retirement income security;
- to supplement an existing defined benefit plan;
- to avoid the long-term funding and liability commitments, as well as the more burdensome regulations, of a defined benefit plan; and
- to create a program that provides benefits for short-term workers.

To illustrate the basic differences between the two approaches, the discussion in this chapter will focus on the major considerations involved in an employer's selection of a plan and the differences for employees. These include achievement of objectives, plan cost, ownership of assets and investment risk, ancillary benefit provisions, postretirement benefit increases, employee acceptance, employee benefits and length of service, plan administration, taxes, and regulations.

Achievement of Objectives

A foremost objective for many employers in adopting a retirement plan is to provide future retirement income to employees. Another is to help to maintain organizational efficiency and vitality. Sometimes a goal is to help reward long-term employees. Such goals usually require plans to be available for long periods of benefit accumulation.

A defined benefit plan can provide a meaningful retirement benefit for employees who remain with one employer throughout their career. An employee's earnings generally grow over the years, and if years of service are calculated, the longer the employee works for one employer, the greater the benefit. In addition, employees who begin employment with a new employer later in life can benefit from a defined benefit plan that is based on final average pay or career earnings.

However, for employees who change jobs frequently, especially at younger ages, a defined contribution plan offers more portability and the ability to accrue a meaningful retirement benefit. A defined contribution plan often has a shorter vesting period—that is, the period of service required before the employee becomes entitled to the benefit. Once vested, if the employee terminates service, he or she can often take the benefit, roll it over into an individual retirement account (IRA), and receive investment earnings. In a defined benefit plan, the benefit often must stay with the employer, where it accrues no interest until retirement.

Plan Cost

In adopting a defined benefit plan, an employer accepts an unknown cost commitment. Numerous factors determine the cost of promised benefits, including the rates of return on investment, the number of employees working until they become vested in a benefit, the nature of future government regulatory changes, and future employee pay levels.

The unknown cost aspect of defined benefit plans is sometimes considered a deterrent. Employers minimize the unknown cost by projecting future interest earnings, mortality rates, personnel turnover, and salary increases; thus, they attempt to establish a reasonably level funding pattern. Moreover, the plan's assets and liabilities are evaluated periodically (usually annually), and contribution adjustments can be made on a regular basis. Within legal limits, the employer is permitted to vary contributions from year to year. Therefore, defined benefit plan sponsors are permitted a certain amount of contribution flexibility.

Defined contribution plan sponsors generally know the plan's cost on a yearly basis. The employer pays a set amount—usually on a regular basis. Future costs are not an issue. This cost control feature appeals to many employers, particularly newer and smaller companies. Some funding flexibility is possible by basing employer contributions on profits, thus allowing the employer to temporarily forgo contributions during economic hardship.

Ownership of Assets and Investment Risk

The ownership of plan assets differs between defined benefit and defined contribution plans. In a defined contribution plan, contributions can be viewed as a deferred wage once an employee has become vested. The full vested value of each participant's account can be considered *owned* by the employee. Vested benefits are often distributable to employees on employment termination. Defined contribution plan sponsors may be committed only to paying a stipulated contribution each year. It is the employee who bears the investment risk. Favorable investment results will increase benefits, while unfavorable results will decrease benefits.

In a defined benefit plan, vested benefits can again be viewed as a deferred wage. It is here, however, that the difference in investment risk becomes important. Defined benefit plan sponsors assume an obligation for paying a stipulated future benefit. Consequently, the employer accepts the investment risk involved in meeting this obligation. If the pension fund established to provide promised benefits earns a lower-than-expected yield over the life of the annuity, the employer will have to make additional contributions. If the pension fund investment results are better than expected, the employer can reduce annual contributions.

Ancillary Benefit Provisions

Although retirement plans are intended first and foremost to provide retirement income, they must, under some circumstances, make some provision for paying benefits in the event of a participant's death (see chapter 4). Most plans provide early retirement and disability benefits as well. To receive ancillary benefits, employees may be required to satisfy certain eligibility requirements, although the law places limits on such requirements.

Defined contribution thrift and profit-sharing plans usually pay a vested employee's individual account balance in full upon death, employment termination, retirement, or disability. Defined benefit plans frequently distribute the vested benefit as a stream of level monthly payments for life or for some stated period beginning at the time the employee retires early, at the normal age, or later. This is called an annuity.

57

Postretirement Benefit Increases

During periods of inflation, the pensioner's financial position is brought into sharp focus. In such periods, retired employees living on fixed pensions, or on incomes derived from investing lump-sum retirement distributions, have been affected by the dollar's declining value. Automatic Social Security benefit increases have helped, but they frequently have not provided total retirement income increases comparable to inflationary increases for above-average earners.

Most employers are concerned about their retired workers' financial problems. However, few sponsors of defined benefit plans can afford the uncertainty of providing automatic cost-of-living adjustments under their plans. If resources are available, many employers are willing to voluntarily grant periodic benefit increases after retirement to help offset inflationary effects; such ad hoc adjustments generally can be made easily.

Defined contribution thrift and profit-sharing plan sponsors usually provide the option of lump-sum distributions at retirement. Money purchase pension plans may require that pension benefits be taken in the form of an annuity.

Employee Acceptance

By nature, defined benefit plans are complex. The formulas are often complicated. The legal documents explaining the plan and employee rights under the plan can be difficult to understand. Numerous government regulations have added more and more complexity to the operation of defined benefit plans, making them more difficult to understand. Sometimes, promised future benefits may seem remote to the employee, and the current dollar value of benefits is not clear.

Defined contribution plans can also be complex, but their complexity is less apparent to employees. Defined contribution plan participants have individual accounts; their accounts usually have known values expressed in dollars rather than benefit formulas. And the ability of employees to take accumulations in a lump sum at employment termination is often appealing.

Pension Benefits and Length of Service

Defined contribution plans offer distinct advantages to employees who change jobs frequently. Vesting provisions in these plans are generally more liberal than for defined benefit plans. Many defined contribution plans provide at least partial vesting of employer con-

58

tributions after two or three years of service. Employee contributions are always immediately and fully vested—as they are in defined benefit plans. Additionally, vested benefits under thrift and profit-sharing plans are normally paid in a lump sum at employment termination, but under defined benefit plans they are usually paid as an annuity.

Alternatively, defined benefit plans often have "cliff" vesting, with no vesting of contributions until employees work a certain number of years (capped by law). And defined benefit plans do not usually provide payment of vested benefits at employment termination; participants receive deferred monthly income when they retire. The benefit amount is usually frozen at termination, however, and the employee is exposed to future inflationary effects unless the benefit is indexed to reflect cost-of-living adjustments.

Defined benefit plan benefit formulas frequently anticipate late-age hirings; some are designed to provide adequate retirement benefits for employees with fewer years of service. This offers an advantage for the employee making a permanent job commitment relatively late in his or her career. Under defined contribution plans, employees hired later in life are less likely to accrue meaningful retirement benefits.

Plan Administration

Both defined benefit and defined contribution plans can be complex to administer; they usually require trained internal staffs and/or outside advisors. Defined contribution plans offer some administrative advantages over defined benefit plans. First, defined benefit plans require the use of actuarial projections that take into account the future number of employees, ages, life span, earnings, and other demographic characteristics. Defined contribution plans do not.

Second, provisions of the tax code and the Employee Retirement Income Security Act of 1974 (ERISA) tend to have less impact on defined contribution plans than on defined benefit plans. For example:

- Defined benefit plans must satisfy both minimum and maximum funding standards. (For more information on funding standards, see chapter 3.) Generally, defined contribution plans do not have to satisfy these standards.
- Most defined benefit plans must calculate and pay insurance premiums to the Pension Benefit Guaranty Corporation (PBGC) to protect pension benefits in the event of plan termination. Defined contribution plans are by nature fully funded; therefore, they do not present the risks of defined benefit plans and are not subject to the pension insurance program. This

also makes it administratively easier to terminate a defined contribution plan because approval by PBGC is not necessary. (For further information on PBGC premiums, see chapter 3.)

- ERISA originally set limits on the maximum benefits that could be paid from defined benefit plans and on maximum contributions to defined contribution plans. Several laws since ERISA have made changes to those benefit limits but with generally fewer and less restrictive limits on defined contribution plans. The calculation of these limits can be quite complicated.

- Defined benefit plans usually must provide more detailed and complicated actuarial disclosure reports than defined contribution plans. But, for defined contribution plans, recordkeeping can also pose complications, especially when employees are allowed different investment options or when loan and/or withdrawal provisions are provided.

Taxes

For employers, the tax impact under defined benefit and defined contribution plans is quite different. Under a defined contribution plan, employer contributions are a deductible business expense in the year they are paid to participants' accounts, subject to certain statutory limits. In a defined benefit plan, an employer must contribute a minimum amount to fund the future benefit, for which a tax deduction is also allowed. But the employer may not "overfund" the plan and has a maximum limit that cannot be surpassed without tax penalty.

For employees, the tax considerations associated with each plan are essentially the same. Employees do not pay taxes on employer contributions, investment income, or capital gains of retirement plan assets until they receive benefits.

Employees, however, have traditionally paid taxes on their own plan contributions in the year such income was earned. Most private defined benefit plans do not require employee contributions, but public-sector defined benefit plans commonly do.

Under defined benefit and defined contribution plans, benefits are subject to income taxation when received by the employee. The tax consequences depend on the form of benefit payment, not on the type of plan. Lump-sum distributions are treated the same, for example, whether paid from a defined benefit or a defined contribution plan.

If the benefit is in the form of an annuity, which is typical under defined benefit plans, ordinary income tax rates apply. (A portion of any employee contribution to the plan is considered a return of the contribution and therefore is not taxable.) The advantage here is that traditionally the employee has been in a lower income tax bracket when retired than during his or her working years, although this has become less likely under current tax laws, which provide only two major tax brackets (15 percent and 28 percent).

A distribution in the form of a lump sum may qualify for special tax treatment. Lump-sum distributions are common in defined contribution plans, especially for smaller amounts. A detailed discussion of the taxation of lump sums and annuities is found in chapter 4.

Legislation and Regulations—Since the passage of ERISA, Congress has enacted many laws that have increased the complexity and administrative burden of pension plans, especially defined benefit plans. Such laws include the Economic Recovery Tax Act of 1981 (ERTA), the Tax Equity and Fiscal Responsibility Act of 1982 (TEFRA), the Deficit Reduction Act of 1984 (DEFRA), the Retirement Equity Act of 1984 (REA), the Consolidated Omnibus Budget Reconciliation Act of 1985 (COBRA), the Tax Reform Act of 1986 (TRA '86), and the Omnibus Budget Reconciliation acts of 1986, 1987, and 1989 (OBRA '86, '87, and '89, respectively). Many observers agree that continuing legislative and regulatory change has added unnecessary complexity and uncertainty to plan sponsorship.

Conclusion

In the past, defined benefit plans were generally adopted as the primary vehicle for meeting employees' retirement income needs. More recently, due to changes in legislation, employee attitudes, and the mobility of the work force, there is more interest in defined contribution plans. Over the last 10 years, the number of defined contribution plans has grown at a much faster rate than that of defined benefit plans (Employee Benefit Research Institute, 1989).

A certain number of employers believe that the most effective retirement program combines the two types of plans, making maximum use of the particular cost and benefit advantages of each.

An employer could, for example, adopt a defined benefit plan that provides a modest level of benefits and supplement these benefits with a defined contribution thrift, profit-sharing, or 401(k) plan. The employer's cost risk under the defined benefit plan is minimized, while the two plans combine benefits to satisfy income adequacy standards.

Employers might also adopt a single plan that incorporates characteristics of both defined benefit and defined contribution plans. One type is a cash balance pension plan (discussed in chapter 14). Relatively new to the field, it is a defined benefit plan with features common to defined contribution plans. Another type is a target benefit plan, which is a defined contribution plan that has defined benefit plan features.

Defined benefit and defined contribution plans have distinctly different features that offer various advantages and disadvantages for both employers and employees. A close examination of all these features is important for employers in deciding whether to adopt a plan and for employees in understanding the plan in which they participate.

Bibliography

Allen, Everett T., Jr., Joseph J. Melone, Jerry S. Rosenbloom, and Jack L. VanDerhei. *Pension Planning.* Homewood, IL: Richard D. Irwin, Inc., 1988.

Andrews, Emily S. *Pension Policy and Small Employers: At What Price Coverage?* Washington, DC: Employee Benefit Research Institute, 1989.

Employee Benefit Research Institute. *What Is the Future for Defined Benefit Pension Plans?* Washington, DC: Employee Benefit Research Institute, 1989.

Pension Benefit Guaranty Corporation. *Employer's Pension Guide.* Washington, DC: Pension Benefit Guaranty Corporation, n.d.

———. *Your Pension: Things You Should Know about Your Pension Plan.* Washington, DC: Pension Benefit Guaranty Corporation, 1988.

U.S. Department of Labor. Bureau of Labor Statistics. "Employee Benefits Focus on Family Concerns in 1989." USDL news release 90-160, 30 March 1990.

6. Multiemployer Plans

Introduction

A multiemployer plan is typically an employee pension or welfare plan that covers the workers of two or more unrelated companies in accordance with a collective bargaining agreement. Contributions to support such plans are negotiated at the initiative of a labor union or a group of labor unions representing the workers of a number of companies, usually in a given geographic area. The workers are usually engaged in the same kind of employment (for example, a skilled craft such as carpentry or acting).

There are two broad types of multiemployer plans. The first, a welfare benefit plan, may provide group life insurance; disability insurance; coverage for hospitalization, surgical, and/or medical costs; prepaid legal services; vacation; or unemployment benefits. The other, a pension plan, is designed to provide retirement income benefits. The multiemployer concept can also be used to provide other benefits. Its collective approach has been used effectively in areas such as employee training.

Multiemployer plans are set up under section 302(c)(5) of the Labor-Management Relations Act of 1947, commonly known as the Taft-Hartley Act. This law requires that the plans be governed by a board of trustees made up of employer and union representatives, each having equal representation.

The first multiemployer plan was probably an employer-funded pension plan started in 1929 by Local 3 of the Brotherhood of Electrical Workers and the Electrical Contractors Association of New York City. Subsequently, certain *negotiated* plans developed in the 1930s and 1940s in industries such as the needle trades and coal mining. Multiemployer pension plans grew after World War II with the passage of Taft-Hartley and a court ruling under federal labor law that established benefits as a mandatory subject of collective bargaining. By 1950, multiemployer pension plans covered 1 million workers. Participation under these plans rose to 3.3 million workers in 1960 and to 9.7 million active workers and retirees in 1987 (Piacentini and Cerino, 1990). The U.S. Department of Labor (DOL) estimates that there are approximately 3,000 multiemployer plans (Turner and Beller, 1989). There is likely at least an equal number of multiemployer welfare plans and a growing number of multiemployer plans that provide annuity funds (individual account plans), supplementary unemployment insurance, and legal benefits.

There are also nonnegotiated multiemployer plans, which have been established by certain employers that have chosen, on their own initiative, to provide their employees with a benefit package. Nonnegotiated plans are common in the nonprofit area among religious, charitable, and educational institutions. They are categorized as "multiple-employer plans" under the Employee Retirement Income Security Act of 1974 (ERISA) and the Internal Revenue Code, and are generally subject to the same legal rules as single-employer plans.

Plan Characteristics

In a multiemployer plan, there must be at least two companies and at least two employees, but there is no maximum limit.

Most participants in multiemployer pension plans are in large defined benefit plans. DOL reports that in 1985, the latest year for which data are available, nearly 80 percent of the 6.5 million active participants were in plans with 1,000 or more participants per plan, and almost 86 percent of participants were in defined benefit plans (Turner and Beller, 1989).

Multiemployer plans are concentrated in certain industries, where there are many small companies each too small to justify an individual plan. They are also found in industries where, because of seasonal or irregular employment and high labor mobility, few workers would qualify under an individual company's plan if one were established. For example, construction workers are commonly hired by a given contractor for only a few weeks or months. When the job is completed, the worker may be unemployed until another contractor needs his or her particular skills or talent.

There is frequently more than one multiemployer plan within each large industry. Multiemployer plans may cover industry employees on a national, regional, or local basis, and some cut across several related industries (e.g., crafts or trades in one geographic area). Many plans cover a trade or craft rather than an entire industry. However, some plans that embrace whole industries or a large part of an industry include those of the American Federation of Television and Radio Artists, Communication Workers of America, International Ladies Garment Workers Union, United Paperworkers International Union, and Amalgamated Clothing Workers.

Many multiemployer plans exist in the following *manufacturing* industries, as defined by DOL: food, baked goods, and kindred products; apparel (or needle trades) and others; printing, publishing, and allied industries; finished textile products; leather and leather products; lumber and wood products; furniture and fixtures; and metalworking.

In *nonmanufacturing* industries, multiemployer plans are common in mining; construction; motor transportation; wholesale and retail trades; services; entertainment; and communication and public utilities.

The construction industry has the highest concentration of multiemployer plan participants. In 1985, 34 percent of all active multiemployer plan participants were in construction, followed by manufacturing at 14 percent (Turner and Beller, 1989).

Qualified Plan Rules

ERISA and the Internal Revenue Code set out rules that multiemployer plans, like single-employer plans, must follow to qualify for preferential tax treatment. The rules govern fiduciary responsibility, disclosure and reporting, eligibility, vesting, benefit accrual, funding, coverage and participation, integration, and plan termination.

Some of the requirements—such as those for fiduciary responsibility and disclosure and reporting—are essentially the same for both types of plans, while other requirements differ. Benefits of the union-represented participants in multiemployer pension plans are generally deemed to meet the tax code's nondiscrimination standards, but the coverage for any other employees (for example, the staff of the sponsoring union or of the fund itself) will have to meet the generally applicable nondiscrimination tests (discussed in chapter 17). Chapters 3, 16, and 17 address most of the multiemployer plan rules.

Establishing the Plan

Once a union and various companies agree to set up a multiemployer plan, the first step is usually to negotiate how much each employer will contribute to the plan. Employer and union representatives then adopt a trust agreement that establishes a board of trustees, defines the board's powers and duties, and covers the affairs of both the trustees and the pension or welfare plan. An attorney and an accountant assist in establishing a trust fund to accept company contributions. Benefit and actuarial consultants assist the trustees in working out plan details and determining a supportable benefit level.

The trustees probably will retain a professional investment advisor or portfolio manager to ensure competent asset management. The trustees may also hire a salaried plan administrator and staff or retain an outside administration firm to manage the plan and handle day-to-day details, such as the collection of employer contributions and employee claims, payments, recordkeeping, and inquiries. Finally, the trustees must adopt a formal plan document and publish a booklet in lay language informing employees of plan benefits, eligibility rules, and procedures for filing benefit claims.

Like a corporation's board of directors, a board of trustees sets overall plan policy and directs the plan's activities. Trustees are responsible for proper fund management. They may delegate certain of their duties and functions, including the management of plan funds, but they bear ultimate responsibility for all actions taken in their names. Fund management is a serious responsibility, since vast sums of money may be involved and pensions or other benefits of hundreds or thousands of people are at stake. Trustees are bound by rigid fiduciary rules of honesty and performance. They are required by both ERISA and the Taft-Hartley Act to act on behalf of plan participants as any prudent person familiar with such matters (that is, financial affairs) would act.

Contributions and Benefits

Plan contributions are normally made by the employers participating in the collective bargaining agreement. Occasionally, employees are required or permitted to make additional contributions to welfare plans (for example, during short unemployment periods). The employer's contribution amount is determined through negotiations and fixed in the bargaining agreement. It is usually based on some measure of the covered employee's work (for example, $1 for each hour worked by each employee). All the contributions are pooled in a common fund that pays for the plan benefits. Investment earnings augment the fund. A multiemployer plan by virtue of its size often can undertake certain forms of investment that are not available to a small fund or a plan established by a single company employing only a few workers.

Companies participating in the same multiemployer plan often make equal contributions. However, some large national or regional multiemployer plans provide several levels of benefits that require different levels of employer contributions. As a result of special circumstances, a company may be required to make higher contributions than other participating companies or its employees may receive lower benefits. For example, a company with a large number of older workers that brings the group into an established multiemployer pension plan might be required to make higher contributions because of the substantial past service liabilities of its older workers who are approaching retirement. However, in general, one hallmark of a multiemployer fund is the cross-subsidy among employers that usually contribute at the same rate for all their employees who are at the same benefit level regardless of their actuarial costs.

Reciprocity—Normally, pension credits cannot be transferred from one multiemployer plan to another unless the trustees of the various plans have negotiated reciprocity agreements. Under such agreements, a worker can shift from employer to employer and among different plans without losing pension credits.

About 75 percent of the workers covered by multiemployer health, welfare, and pension programs in the construction industry were covered by reciprocity agreements in 1983. Many other multiemployer plans are also industrywide. Still others are adopting reciprocity agreements at an accelerating rate as international unions continue to encourage these arrangements.

Benefits—Benefit formulas under multiemployer plans may vary: they may be a flat-dollar amount for each year of service, or they may base benefits on earnings (see chapter 4). About 75 percent of multiemployer plans (with 65 percent of multiemployer plan workers) base benefits on length of service and not on earnings level. This is partly because the range of earnings for workers covered by multiemployer plans tends to be narrower than that for workers covered by single-employer plans. Under multiemployer plans that do not base benefits on pay, the need to keep individual earnings records is eliminated; the contribution rate for all employees at a given benefit level is usually identical.

Most multiemployer plans suspend pension benefit payments to retirees in their jurisdictions who work in the same trade or industry while receiving pensions. The restriction is intended to prevent retirees from competing for jobs with active workers or practicing their skills in the nonunion sector of the industry. Under rules issued by DOL, a multiemployer plan may suspend benefits for a retiree who completes 40 or more hours of service in one month under certain circumstances, such as: in an industry where other employees covered by the plan were employed and accrued benefits under the plan, at the time benefit payments commenced or would have commenced if the retired employee had not returned to employment; in a trade or craft where the retiree was employed at any time under the plan; and in the geographic area covered by the plan at the time benefit payments commenced or would have commenced if the retired employee had not returned to employment.

Advantages of Multiemployer Plans

Multiemployer plans offer attractive portability features. Employees may carry pension credits with them as they move from company to company. Thus, they can earn pensions based on all accumulated credits, even if some of their former employers have gone out of business or stopped making plan contributions. Similarly, continuity of coverage can be assured for other benefits, such as medical insurance, when the worker switches jobs within the same industry.

Multiemployer plans may also provide an incalculable advantage to employees of small companies, who might not receive benefits if multiemployer plans did not make benefit programs more affordable for their employers.

There are several advantages for employers who participate in multiemployer plans. First, economies can be achieved through group purchasing and simplified administration. Second, benefit and labor costs throughout a region or even an industry may be stabilized. This can help reduce employee turnover, because workers will not be attracted to other jobs by the promise of better benefits elsewhere. As with all benefit plans qualified under the Internal Revenue Code, company contributions to a multiemployer plan are generally tax deductible.

Conclusion

The years of heavy multiemployer plan growth are probably over. The decline of unionized workers in many sectors is clearly one reason. Another is the general leveling off of pension plan establishment among all employers. In the future, minimal growth will likely occur in the aggregate as small numbers of new workers come under multiemployer plan protection. Certain industries, such as entertainment, where employees work irregularly, and small manufacturers, retail trade, and transportation—particularly mass transit—may experience heavier than average growth.

Bibliography

Employee Benefit Research Institute. *EBRI Quarterly Pension Investment Report*. Washington, DC: EBRI, 1986–1990.

_____. "Reciprocity and Multiemployer Plans." *Employee Benefit Notes* (February 1987): 5–7.

Martin E. Segal Company. *1989 Survey of the Funded Position of Multiemployer Plans*. New York: Martin E. Segal Company, 1989.

Turner, John A., and Daniel J. Beller, eds. U.S. Department of Labor. Pension and Welfare Benefits Administration. *Trends in Pensions*. Washington, DC: U.S. Department of Labor, 1989.

U.S. General Accounting Office. *1980 Multiemployer Pension Amendments: Overview of Effects and Issues*. HRD-86-4. Washington, DC: U.S. Government Printing Office, February 1986.

Additional Information

International Foundation of Employee Benefit Plans
P.O. Box 69
Brookfield, WI 53005
(414) 786-6700

National Coordinating Committee for Multiemployer Plans
815 16th Street, NW, Suite 603
Washington, DC 20006
(202) 347-1461

7. Profit-Sharing Plans

Introduction

A profit-sharing plan is a type of defined contribution plan that is often used as a supplement to a primary defined benefit plan. Through these plans, employees share in their companies' profits and potentially gain a greater interest in their firms' success.

About 100 years ago, Pillsbury Mills and Procter & Gamble each established a *cash* (defined below) profit-sharing plan. In 1916, Harris Trust & Savings Bank in Chicago established the first *deferred* (defined below) profit-sharing plan. In 1939, legislation clarified the tax status of deferred plans. This legislation and the World War II wage freeze resulted in rapid growth of profit-sharing plans in the 1940s. The Employee Retirement Income Security Act of 1974 (ERISA) furthered the growth by imposing less burdensome regulations on profit-sharing plans than on defined benefit pension plans, thus increasing their attractiveness.

Today, profit-sharing plans continue in popularity. The Profit Sharing Research Foundation estimates that by 1988 there were approximately 435,000 companies maintaining deferred or combination deferred and cash profit sharing and that approximately 100,000 companies were offering cash profit-sharing plans. The U.S. Department of Labor (DOL) reports that 18 percent (or 5.6 million) full-time employees in medium-sized and large private establishments participated in profit-sharing plans in 1988 (U.S. Department of Labor, 1989).

Types of Plans

There are three basic types of profit-sharing plans.

Cash Plan—At the time profits are determined, contributions are paid directly to employees in the form of cash, checks, or stock. The amount is taxed as ordinary income when distributed.

Deferred Plan—Profit-sharing contributions are not paid out currently but rather are "deferred" to individual accounts set up for each employee. Benefits—and any interest accrued—are distributed at retirement, death, disability, and sometimes at separation from service and other events. This appears to be the most popular type of profit-

71

sharing arrangement, with 78 percent of plan participants in a deferred plan, according to DOL.

Combination Plan—In this type of plan the participant has the option of deferring all or part of the profit-sharing allocation. That portion taken as a deferral is placed into the participant's account, where it and investment earnings accrue tax free until withdrawal. Any amount taken in cash is taxed currently.

For tax purposes, Internal Revenue Service (IRS) qualification of profit-sharing plans is restricted to deferred or combination plans. Therefore, the remainder of this chapter will focus primarily on these two types of profit-sharing arrangements.

Plan Qualification Rules

Profit-sharing plans, as other retirement plans, must meet a variety of requirements to qualify for preferential tax treatment. These rules, created under ERISA and discussed in chapter 3, are designed to protect employee rights and to guarantee that pension benefits will be available for employees at retirement. The rules govern requirements for reporting and disclosure of plan information, fiduciary responsibilities, employee eligibility for plan participation, vesting of benefits, form of benefit payment, and funding. In addition, qualified plans must satisfy a set of IRS nondiscrimination rules (under IRC sections 401(a)(4), 410(b), and, in some cases, 401(a)(26)) designed to insure that a plan does not discriminate in favor of highly compensated employees.

Contributions

Employer Contributions—Plans must define how employer contributions will be allocated to employee accounts. The allocation formula is generally based on compensation. Sometimes the allocation is a flat percentage of pay, or it may be determined by calculating the proportion of each employee's compensation relative to the total compensation of all plan participants. For example, if the employee earns $15,000 annually and total annual compensation for all participants is $300,000, he or she would receive 5 percent of the employer's annual contribution.

Some plans base their allocations on compensation *and* service credits. These plans must be careful to assure that the wage/service formula meets the regulatory scheme for demonstrating that the formula does not discriminate in favor of highly compensated employees. Whether a plan uses compensation or both compensation and service in determining allocations depends on an employer's objectives. If employee retention is a primary goal, this can be reflected in a pay-and-service allocation formula. Allocation formulas may be integrated with Social Security within prescribed limits. (For more information about integration, see chapter 16.)

Maximum annual contributions (employer and employee, if any) on behalf of each plan participant are limited by the defined contribution limits under section 415 of the IRC—the lesser of 25 percent of compensation or $30,000 (see chapter 4 for further details). But the total amount of contributions for all employees that an employer may *deduct* for federal tax purposes is limited to 15 percent of all covered employees' compensation. If a company has both a profit-sharing and a defined benefit pension plan covering the same employees, the combined tax-deductible contributions to both plans generally cannot exceed 25 percent of all covered employees' compensation.

Until recently, an employer's contribution to a profit-sharing plan was limited to the extent of an employer's current or accumulated profits. Currently, an employer does not have to have profits to establish a profit-sharing plan, and total contributions are not restricted to total profits. Plan documents, however, must specify that the plan is a profit-sharing plan.

If an employer's contribution for a particular year is less than the maximum amount for which a deduction is allowed, the unused limit may not be carried forward to subsequent years unless the carryforward existed as of December 31, 1986. These "limit" carryforwards may be used to increase the general deduction limit to 25 percent until the carryforwards are exhausted.

A "deduction" carryforward of contributions in excess of the deduction limit for a particular year may be deductible in succeeding taxable years to the extent allowed. Such contributions, however, may be subject to a 10 percent nondeductible excise tax. Excess contributions are defined as the sum of total amounts contributed for the taxable year over the amount allowable as a deduction for that year plus the amount of excess contributions for the preceding year, reduced by amounts returned to the employer during the year, if any, and the portion of the prior excess contribution that is deductible in the current year. In other words, if an excess contribution is made during a taxable year, the excise tax would apply for that year and for each succeeding year to the extent that the excess is not eliminated. Excess contributions for a year are determined at the close of the employer's taxable year and the tax is imposed on the employer.

Employee Contributions—Pure profit-sharing plans do not require employee contributions, but some may permit voluntary employee contributions up to certain limits. The plan then generally looks more like a thrift plan (discussed in chapter 8). Employee contributions in the form of a salary reduction are becoming increasingly popular. When pretax salary reduction is allowed, the plan must follow rules for 401(k) arrangements (discussed in chapter 9).

Taxation—Employer contributions to a profit-sharing plan are deductible by the company as a business expense (up to the limits noted above). Employees are not taxed on the deferred contributions—and any interest accrued—until distribution. Any allocation (all or part) taken in cash is taxed on a current basis.

Investments

Profit-sharing funds may be invested in a wide variety of vehicles including corporate stocks, bonds, real estate, insurance products, and mutual funds. In general, retirement plans may not hold more than 10 percent of their assets in employer securities. However, an exception exists for profit-sharing plans, stock bonus plans, thrift plans, and employee stock ownership plans, as well as money-purchase plans that were in existence before ERISA's enactment and invested primarily in employer securities at that time. Therefore, contributions are frequently invested in employer securities. This practice may give participants an increased interest in the firm's success.

Individual account assets can be held in one fund or in several funds. The plan sponsor usually has responsibility for developing broad investment policies. The trustee (for example, a bank) is usually responsible for the actual investment of plan assets. Some employers permit participants to select among several investment options. In addition, participants may be given individual direction within certain limits set forth in DOL regulations.

Distributions

Retirement, Disability, and Death Benefits—The law requires that participants' account balances fully vest at retirement. In addition, plans generally provide for benefits upon death and disability. The plan's vesting provisions determine whether an employee will receive full or partial benefits upon other types of employment termination. However, if the plan is *contributory* (that is, employees make contributions), the employee will always receive the benefits that are attributable to his or her own contributions.

Profit-sharing plans typically give retiring participants and bene-ficiaries of deceased participants a choice between a lump-sum pay-ment and installments. Usually, those who terminate employment for reasons other than retirement, death, or disability receive lump-sum distributions, although if the benefit exceeds $3,500, the partic-ipant cannot be forced to take an immediate benefit.

Distributions from profit-sharing accounts must follow the general distribution rules for all qualified retirement plans. Distributions must begin by the year following the attainment of age 70½ even if the individual has not retired. There are minimum and maximum limits on the amount of annual distribution, both subject to penalty taxes if not followed. (See chapter 4 for a complete description.)

In-Service Withdrawals—Some profit-sharing plans provide for par-tial account withdrawals during active employment. Plans allowing participants to elect account withdrawals impose certain conditions, which vary widely. But generally the funds must be held in the plan for two years before a withdrawal is allowed.

A 10 percent additional income tax applies to most early distri-butions made before age 59½. The 10 percent additional tax does not apply to distributions that are: (1) due to the participant's death or disability; (2) in the form of an annuity or installments payable over the life or life expectancy of the participant (or joint lives or life expectancies of the participant and the participant's beneficiary); (3) made after the participant has separated from service on or after age 55; (4) used for payment of medical expenses deductible under federal income tax rules; (5) made to or on behalf of an alternate payee pursuant to a qualified domestic relations order; or (6) rolled over to an individual retirement account or another qualified plan within 60 days.

Loans—Some plans permit employees to borrow a portion of their vested benefits. In general the employee must repay the loan accord-ing to a level amortization schedule with payments made at least quarterly. If loans are permitted, they must be available to all par-ticipants on a comparable basis, and must bear a reasonable interest rate (see chapter 4 for a detailed explanation).

Conclusion

Profit sharing offers employees a chance to share in their company's success. The level of company success is directly related to profits, which often define the amount of profit-sharing allocation. So the greater the profits of the company, the larger the potential allocation.

However, profit-sharing plans can serve several goals. If the plan is cash only, it is generally viewed as a form of bonus. If profits are good, benefits are paid. However, these can become viewed as certain, and employees may *spend* anticipated benefits before they materialize. Deferred plans are generally intended to supplement other pension plans and thus are generally more appropriate for retirement purposes.

Because of their advantages to both employees and employers, profit-sharing plans will probably continue to play an important role in employee benefits planning.

Bibliography

Allen, Everett T., Jr., Joseph J. Melone, Jerry S. Rosenbloom, and Jack L. VanDerhei. *Pension Planning.* Homewood, IL: Richard D. Irwin, Inc., 1988.

U.S. Department of Labor. Bureau of Labor Statistics. *Employee Benefits in Medium and Large Firms, 1988.* Washington, DC: U.S. Government Printing Office, 1989.

The Wyatt Company. *Top 50: A Survey of Retirement, Thrift and Profit Sharing Plans Covering Salaried Employees at 50 Large U.S. Industrial Companies as of January 1, 1989.* Washington, DC: Wyatt Research and Information Center, n.d.

Additional Information

Profit Sharing Council of America
20 N. Wacker Drive
Chicago, IL 60606
(312) 372-3411

Profit Sharing Research Foundation
1718 Sherman Ave.
Evanston, IL 60201
(312) 869-8787

8. Thrift Plans

Introduction

A thrift, or savings, plan is a type of defined contribution plan. The Internal Revenue Code (IRC) qualifies thrift plans as a type of profit-sharing plan, and they are similar in many ways. The chief differences from an employer's perspective are that thrift plans generally *require* participants to make contributions, while profit-sharing plans do not. And because thrift plans often require employee contributions, they normally cost the employer less than profit-sharing plans.

Employees generally make periodic contributions to thrift plans. Employee contributions are sometimes matched (completely or in part) by employer contributions. These contributions are placed in a trust fund and invested. For recordkeeping purposes, each participant's savings and earnings are assigned to an individual account.

The tax-favored treatment of employer contributions and employer and employee investment gains make these plans attractive and effective vehicles for retirement savings.

Plan Qualification Rules

Thrift plans, like other retirement plans, must satisfy a set of rules to qualify for tax-favored treatment. These rules, created under the Employee Retirement Income Security Act of 1974 (ERISA) and discussed in chapter 3, are designed to protect employees' rights and to guarantee that pension benefits will be available for employees at retirement. The rules govern requirements for reporting and disclosure of plan information, fiduciary responsibilities, employee eligibility for plan participation, vesting of benefits, form of benefit payment, and funding.

In addition, qualified plans must satisfy a set of Internal Revenue Service (IRS) nondiscrimination rules (under IRC sections 401(a)(4), 410(b), and, in some cases, 401(a)(26)) designed to insure that a plan does not discriminate in favor of highly compensated employees. These are described in chapter 17.

Contributions

Employee Contributions—Most thrift plans are *contributory*; that is, to participate, eligible employees agree to make voluntary contributions. Employee contributions to thrift plans are of two types: basic contributions, which are sometimes matched by employer contributions; and supplemental contributions, which are not matched by employer contributions. Depending on the plan's structure, the employee's contributions can be made from after-tax income or through pretax income in the form of salary reduction. Employee contributions are generally made through payroll deductions. If the thrift plan utilizes this salary reduction feature, the plan must follow special rules for 401(k) arrangements (discussed in chapter 9).

Sometimes the employer requires participants to contribute a specified percentage of pay. Alternately, the employer may be able to choose a contribution level between certain limits—say between 1 percent and 10 percent of pay. Employees are usually permitted to change or suspend contributions at some time during the plan year.

Employer Contributions—Employers can make contributions to a thrift plan through a number of arrangements. Employer contributions usually are defined as a fixed percentage of each dollar of basic employee contributions, although they can be defined as a flat dollar amount. The matching percentage may be the same for all employees, or it may increase with years of service or participation. Employer matching contributions, together with employee contributions, are subject to a special nondiscrimination rule under section 401(m).

Under a different approach, employers may provide a contribution matched (partially or fully) to an employee's contribution and a supplemental contribution based on profits. Under a relatively uncommon approach, employer contributions are based entirely on profits. Many surveys suggest that the level of the employer's matching contribution is an important factor in determining employees' participation and their level of contributions.

Limits—As with other defined contribution plans, annual employer and employee contributions to thrift plans are limited under IRC section 415. Annual contributions per participant cannot exceed 15 percent of compensation, or $30,000, whichever is less. Compensation up to $200,000 (indexed annually beginning in 1990; the amount in 1990 is $209,200) is used in computing the limit. The $30,000 will be indexed when the dollar limit for defined benefit plans reaches $120,000 (in 1990 this limit is $102,582). A further limit applies if an employee participates in both a defined benefit and a defined contribution plan.

Employee contributions are limited separately. In practice, any employee contributions—and matching employer contributions—are limited by nondiscrimination rules under IRC section 401(m). These rules limit the employee after-tax contributions of highly compensated employees and the employer contributions for highly compensated employees to a proportion of the amount nonhighly compensated employees contribute. The rules are very similar to those for 401(k) cash or deferred arrangements (see chapter 9), and include a prescribed method for distributing to highly compensated participants amounts exceeding the permitted limits.

An employer is also limited in the amount of contributions that are eligible for a tax deduction. Each year total employer contributions are deductible as a business expense up to 15 percent of total employee compensation (IRC section 404).

Taxation—Employer contributions to a thrift plan are deductible by the company as a business expense up to the limits noted above. Employees generally make contributions with after-tax money; therefore, income, Social Security, and other payroll taxes apply. However, any employer contributions and investment earnings on all contributions accrue tax free until distribution.

Investments

Most thrift plans offer the participant several investment options. In some cases, employer contributions must be placed in a designated investment vehicle, and flexibility is permitted only with regard to employee contributions. Common investment vehicles include guaranteed investment contracts through insurance companies; company stock; balanced funds, which invest in a mix of stocks and bonds; equity funds; and bond funds.

Many plans permit employees to change their investment vehicles. Where permitted, such changes may be limited to investment of future contributions or may apply to both past and future contributions. Often there is a restriction on the frequency of change.

Distributions

Retirement, Disability, and Death Benefits—The law requires that participants' account balances fully vest at retirement. In addition, plans generally provide for benefits upon death and disability. The plan's vesting provisions determine whether an employee will receive full or partial benefits upon other types of employment termination. However, if the plan is *contributory* (that is, employees make contributions), the employee will always receive the benefits that are attributable to his or her own contributions.

Profit-sharing plans typically give retiring participants and beneficiaries of deceased participants a choice between a lump-sum payment and installments. Usually, those who terminate employment for reasons other than retirement, death, or disability receive lump-sum distributions, although if the benefit exceeds $3,500, the participant cannot be forced to take an immediate benefit.

Distributions from profit-sharing accounts must follow the general distribution rules for all qualified retirement plans. Distributions must begin by the year following the attainment of age 70½ even if the individual has not retired. There are minimum and maximum limits on the amount of annual distribution, both subject to penalty taxes if not followed. (See chapter 4 for a complete description.)

In-Service Withdrawals—Some profit-sharing plans provide for partial account withdrawals during active employment. Plans allowing participants to elect account withdrawals impose certain conditions, which vary widely. But generally the funds must be held in the plan for two years before a withdrawal is allowed.

A 10 percent additional income tax applies to most early distributions made before age 59½. The 10 percent additional tax does not apply to distributions that are: (1) due to the participant's death or disability, (2) in the form of an annuity or installments payable over the life or life expectancy of the participant (or joint lives or life expectancies of the participant and the participant's beneficiary); (3) made after the participant has separated from service on or after age 55; (4) used for payment of medical expenses deductible under federal income tax rules; (5) made to or on behalf of an alternate payee pursuant to a qualified domestic relations order; or (6) rolled over to an individual retirement account or another qualified plan within 60 days.

Loans—Some plans permit employees to borrow a portion of their vested benefits. In general the employee must repay the loan according to a level amortization schedule with payments made at least quarterly. If loans are permitted, they must be available to all participants on a comparable basis, and must bear a reasonable interest rate (see chapter 4 for a detailed explanation).

Plan Administration

The administrative complexity of a thrift plan depends on its design. Individual participant account records must be maintained, and annual account statements must be provided to employees. Administrative complexity varies with the number of options (e.g., contribution rates, investment vehicles, and the frequency of permitted changes). Administrative responsibilities are often divided between the employer and an outside organization. As a plan matures and its trust fund grows, it is frequently necessary to hire an investment manager and an internal liaison.

Conclusion

Thrift plans can play an important role in a firm's total benefit program. They may function as the principal retirement income vehicle, or they may provide supplemental retirement income. While employer contributions are not required, they provide an incentive for employee participation and add to the retirement savings potential of employees. Nevertheless, even without employer contributions thrift plans are a tax-effective way for employees to save and are less costly for employers in such cases.

Bibliography

Allen, Everett T., Jr., Joseph J. Melone, Jerry S. Rosenbloom, and Jack L. VanDerhei. *Pension Planning*. Homewood, IL: Richard D. Irwin, Inc., 1988.

U.S. Department of Labor. Bureau of Labor Statistics. *Employee Benefits in Medium and Large Firms, 1988*. Washington, DC: U.S. Government Printing Office, 1989.

The Wyatt Company. *Top 50: A Survey of Retirement, Thrift and Profit Sharing Plans Covering Salaried Employees at 50 Large U.S. Industrial Companies as of January 1, 1989*. Washington, DC: Wyatt Research and Information Center, n.d.

9. 401(k) Cash or Deferred Arrangements

Introduction

A qualified cash or deferred arrangement under section 401(k) of the Internal Revenue Code (IRC) allows an employee to elect to have a portion of his or her compensation (otherwise payable in cash) contributed to a qualified retirement plan. The employee contribution is treated not as current income but most commonly as a pretax reduction in salary, which is then paid into the plan by the employer on behalf of the employee. In some cases, an employer allows employees to elect to have profit-sharing allocations contributed to the plan. In both instances, the employee defers income tax on the 401(k) plan contribution until the time of withdrawal. Whatever portion is not contributed to the 401(k) arrangement may be taken in cash, which is considered current income and taxed accordingly.

Various forms of deferred compensation have existed for many years. As early as the mid-1950s, cash or deferred profit-sharing plans using pretax employee contributions were permitted by the Internal Revenue Service (IRS) as long as at least one-half of the participants electing to defer were in the lowest paid two-thirds of all plan participants. It was not until the late 1970s that the U.S. Congress acted to sanction cash or deferred arrangements, formalize their design, and provide for regular guidance. The Revenue Act of 1978 added section 401(k) to the IRC—hence the commonly used reference to this type of arrangement as a "401(k)" plan. These arrangements are a popular vehicle for retirement savings. They provide employees the ability to save on a tax-effective basis by deferring current taxes until a future time when taxes might be lower and permit employers some flexibility in pension plan design and contribution levels.

More than 27.5 million workers were covered by 401(k) or 401(k)-type arrangements in 1988, up from 7.1 million in 1983.[1] Growth in

---

[1] These numbers are derived from the employee benefit supplements to the Census Bureau's May 1983 and May 1988 Current Population Surveys cosponsored by the Employee Benefit Research Institute and various federal agencies. Further references to 1988 data are from the latter survey. "401(k)-type" arrangements include salary deferral plans of state and local governments (section 457 plans) and tax-exempt organizations (403(b) plans). For further information on the surveys and participation in 401(k) arrangements, see Salisbury, 1989.

401(k)s has been broad based, occurring across industries, earnings groups, and firm sizes. Nevertheless, 401(k) arrangements are most popular in larger firms. A Hewitt Associates survey of large employers reports that by 1988, 96 percent of firms surveyed offered 401(k)s, up from 68 percent in 1984 and 2 percent in 1982 (Hewitt Associates, 1988, 1989). In smaller firms, where there is less likely to be a pension of any kind, 401(k) arrangements are less prevalent. In 1988, 8 percent of workers in firms with between 10 and 24 employees were covered by 401(k)s, while among workers in firms with more than 250 employees, 42 percent were covered (Salisbury, 1989).

Eligibility

Most private for-profit firms may establish 401(k) arrangements. However, nonprofit organizations cannot maintain 401(k)s unless they were adopted before July 2, 1986. Many may be able to establish similar plans, known as tax-deferred annuity programs, under IRC section 403(b) (discussed in chapter 11). State and local governments may not maintain 401(k) arrangements unless adopted before May 6, 1986, but can set up somewhat similar plans under IRC section 457.

Employees become eligible to participate in 401(k) arrangements usually after meeting age and service requirements. The maximum number of years and the age that a plan may set for eligibility is stipulated in the Employee Retirement Income Security Act of 1974 (ERISA). For a 401(k) arrangement, the maximum service period is one year. Vesting—the employee's attainment of nonforfeitable rights to benefits—of employee contributions and some employer contributions must be immediate. Other types of contributions are subject to minimum vesting standards in ERISA. (See chapter 3 for more information on eligibility and vesting rules.)

Types of 401(k) Arrangements

There are essentially two ways a 401(k) arrangement is designed: through an actual salary reduction or through a profit-sharing distribution.

In a salary reduction arrangement, the employee may elect to have a percentage of salary contributed to the plan (otherwise payable in cash), thereby reducing current salary and reducing the base upon which federal income and some state taxes are based. These arrangements must be included in an employer's profit-sharing, stock bonus, pre-ERISA money-purchase, or rural electric cooperative plan. They can be designed to include employee contributions only, employer contributions only, or both employee and employer contributions.

In a cash or deferred profit-sharing arrangement, the employee is offered the option of deferring a profit-sharing distribution (or some portion of it) to a trust account or taking the distribution in cash.

In both arrangements, the deferral and any income thereon accrue tax free until distribution. Any distribution taken in cash from the profit-sharing arrangement is currently taxed.

Contributions

There are four types of contributions that are normally paid to 401(k) plans.

- *Elective*—tax-deferred *employee* contributions (made by the employer on behalf of the employee) in the form of a salary reduction.

- *Matching*—employer contributions that "match" employee contributions, although the employer does not always provide a full dollar-for-dollar match.

- *Nonelective*—contributions other than matching made by the *employer* from employer funds. Sometimes these are made to help satisfy non-discrimination tests (see discussion below).

- *Voluntary*—after-tax *employee* contributions not made through a salary reduction.

Plan participants may be allowed to direct the investment of 401(k) contributions (sometimes just their own contributions; sometimes the employer contributions as well). Investment options commonly include: a fixed (or guaranteed investment contract (GIC)) fund, which invests in a guaranteed interest contract with an insurance company; a balanced fund, which is designed to provide stability as well as growth through an investment mix of stocks and bonds; and an equity fund, which has the most potential for growth but also the most risk. Investments in this fund are made in common stocks. The different funds allow the participant the option to direct investments toward his or her individual retirement planning goal. Other options sometimes available include bond funds, money market funds, fixed income securities, and company stock. Most employers offer fairly conservative investment options, with few offering more risky investments such as real estate or commodities (Newton, 1989).

Employee elective contributions to a 401(k) arrangement are limited (to $7,979 in 1990) and are coordinated with elective contributions to simplified employee pensions, section 457 state and local government plans, tax-deferred 403(b) annuities, and section 501(c)(18) trusts.[2] The limit is adjusted annually for inflation to reflect changes in the consumer price index. Employee after-tax contributions are limited under IRC section 401(m).

The limit on total employer and employee contributions to a qualified 401(k) plan is governed by the same rules as other defined contribution plans under IRC section 415. In general, the sum of the *employer's* contribution (including the amount the employee elected to contribute through salary reduction plus any employer "matching" contributions), any *after-tax employee* contributions, and any forfeitures may not exceed the lesser of 25 percent of an employee's compensation or $30,000.[3] Only compensation up to $209,200 (in 1990, indexed annually) is used in determining the limit.

Nondiscrimination Requirements

Like other qualified retirement plans, 401(k) arrangements must be designed to insure that a plan does not discriminate in favor of "highly compensated" employees in terms of coverage and participation in the plan and contributions provided. The rules for coverage and participation are the same as those for other qualified retirement plans (under sections 410(b) and 401(a)(26)). However, a special test for 401(k)s that limits elective contributions of highly compensated employees replaces the general plan rules prohibiting discrimination in contributions and benefits (under section 401(a)(4)). The test, known as the ADP (or actual deferral percentage) test, must be run annually. Certain of the other rules under the section 401(a)(4) regulatory scheme may be applicable to 401(k) arrangements.

The ADP test works this way: The eligible group of employees (defined as those employees who are eligible for employer contributions under the plan for that year) is divided into the highly compensated and the nonhighly compensated. Then, within each group, the percentage of compensation that is contributed on behalf of each employee is determined. The percentages for each employee are totaled and averaged to get an "actual deferral percentage" (ADP) for the

---

[2] Section 501(c)(18) trusts are essentially trusts created before June 25, 1959, forming part of a plan funded only by employee contributions and satisfying certain restrictions defined in the code.

[3] If a plan participant terminates, the nonvested benefits are "forfeited" and become available for other plan uses. They may be reallocated among employees or used to reduce employer contributions. Section 415 limits are discussed in more detail in chapter 4.

group. The ADP for the highly compensated group is then compared with the ADP for the nonhighly compensated group.

The ADP test may be satisfied in one of two ways:

Test 1: The ADP for the eligible highly compensated may not be more than the ADP of the other eligible employees multiplied by 1.25 (the "basic" test).

Test 2: The excess of the ADP for the highly compensated over the nonhighly compensated may not be more than 2 percentage points, and the ADP for the highly compensated may not be more than the ADP of the nonhighly compensated multiplied by 2 (the "alternative" test).

For example, if the ADP for the nonhighly compensated group is 4 percent and the ADP for the highly compensated group is 6 percent, are the nondiscrimination rules satisfied?

Test 1: Because 6 percent (the ADP of the highly compensated) is greater than 5 percent (4 percent × 1.25), test 1 is *not* satisfied.

Test 2: Because 6 percent (the ADP of the highly compensated) is not more than 2 percentage points more than 4 percent (the ADP of the nonhighly compensated) *and* 6 percent is not more than 8 percent (the ADP of the nonhighly compensated multiplied by 2), test 2 *is* satisfied.

Because one of the tests has been satisfied, the nondiscrimination rules are, therefore, satisfied. As mentioned earlier, these rules apply to employee elective deferrals.

Employee after-tax and employer matching contributions in 401(k) arrangements and any other qualified retirement plan are subject to a parallel rule called the actual contribution percentage (ACP) test under IRC section 401(m). The test is essentially the same as the ADP test applied to elective contributions. If the 401(k) arrangement consists of both elective and nonelective contributions, there are further tests that must be satisfied.

Table 9.1 illustrates the maximum ADPs allowed for the highly compensated employees, assuming various ADPs for the nonhighly compensated.

Distributions

The ability to withdraw funds is more restricted in a 401(k) arrangement than in other types of pension plans. In general, distri-

TABLE 9.1
Maximum Actual Deferral Percentages (ADPs) for Top-Paid Employees

If the Average ADP and Any Employer Contribution for the Lower Paid Is:	The Maximum Average ADP (Including Any Employer Contribution) for the Top Paid Will Be:	
	Test 1	Test 2
½%	⅝%	1%
1	1¼	2
2	2½	4
3	3¾	5
4	5	6
5	6¼	7
6	7½	8
7	8¾	9
8	10	10
9	11¼	11
10	12½	12

butions of employee elective contributions (and any nonelective or matching contributions used to satisfy the ADP test) may be made before age 59½ only in the case of death, disability, separation from service, plan termination if there is no establishment or maintenance of another defined contribution plan (other than an ESOP), sale of a subsidiary or substantially all the business' assets (as long as the employee remains in employment with the corporation acquiring the assets), or "financial hardship." Voluntary employee after-tax contributions and applicable earnings are not subject to these rules.

Hardship Defined—When the term "financial hardship" was originally defined in 1981 by the IRS in proposed regulations, a two-part definition was set out that said that the participant must (1) have an "immediate and heavy" financial need and (2) have no other resources "reasonably" available. These rules required the employer to investigate the individual circumstances of the hardship applicant. Until 1988, the only other regulatory guidance came from individual plan IRS revenue rulings.

In August 1988, IRS issued final regulations in which it retained the two-part definition of hardship but clarified the conditions under which each of these would be met. Each part may be satisfied through either a "facts and circumstances" test or safe harbor rules. The safe harbors provide a set of events that may be deemed automatically to cause an "immediate and heavy financial need" and that would satisfy the "other resources" provision.

Immediate and Heavy Need—Under the facts and circumstances rule, a need is defined as "immediate and heavy" if the need can be determined by the facts and circumstances surrounding the hardship request. Under the safe harbor test a distribution will be deemed to be "immediate and heavy" if it is for medical expenses; purchase of a principal residence for the employee; tuition for post-secondary education, but only for the next quarter or semester; and prevention of eviction or mortgage foreclosure.

Determining Financial Need from Reasonably Available Resources— To determine that a financial need cannot be met by other "reasonably available" resources under the facts and circumstances test, the employee must show that (1) the distribution does not exceed the amount required to meet the need and (2) the need cannot be met from other reasonably available resources (including assets of the employee's spouse and minor children).

An employer may demonstrate that these provisions are met without an independent investigation of the applicant's financial affairs if the employer "reasonably relies" on the participant's representation that the need cannot be "relieved" by insurance, reasonable liquidation of other assets, the cessation of employee contributions under the plans, and other plan distribution or loans from either the plan or commercial sources.

The safe harbor rules for establishing financial need are satisfied if:

- the hardship withdrawal does not exceed the amount needed;

- the employee has obtained all distributions (other than for hardship) and all nontaxable loans available from all of the employer's plans;

- the employee's contributions under all other employer plans are suspended for 12 months after the hardship withdrawal; and

- the dollar limit on pretax contributions for the year after the hardship withdrawal is reduced by the amount of pretax contributions made during the year in which the hardship occurred.

Furthermore, the amount available for a hardship distribution consists only of employee elective contributions and investment earnings that have accrued through December 31, 1988. Most hardship withdrawals are subject to the early distribution penalty tax, discussed later in this chapter.

Loans—An employee may be able to borrow funds from the plan if the plan permits. The rules governing loans from a 401(k) are essentially the same as those for other qualified plans. However, certain of the restrictive distribution rules with respect to 401(k) accounts may come into play. (For more details, see chapter 4.) However, no income tax deduction for interest paid on loans secured with 401(k) elective contributions is permitted, and no deduction for interest paid on a loan from any type of retirement plan (including from a 401(k)) made to a "key employee" (defined in chapter 4) is permitted.

Taxation

Contributions—Elective, nonelective, and matching contributions to a qualified section 401(k) arrangement are excludable from the employee's gross income until distribution. The employee thus defers federal income tax until the time the benefit is distributed. The deferral of taxation applies also to most state[4] and municipality tax provisions but not to Social Security and unemployment taxes. Voluntary employee after-tax contributions are taxable on a current basis. Earnings generated by any of these contributions are not taxed until withdrawal.

An employer may claim a business deduction for contributions to a 401(k) plan up to statutory limits defined under IRC section 404(a). If the 401(k) is part of a profit-sharing plan, the maximum annual deduction is generally limited to 15 percent of the total compensation of participating employees. (See chapter 7 for complete discussion of deduction limits.)

Distributions—Distributions of 401(k) funds prior to age 59½ are subject to a 10 percent penalty tax (in addition to regular income tax) unless the distribution is (1) upon the participant's death or disability, (2) in the form of an annuity payable over the life or life expectancy of the participant (or the joint lives or life expectancies of the participant and the participant's beneficiary), (3) made after the participant has separated from service after attainment of age 55, (4) made to or on behalf of an alternate payee pursuant to a qualified domestic relations order, (5) for payment of a medical expense to the extent deductible for income tax purposes under IRC section 213 (expenses that exceed 7½ percent of adjusted gross income), or rolled over to an individual retirement account or another qualified plan within 60 days.

---

[4]At this writing, the only exception is Pennsylvania.

90

Hardship distributions *are* subject to the 10 percent penalty tax unless for medical expenses to the extent deductible for federal income tax purposes.

Distributions of 401(k) accumulations received after the attainment of age 59½ are taxed just as other qualified plan distributions. (See chapter 4 for a detailed discussion of these rules.)

Plan Administration

The installation and operation of a qualified 401(k) plan can require detailed recordkeeping and account maintenance procedures. Proposed regulations set forth specific requirements for the administration of each plan participant's 401(k) account. Under the regulations, a 401(k) plan must maintain separate accounting between the portion of the employee's accrued benefit that is subject to the special vesting and withdrawal rules and any other (after-tax) benefits.

In each participant's account, depending on the structure of the plan, there may need to be a separate record for deductible "employer" contributions (elective and nonelective), nondeductible "voluntary" employee contributions, and vested and nonvested company contributions. Special rules exist for contributions made before 1980.

Conclusion

In today's mobile society, 401(k) arrangements can be particularly effective in meeting retirement income needs among workers who change jobs frequently and workers with intermittent labor force participation. Employee elective contributions to the plans are fully and immediately vested. When employees terminate employment or change jobs, they can "roll over" the accumulated contributions and earnings of the plan to an IRA or another qualified plan. As a result, 401(k) arrangements may particularly benefit young workers with high labor force mobility and women who leave the labor force for a protracted time. Section 401(k) arrangements are also used by employers as a way to provide supplemental retirement security for their employees without increasing overall pension costs. This may be accomplished by supplementing the employer's primary pension (often a defined benefit) plan with a 401(k) arrangement that has little or no employer contribution.

Bibliography

Allen, Everett T., Jr., Joseph J. Melone, Jerry S. Rosenbloom, and Jack L. VanDerhei. *Pension Planning*. Homewood, IL: Richard D. Irwin, Inc., 1988.

Canan, Michael. *Qualified Retirement and Other Employee Benefit Plans*. St. Paul, MN: West Publishing Company, 1989.

Hewitt Associates. *Salaried Employee Benefits Provided by Major U.S. Employers: A Comparison Study*, 1982–1987 and 1984–1988 eds. Lincolnshire, IL: Hewitt Associates, 1988 and 1989.

Newton, Bonnie. Employee Benefit Research Institute. "Surveys Explore 401(k) Investment Options." *Employee Benefit Notes* (June 1989): 4–7.

Salisbury, Dallas L. Employee Benefit Research Institute. "Individual Saving for Retirement: The 401(k) and IRA Experiences." *EBRI Issue Brief* no. 95 (October 1989).

U.S. Department of Labor. Bureau of Labor Statistics. *Employee Benefits in Medium and Large Firms, 1988*. Washington DC: U.S. Government Printing Office, 1989.

U.S. General Accounting Office. *401(k) Plans: Incidence, Provisions and Benefits*. Pub. no. GAO/PEMD-88-15BR. Washington, DC: U.S. Government Printing Office, 1988.

VanDerhei, Jack L. "Cash or Deferred Plans." In Jerry S. Rosenbloom, ed., *Handbook of Employee Benefits*, 2nd ed. Homewood, IL: Dow Jones-Irwin, 1988.

10. Employee Stock Ownership Plans

Introduction

An employee stock ownership plan (ESOP) allows companies to share ownership with employees without requiring the employees to invest their own money. Through an ESOP, employers contribute shares of company stock to their employees. Although other employer-sponsored plans, such as stock bonus and profit-sharing plans (see chapter 7), may contain company stock, an ESOP is required to invest *primarily* in company stock.

ESOPs are unique among employee benefit plans in another way: they may borrow money. This feature can be beneficial as a corporate finance tool. Because of special tax benefits accorded ESOPs, they can also lower the cost of financing corporate transactions.

The concept of employee ownership is popular. A nationwide public opinion poll in 1989 showed that nearly one-half of respondents would trade in their next pay increase for a share in the ownership of the company in which they worked (Employee Benefit Research Institute/ The Gallup Organization, Inc., 1989). And many companies have established employee ownership plans; the National Center for Employee Ownership estimates that companies have established nearly 10,000 employee ownership plans since the mid-1970s, covering about 11 million employees (table 10.1).

Louis O. Kelso is generally credited with creating the ESOP concept. Kelso believed that by providing employees with access to capital credit, ESOPs would broaden the distribution of wealth through free enterprise mechanisms. Employees who were made owners of the productive assets of the business where they work, Kelso reasoned, would benefit from the wealth produced by those assets and would thus acquire both a capital income and an incentive for being more productive.

Kelso attracted a powerful ally in Sen. Russell Long (D-LA), who used his influence to spearhead legislative efforts to promote ESOPs. Political support for the ESOP concept has grown steadily, and through the end of the 1980s Congress encouraged ESOPs through a number of favorable laws, including the Employee Retirement Income Security Act of 1974 (ERISA), the Tax Reduction Act of 1975, the Tax Reform Act of 1976, the Revenue Act of 1978, the Economic Recovery

TABLE 10.1
Growth of Employee Ownership Plans, 1975–1989

Year	Cumulative Number of Plans	Cumulative Number of Employees
1975	1,601	248,000
1976	2,331	503,000
1977	3,137	1,658,000
1978	4,028	2,800,000
1979	4,551	3,039,000
1980	5,009	4,048,000
1981	5,680	4,537,000
1982	6,082	4,745,000
1983	6,456	5,397,000
1984	6,904	6,576,000
1985	7,402	7,353,000
1986	8,046	7,860,000
1987	8,777	8,860,000
1988	9,407	9,630,000
1989	10,237	11,530,000

Source: National Center for Employee Ownership.

Tax Act of 1981, the Deficit Reduction Act of 1984, and the Technical and Miscellaneous Revenue Act of 1988. However, in 1989 ESOPs came under congressional scrutiny when the large amount of debt incurred by some ESOPs was connected with heavy corporate take-over activity. Congress considered major ESOP changes that would have dramatically reduced their attractiveness to corporations, but ultimately passed relatively minor tax changes in the Omnibus Budget Reconciliation Act of 1989 (OBRA '89). These changes are discussed later in this chapter.

Types of ESOPs

Leveraged ESOPs—An ESOP that borrows funds to acquire stock is called a leveraged ESOP and usually works in the following way.

Funds are borrowed to acquire employer securities. This can be accomplished in one of two ways (chart 10.1). An employer may arrange to sell the ESOP a specified amount of qualified employer securities at fair market value. The ESOP then borrows the funds needed to purchase the stock. The lender may be a bank or regulated investment company or the employer or shareholders in the employing company. The loan may be guaranteed by the employer, or the

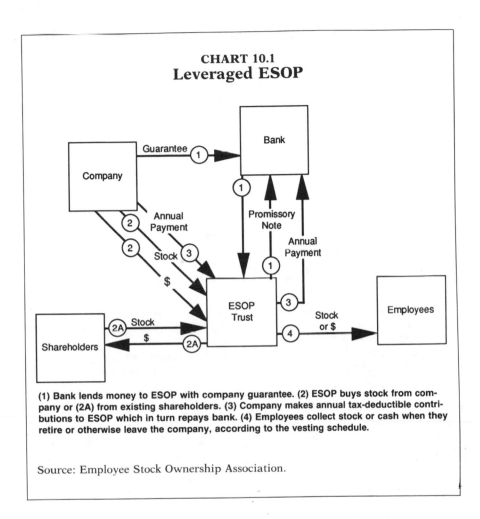

CHART 10.1
Leveraged ESOP

(1) Bank lends money to ESOP with company guarantee. (2) ESOP buys stock from company or (2A) from existing shareholders. (3) Company makes annual tax-deductible contributions to ESOP which in turn repays bank. (4) Employees collect stock or cash when they retire or otherwise leave the company, according to the vesting schedule.

Source: Employee Stock Ownership Association.

stock may be pledged as collateral. The loan is repaid with the employer's tax-deductible contributions to the ESOP. As the ESOP loan is repaid, shares of stock are allocated to participants' accounts. Unallocated shares remain in the ESOP trust and can continue to serve as collateral for the remaining loan balance.

Alternatively, the employer may borrow the money and transfer stock to the ESOP in exchange for the promissory note. The employer makes deductible contributions to the ESOP, which uses these contributions to pay off the note. These repayments to the employer, in turn, are used to pay off the employer's loan.

In contrast to a nonleveraged ESOP, where stock is acquired slowly through employer contributions, a leveraged ESOP generally acquires a large block of stock purchased with the borrowed funds; the shares are held in trust and allocated to participants as the loan is repaid. Unlike a nonleveraged ESOP, a leveraged ESOP can acquire a large share of ownership in a company much faster than a nonleveraged ESOP. Furthermore, if the loan is used to buy stock from the employer (rather than from outside existing stockholders), the ESOP transaction provides a cash infusion for the employer.

Leveraged ESOPs have been responsible for much of the overall growth of ESOPs over the past several years. The National Center for Employee Ownership attributes this growth to several factors.

- There was a general increase at the end of the 1980s in merger and acquisition activity, of which leveraged ESOPs are sometimes a part.
- Tax incentives passed in 1984 and 1986 have made leveraged ESOPs a more attractive means of borrowing money, and nonleveraged ESOPs less attractive in general.
- For a minority of the companies (probably under 1 percent of all ESOPs and 15 percent of public company ESOPs), ESOPs are part of a defense against hostile takeovers.
- Many employers have come to believe that sharing ownership with employees helps to create a more productive work environment.

Other ESOPs—Some companies establish ESOPs that are not leveraged. A company sets up a trust, to which it periodically contributes. The company may contribute stock directly or cash, which the fund uses to purchase the stock. The stock is allocated to individual accounts for employees. ESOPs that are not leveraged but can be are sometimes called "leverageable ESOPs."

The Tax Reduction Act of 1975 allowed an extended investment tax credit equal to qualified contributions to a special nonleveraged ESOP called a TRASOP (Tax Reduction Act stock ownership plan); the allowed credit was increased in the Tax Reform Act of 1976. Under the Economic Recovery Tax Act of 1981, beginning in 1983 the basis for the allowed tax credit was shifted from investment to payroll, replacing the TRASOP with the PAYSOP (payroll-based employee stock ownership plan). The Tax Reform Act of 1986, however, repealed the PAYSOP tax credit for compensation paid or accrued after December 31, 1986.

Plan Qualification Rules

ESOPs are a type of defined contribution plan and qualify with the Internal Revenue Service as either a stock bonus plan or a stock

96

bonus/money-purchase pension plan combination. As with all tax-qualified plans, ESOPs must establish a trust to receive the employer's contributions to the plan, and the plan must be created exclusively for the benefit of employees.

ESOPs are subject to the general ERISA rules governing eligibility, vesting, participation and coverage, and reporting (see chapters 3 and 17). But ESOPs also must comply with additional requirements aimed at the specific characteristics of the plans.

Investment of Assets—As mentioned earlier, ESOPs must invest primarily in qualified securities of the employer. In practical terms, this means that at least 51 percent of a plan's assets must be so invested. Qualified employer securities may include readily tradeable common stock, stock with voting power and dividend rights, preferred stock that is convertible into qualified common stock, and stock of affiliated corporations if certain requirements are met. Debt instruments are not included.

Diversification—For stock acquired after 1986, ESOPs must provide means for qualified participants nearing retirement to diversify part of their ESOP account balance. In general, beginning with the plan year following the participant's attainment of both age 55 and 10 years of participation, the participant must be provided the opportunity to diversify at least 25 percent of the total account. Five years later, the participant must be allowed to diversify at least 50 percent. Alternatively, the ESOP may distribute the amount that could be diversified.

Voting Rights—ESOP participants must be allowed certain voting rights. For stock that is readily tradeable (stock of a public company), full voting rights for all allocated shares must be passed through to participants. For stock of closely held companies (those whose voting stock is held by a few shareholders), voting rights must be passed through on all *major* corporate issues, specifically those that must be decided by more than a majority vote. Shares not voted by participants are voted by the ESOP trustee.

Distributions—ESOPs are permitted to make distributions in either stock or cash. Unless the sponsoring company's charter or bylaws require that substantially all of the company's stock be owned by employees, participants must be allowed to take their distributions in stock.[1] Generally, the full amount must be paid out over no more

---

[1] Unless the separating participant elects otherwise, distributions attributable to stock acquired after December 31, 1986, must begin within one year following the plan year in which the participant retires, dies, or becomes disabled or within five years

than five years, although the participant can elect to extend this period. Also, the period can be extended up to an additional five years for account balances in excess of $500,000, as indexed.

A participant receiving nonpublicly traded stock must be given an option to sell the stock to the employer at an independently appraised fair market value (a put option). For stock acquired after 1986, the employer can pay for the stock in annual installments, over a period of up to five years (beginning no later than 30 days after the sale), and pay interest at a reasonable rate. The employer must provide security for the unpaid balance of deferred payments. The employer and the ESOP may exercise a right of first refusal to repurchase nonpublicly traded stock distributed by the ESOP.

Special Tax Advantages

ESOPs enjoy a variety of tax advantages over other defined contribution plans.

Deductions for Contributions—ESOP contributions that are used to repay an ESOP loan are not subject to the usual 15 percent of covered compensation deduction limit (see chapter 4). Instead, employers can deduct contributions used to pay the loan principal, up to 25 percent of compensation. Unlimited deductions are permitted for contributions used to pay loan interest.

Dividend Deduction—Employers generally may also deduct dividends paid on ESOP stock to the extent that the dividends are distributed in cash to participants or used to repay the principal on the ESOP loan. However, new rules in OBRA '89 require that to be deductible, the dividends must be on employer securities acquired with the ESOP loan (generally effective for securities acquired after August 4, 1989). These liberal deduction limits are designed to help accelerate the rate at which ESOPs can repay loans, thereby allowing more rapid allocation of ESOP stock to participants' accounts.

Lender Incentive—Until 1989, qualified lenders—banks and regulated investment companies—could exclude from gross income 50 percent of the interest earned on ESOP loans. Some of this advantage was passed on to the ESOP through lower interest rates. OBRA '89 permits this interest exclusion, however, only if three conditions are satisfied: (1) the ESOP owns more than 50 percent of each class of outstanding stock of the corporation issuing the securities or more

---

after the participant separates from service for any other reason (if not reemployed with the same company).

than 50 percent of the total value of all outstanding stock of the corporation immediately after the acquisition of employer securities with the proceeds of such loans; (2) the term of the loan is not more than 15 years; and (3) voting rights on allocated shares are passed through to participants. The provision is generally effective for loans made after July 10, 1989. Certain exceptions apply for loans pursuant to certain written binding commitments in effect on that date (or on June 6, 1989) and for loans after which the ESOP owns at least 30 percent of the company and the loan was made by November 17, 1989.

A number of other tax incentives are provided to encourage the use of ESOPs to broaden corporate ownership, as follows.

Incentives for Sale of Stock to an ESOP—Shareholders of corporate stock can defer taxes on the gain from the sale of stock to an ESOP if, upon the completion of the sale, the ESOP owns at least 30 percent of the company and the seller reinvests the proceeds from the sale in qualified domestic securities within one year after (or three months before) the sale. In addition, the seller must have held the securities for at least three years before the sale of the stock (effective for sales after July 10, 1989). This provision allows owners of closely held businesses who are approaching retirement age to, in essence, create a market for their stock and to diversify their investments, on a tax-deferred basis, while providing their employees with a significant benefit and assuring the continued independence of the business.

Until 1989, estates that sold employer stock to an ESOP could exclude from taxes 50 percent of the proceeds received on the sale, up to $750,000. This was repealed in OBRA '89, effective for estates of decedents dying after December 19, 1989.

Early Distribution Tax—Lump-sum distributions paid to ESOP participants prior to January 1, 1990, are exempt from the 10 percent penalty tax to employees for early withdrawal (prior to age 59½).

Conclusion

ESOPs can provide employees with substantial financial benefits through stock ownership while providing companies with attractive tax advantages and a powerful corporate finance tool. By making employees partial owners of the business, a company also may realize productivity improvements, since workers benefit directly from corporate profitability and are thus working in their own interest.

Although the advantages of ESOPs are attracting growing numbers of companies, there is also some risk to consider. Because the ESOP is invested primarily in employer securities, the success of the ESOP depends on the long-term performance of the company and its stock. There is, therefore, a greater degree of risk involved because of the concentration of employee capital.

An ESOP is not appropriate in every circumstance, but the many benefits of employee ownership and ESOP financing merit close consideration of this concept.

Bibliography

Blasi, Joseph R. *Employee Ownership*. Cambridge, MA: Ballinger, 1988.

Bureau of National Affairs. *Employee Ownership Plans*. Washington, DC: Bureau of National Affairs, 1987.

Case, John. "Every Worker an Owner?" *Inc.* (May 1987): 14–16.

Employee Benefit Research Institute/The Gallup Organization, Inc. *Public Attitudes on Employee Ownership and Participation* (Washington, DC: Employee Benefit Research Institute, 1989).

Farrell, Christopher. "ESOPs: Are They Good for You?" *Business Week* (15 May 1989): 116–123.

Kelso, Louis O. *Democracy dnd Economic Power*. Cambridge, MA: Ballinger, 1986.

Korczyk, Sophie. "Employee Stock Ownership and Recent Policy Changes." Peat Marwick *Spectrum 9* (November 1986).

Piacentini, Joseph S. Employee Benefit Research Institute. "Employee Stock Ownership Plans: Impact on Retirement Income and Corporate Performance." *EBRI Issue Brief* no. 74 (January 1988).

Smiley, Robert W. *Employee Stock Ownership Plans*. New York: Prentice Hall/ Rosenfeld Launer Publishers, 1989.

Super, Nora. Employee Benefit Research Institute. "ESOPs: Will Congress Restrict Their Tax Advantages?" *Employee Benefit Notes* (July 1989): 1–4.

U.S. General Accounting Office. *Employee Stock Ownership Plans: Allocation of Assets in Selected Plans*. Washington, DC: U.S. General Accounting Office, 1989.

———. *Employee Stock Ownership Plans: Benefits and Costs of ESOP Tax Incentives for Broadening Stock Ownership*. Washington, DC: U.S. General Accounting Office, 1987.

Additional Information

Employee Stock Ownership Association
1100 17th Street, NW, Suite 310
Washington, DC 20036
(202) 293-2971

National Center for Employee Ownership
426 17th Street, Suite 650
Oakland, CA 94612
(415) 272-9461

11. Section 403(b) Plans

Introduction

A unique type of tax-deferred retirement arrangement is available to certain nonprofit organizations and public school systems. Since 1942, the Internal Revenue Code (IRC) has permitted such employers to purchase annuities for their employees on a tax-deferred basis. However, it was not until 1958, through the Technical Amendments Act of 1958 and a later series of IRC amendments, that Congress established the ground rules for today's "section 403(b)" plans. Two distinct retirement arrangements are governed by section 403(b) of the IRC. In the first, the employee is typically required to make a contribution, usually not exceeding 5 percent of salary. The employer then typically contributes a fixed percentage of salary for each participating employee. This arrangement is referred to in this chapter as a *section 403(b) pension plan*. The second provides a vehicle for voluntary employee tax-deferred savings, generally to supplement institutional plans. This arrangement is referred to in this chapter as a *tax-deferred annuity (TDA)*.

To be eligible, nonprofit organizations must qualify as "charitable" under IRC section 501(c)(3). These organizations include hospitals, churches, social welfare agencies, and educational institutions. Publicly sponsored schools, colleges, and universities are also eligible. A number of nonprofit organizations, however, do not qualify, including some federal, state, and local government offices; civic leagues; labor organizations; recreational clubs; fraternal societies; credit unions; business leagues; and cooperatives.

Until 1989, employers could adopt section 403(b) plans for one or more employees on a selective basis; unlike other qualified retirement plans, nondiscrimination rules were generally not applicable, although certain limited restrictions did apply.

In plan years beginning after December 31, 1988, however, section 403(b) plans (except those maintained by churches) must satisfy essentially the same nondiscrimination rules as other qualified retirement plans, as changed by the Tax Reform Act of 1986 (TRA '86) (see chapter 17). For plans involving employee salary reduction contributions, special coverage and participation rules apply, similar to those for 401(k) arrangements (see chapter 9).

Since many organizations (for example, hospitals) have contracts with professional persons, 403(b) plan sponsors must determine the true employer/employee relationship. If the employer is not paying Social Security taxes and is not withholding federal income taxes for a particular individual, it is likely that he or she is not considered an employee eligible for a 403(b) plan. Radiologists, pathologists, and anesthesiologists working at a hospital, for example, might fall into this category.

Originally, 403(b) plan contributors were required to purchase an annuity contract or similar policy from a life insurance company. The IRC has been modified and now allows investment in mutual funds. Section 403(b) funding vehicles include: individual and group fixed and variable annuity contracts; custodial accounts held by banks, credit unions, investment companies, and loan associations; and for churches, certain retirement income accounts. Most employers specify the available funding arrangements, particularly in 403(b) pension plans. Under TDA plans, some employers have no restrictions and permit employees to select the type of arrangement they prefer, as long as they meet the legal requirements of section 403(b).

Plan Features

Salary Reduction Agreement—Under section 403(b) pension plans providing employee salary reduction contributions, the employee and the employer enter into an agreement to reduce the employee's salary by a specified amount. The employer then remits these contributions together with employer contributions to an insurance company, custodian, or mutual fund. Under TDAs, the amount of the salary reduction is determined by the employee, as long as it falls within IRC limits. Instead of reducing current pay, employee TDA contributions may be derived from what otherwise would have become a pay increase. In this case, the employee agrees to forgo the pay increase in order for the employer to make TDA contributions of the same amount. In either situation, the language in the agreement must specifically state the level of the contribution, the date the contribution will become effective, and the investment vehicle in which the contribution will be placed.

A salary reduction agreement under a 403(b) pension plan or a TDA must follow the requirements outlined below.

- The agreement must be in writing.
- Contributions can be derived only from money earned after the date of the agreement.

- The employee can make only one agreement with the employer during a taxable year.

- The agreement must specify the amount of the contribution (either as a dollar amount, percentage of pay, or as the maximum permitted by law).

Contributions—Annual contributions to a 403(b) plan cannot exceed a maximum limit, referred to as the exclusion allowance. The exclusion allowance is generally equal to 20 percent of the employee's includable compensation from the employer, multiplied by the number of the employee's years of service with that employer, reduced by section 403(b) contributions paid in prior years through the same employer.

Because the employee's includable compensation is, in turn, based on taxable income (that is, income after making a salary reduction), the specific calculation can be complex. In addition to the limit imposed by the exclusion allowance, employee contributions made by salary reduction are limited to $9,500 annually, coordinated with any contributions to a 401(k) arrangement and/or a simplified employee pension (SEP; see chapter 12). The limit applies until the $7,000 limit for 401(k)s, adjusted annually for changes in the cost of living, reaches $9,500, at which time the 403(b) salary reduction limit will be indexed in the same manner. (In 1990, the annual limit for 401(k) arrangements is $7,979.) If an employee is required to contribute a set percentage of compensation to an institutional pension plan by salary reduction as a condition of employment, or if the employee contribution is made as a one-time irrevocable election, this contribution is not necessarily applied toward the $9,500 annual limit.

A special annual catch-up election is available for employees of educational organizations, hospitals, home health agencies, health and welfare service agencies, and churches or conventions of churches. Under this provision, any eligible employee who has completed 15 years of service with the employer is permitted to make an additional catch-up salary reduction contribution equal to the lesser of:

- $3,000;

- $15,000 reduced by the total amount of prior contributions that, in any year, exceed $9,500; or

- $5,000 multiplied by the number of years of service the individual has with the employer, minus an individual's lifetime elective deferrals under a 401(k), 403(b), and/or a SEP.

ERISA's overall limits on defined contribution plans under section 415 of the IRC also apply to total amounts that can be contributed on behalf of each employee in any one year (see chapter 4).

Employee Rights—A participant in a section 403(b) plan has a variety of rights and privileges. Some important rights provided to participants in 403(b) plans that are not generally required in other retirement plans include the right to select among investment vehicles offered under the plan (depending on the terms of the plan) and the right to select from a variety of settlement options at termination. If salary reduction is involved, participants must have the right to determine the contribution amount and the date contributions will begin.

Taxation

Employer contributions and employee salary reduction contributions to section 403(b) plans are excluded from reportable income at the time they are set aside. During the savings accumulation period, investment earnings on these funds are also exempt from current income taxes. When the employee withdraws funds, they are reported as ordinary income for federal tax purposes. However, the ultimate tax impact may be reduced for individuals who make withdrawals after retirement if their yearly retirement incomes are lower than their working year incomes.

Social Security—Employees' contributions that are attributable to voluntary salary reduction agreements are subject to Social Security taxes, even though they are excluded from employees' federal income taxes. Future Social Security benefits are then based on the higher income (that is, not reflecting the salary reduction); thus, retired employees will not receive lower Social Security benefits as a result of participation in a section 403(b) plan.

Regular Distributions—Distributions from a 403(b) plan are generally taxed as ordinary income in the year received. If an employee rolls a lump-sum distribution into another qualified plan or into an individual retirement account (IRA) within 60 days, no tax applies until distribution. For benefits accrued after December 31, 1986, a 403(b) plan must generally comply with the standard distribution rules governing timing and payouts applicable to qualified retirement plans (see chapter 4).

Early Distributions—A 10 percent penalty tax is generally imposed on early distributions (those made before age 59½) from all 403(b) plan accumulations. The tax is in addition to the regular income tax applicable for the year in which the distribution is taken. Some distributions are exempt from the additional tax, including amounts rolled over to an IRA or other qualified plan within 60 days, as are most distributions in the form of an annuity. Payments made upon the participant's death or disability, made after the participant has separated from service on or after age 55, used for medical expenses to the extent deductible for federal income tax purposes (under IRC section 213), or made to or on behalf of an alternate payee pursuant to a qualified domestic relations order are also exempt from the penalty tax.

Until the end of 1988, the IRC permitted withdrawals at any age, for any reason, from TDAs funded through annuities (although not from those funded through custodial accounts such as mutual funds). As of January 1, 1989, TDAs funded through either annuity or custodial accounts must follow the same early withdrawal rules as 401(k) arrangements. Participants may not make withdrawals prior to age 59½ from TDA accumulations attributable to salary reduction contributions except on account of separation from service, death, disability, or "financial hardship." Withdrawals due to hardship are limited to contributions only; earnings may not be withdrawn. The limits on distributions are not applicable to amounts accrued in annuity contracts, but are applicable to custodial accounts, prior to January 1, 1989.

Hardship has been defined in IRS regulations, but at present these regulations only apply to section 401(k) arrangements. Although IRS may provide different regulations for section 403(b) plans, legislative history suggests that it intends to apply the same criteria for 403(b) hardship distributions (see chapter 9 for more information on hardship).

Bibliography

NEA Special Services. *Tax-Deferred Annuities*. Rockville, MD: NEA Special Services Response Center, 1987.

Employee Benefit Research Institute. *Fundamentals of Employee Benefit Programs for Education Employees*. Washington, DC: Employee Benefit Research Institute, 1987.

12. Simplified Employee Pensions

Introduction

Many small businesses have been reluctant to establish a qualified retirement plan for their employees. Some fear the potential burdens associated with administering a plan and complying with complex federal regulations. The U.S. Congress sought to remove some of these obstacles for small businesses in the Revenue Act of 1978, which established a new tax-favored retirement plan aimed primarily at small employers—the simplified employee pension (SEP).

SEPs are arrangements under which an individual retirement account (IRA) is established for each eligible employee. The employee is immediately vested in employer contributions and generally directs the investment of the money. These arrangements are sometimes called SEP-IRAs.

A principal difference for individuals between a SEP and an employer-sponsored IRA is the larger annual contribution available for a SEP (discussed below). SEPs must also meet some qualified retirement plan rules for eligibility, coverage, vesting, and contributions that do not exist for employer-provided IRAs (IRAs are discussed in chapter 15).

SEPs offer employers an alternative to more complex and costly qualified pension plans. Paperwork, recordkeeping, and reporting requirements are kept to a minimum.

Acceptance of SEPs has been slow. To increase their attractiveness, Congress added a salary reduction feature in the Tax Reform Act of 1986 (TRA '86), under which employees in small firms may elect to have a portion of their pretax salary contributed to a SEP (see "Contributions"). An employer may offer both an employer-funded SEP and a salary reduction SEP as long as the total amount contributed per employee does not exceed certain limits. Salary-reduction SEPs are not available to tax-exempt organizations or to state or local governments.

SEPs may be set up by corporations, unincorporated businesses and partnerships, and self-employed persons. Although companies of any size may create SEPs, the simplicity of the arrangement is designed to interest small businesses.

Eligibility

Employer contributions must be made for each employee who has reached age 21, has worked for the employer during at least three of the preceding five years, and has received at least $300 in compensation from the employer during the year. The $300 figure is indexed to increases in the cost of living. The indexed amount for 1990 is $342.

Any period of service during a year, even if only one day, qualifies as work for the year. The employer must contribute for employees who worked some period during the year even if they have left the company by the time the employer makes the contribution. Employees covered by collective bargaining agreements and nonresident aliens may be excluded from eligibility.

All eligible employees must participate in the SEP, including eligible part-time employees. If at least one eligible employee elects not to participate, the employer is not permitted to contribute to accounts for the other employees.

Contributions

Employers—Under the Revenue Act of 1978, the maximum an employer could contribute for each employee was the lesser of $7,500 or 15 percent of compensation. The limit on compensation that could be considered for calculating the annual contribution was $100,000.

The dollar limit on contributions to SEPs was raised to $15,000 and the compensation limit to $200,000 by the Economic Recovery Tax Act of 1981. The Tax Equity and Fiscal Responsibility Act of 1982 raised the dollar limit on contributions to $30,000. The limit includes the amount an employee elects to contribute through salary reduction. The $200,000 compensation limit is indexed to the cost of living. In 1990 the limit is $209,200.

Contributions must be made according to a formula that does not discriminate in favor of officers, shareholders, or highly compensated employees. Employer contributions are considered discriminatory unless the same percentage of compensation is allocated to all eligible employees. In plans integrated with Social Security, a limited disparity is permitted (see "Plan Design").

An employer may contribute to a SEP in addition to contributing to other qualified pension plans. However, SEP contributions are included in the total contribution and deduction limits on all qualified plans, under sections 415 and 404 of the Internal Revenue Code.

One of the most flexible features of a SEP from an employer's standpoint is that there is no required annual contribution. For example, if a company has a poor year and profits are low, the employer can decrease the contribution or simply not make one.

Employees are fully and immediately vested in the employer's contributions and investment earnings on the contributions. Therefore, the employee has nonforfeitable rights to the funds and will not lose any upon separation from service.

Employees—When SEPs were first created, if the employer contribution was less than the maximum contribution permitted for IRAs that year, the employee was permitted to make up the difference with a tax-deductible contribution to the SEP. In addition, an employee could also contribute up to the maximum tax-deductible level to his or her own IRA. Under rules established by TRA '86, an employee covered under a SEP may not be able to make the full $2,000 deductible contribution to his or her own IRA if his or her adjusted gross income exceeds $25,000 (single) or $40,000 (married filing jointly). (See chapter 15 for more detail.)

TRA '86 considerably broadened the incentives for employee participation in a SEP by providing the salary reduction option. The option is available only to employees in firms with 25 or fewer employees, at least 50 percent of whom must elect to have amounts contributed to the SEP.

Employees may elect to defer up to $7,000 annually, indexed to the cost of living. The limit is reduced by any salary deferral made to a 401(k) arrangement or tax-deferred annuity (section 403(b) plan). The indexed amount in 1990 is $7,979.

There is also a special nondiscrimination test for elective deferrals to a SEP. The deferral percentage for *each* "highly compensated" employee cannot exceed 125 percent of the average deferral percentage for all other eligible employees (see chapter 9). Thus, if all employees of a firm on average contribute 10 percent of their pay to a SEP, the owner of the firm cannot contribute more than 12.5 percent of compensation to his or her own account (not to exceed $30,000).

Excess contributions made by highly compensated employees are subject to a 10 percent excise tax on the employer if they are not distributed within 2½ months following the plan year in which the excess was deferred. Any excess contribution distributed to an employee is includable in the employee's taxable income for the year in which the contribution is made.

Distributions

From their inception, SEPs have been subject to the same penalties on early withdrawals (those made prior to age 59½) that have applied to IRAs. In 1986, this tax was expanded to apply not only to SEPs and IRAs but to all qualified employer-sponsored retirement plans. A 10 percent excise tax is imposed on amounts withdrawn before age 59½, unless in the form of an annuity, or upon the death or disability of the covered worker. SEP distributions must begin by April 1 of the calendar year following the calendar year in which an individual attains age 70½. Loans cannot be made from SEPs.

Taxation

Until the end of 1986, employees had to include as gross income on their tax returns the amounts contributed by their employers to a SEP account and claim an offsetting deduction for the amount; employers included the contributions on employees' W-2 forms. Effective in 1987, employer contributions and employees' elective deferrals to SEPs are excluded from employees' taxable income. Contributions and earnings accumulate tax free until withdrawn.

Employer contributions to a SEP are not subject to Social Security (FICA) taxes or to unemployment (FUTA) taxes, but employee elective deferrals are included as wages for FICA and FUTA purposes.

An employer may elect to operate a SEP on the basis of a calendar year or the employer's taxable year. Contributions for a taxable year may be made no later than the due date (including extensions) for filing the return for that taxable year.

Integration

Until 1989 employers were permitted to take a portion of the Social Security taxes paid by the employer for each employee into account in calculating the SEP contribution for the employee. That is, the employer could subtract a portion of the Social Security tax paid in a given year from the SEP contribution. This enabled employers to make SEP contributions that were a higher percentage of compensation for higher-paid employees (assuming that their compensation exceeded the maximum taxable wage base) because the Social Security tax is a smaller percentage of their total compensation than it is for lower-paid workers.

Effective in 1989, TRA '86 prescribed new integration rules for defined contribution plans that also apply to the nonelective portion of SEP contributions. These rules permit a limited disparity between the percentage contribution above and below the Social Security wage base. (Refer to chapter 16 for a discussion of integration requirements.)

Plan Administration

The Internal Revenue Service (IRS) provides a short model form (5305-SEP) that constitutes an agreement between employer and employee. The model form includes instructions and questions and answers. The form cannot be used if the SEP is to be integrated with Social Security or if the employer maintains any tax-qualified pension, profit-sharing, or stock bonus plan. An employer also cannot use a model SEP if it has any leased employees or if the employer is part of a controlled group of employers, unless all eligible employees of the controlled group participate in a SEP.

The model form is not filed with the federal government. The employer retains it and furnishes a copy with explanatory material to each employee.

The employer also must draw up a "written allocation formula" that explains the percentage of salary used for making contributions. Employees may designate the kind of investment vehicle they want to use for the SEP contribution, such as stocks, bonds, mutual funds, certificates of deposit, and other similar types of investment vehicles. They are also free to subsequently change investment vehicles. Employers themselves may select the investments, but in practice most leave the decision to the employees.

The employer then forwards the contributions directly to the SEP fiduciary, which is generally a bank, insurance company, or investment firm.

The employer does not have to file detailed annual reports with the U.S. Department of Labor, as are required for other qualified pension plans, but must keep track of the names of the employees for whom contributions are made, the amounts of the contributions, and the institutions to which the amounts have been paid.

An employer may also set up a nonmodel SEP. In this case, an employer must either file form 5306-SEP with IRS or adopt a prototype plan sponsored by banks or insurance companies and approved by IRS.

Conclusion

Pension coverage is less common among small businesses than among medium-sized and large businesses. In 1988, only 17 percent of workers in firms with fewer than 25 employees were covered by an employer pension plan, compared with 44 percent among firms with 25 to 99 employees and 79 percent among firms with 100 or more (Piacentini, 1989). Despite attempts by Congress since 1978 to stimulate interest in SEPs by increasing contribution limits, many of the very firms to whom SEPs are targeted know little about them.

Among employers that have heard of SEPs, interest in flexibility of contributions and simplicity of administration may be tempered by concern about the nondiscrimination requirements. The employer must make contributions on behalf of employees who may not remain long with the employer, thus diverting funds the employer might wish to use to reward longer-service employees. Because employees vest immediately in employer contributions, employers may feel that such a retirement arrangement does little to encourage employees to remain with the employer.

Employees have the advantage of immediate vesting, but as with other retirement arrangements face penalties and taxation if they withdraw the contributions and earnings before age 59½. Employees also have the opportunity to contribute to their SEPs through salary reduction, but the requirement for 50 percent participation by eligible employees may limit this option.

Bibliography

Andrews, Emily S. *Pension Policy and Small Employers: At What Price Coverage?* Washington, DC: Employee Benefit Research Institute, 1989.

Commerce Clearing House, Inc. *Tax-Saving Plans for the Self-Employed Reflecting the Technical and Miscellaneous Revenue Act of 1988*. Chicago: Commerce Clearing House, Inc., 1989.

_____. *Individual Retirement Plans*. Chicago: Commerce Clearing House, Inc., 1987.

Piacentini, Joseph S. Employee Benefit Research Institute. "Pension Coverage and Benefit Entitlement: New Findings from 1988." *EBRI Issue Brief* no. 94 (September 1989).

Samuelson, John L. "Simplified Employee Pensions." *Management Accounting* (September 1988): 29–31.

U.S. Department of Labor and U.S. Small Business Administration. *Simplified Employee Pensions: What Small Businesses Need To Know*. Washington, DC: Pension Rights Center, n.d.

13. Retirement Plans for the Self-Employed

Introduction

Self-employment has long been part of the American dream. The continued willingness of entrepreneurs to accept the risks of starting their own business is testament to the strength of this dream.

Since 1962, federal policy has encouraged the provision of pensions for the self-employed and their employees through the Self-Employed Individuals Tax Retirement Act. This law created "Keogh" plans, named for U.S. Rep. Eugene J. Keogh of New York, who sponsored the original legislation. (Sometimes these plans are referred to as H.R. 10 plans, after the number assigned to an early version of the bill.) The act allowed unincorporated small business owners, farmers, and those in professional practice to establish and participate in tax-qualified plans similar to those of corporate employers. The self-employed may either be sole proprietors or members of a partnership.[1]

Prior to 1962, many small business owners found that their employees could participate in a tax-qualified pension plan, but the employers themselves could not. Self-employed individuals without employees also could not participate in a tax-qualified plan. Furthermore, where two people operated similar businesses and realized similar profits—but one was a sole proprietor and the other was incorporated—the corporate operator could benefit from a pension plan even though he or she was the only employee of the corporation, but the sole proprietor could not.

Legislative History

Keogh plans originally were subject to tighter limits on contributions and benefits and stricter rules governing plan operation than corporate retirement plans. Self-employed individuals were limited to a contribution of $2,500 per year, while (at that time) there was no limit imposed on corporate plans. This provision led to otherwise

---

[1]In addition to Keogh plans, the self-employed are also eligible for simplified employee pensions, discussed in chapter 12.

unnecessary incorporation by self-employed persons solely for the purpose of obtaining the tax benefits for retirement savings. In addition, Keogh plans had stricter limits on vesting and contributions for owner-employees (those with a certain percentage ownership interest).

To achieve somewhat greater equity with corporate plans, the Employee Retirement Income Security Act of 1974 (ERISA) increased the annual limit for deductible contributions to Keogh plans to 15 percent of earned income or $7,500, whichever was lower.

In 1981 Congress reviewed Keoghs at the same time that it expanded eligibility for individual retirement accounts (IRAs). The Economic Recovery Tax Act of 1981 retained the 15 percent of compensation deduction limit but increased the dollar maximum to $15,000, effective January 1, 1982.

In the Tax Equity and Fiscal Responsibility Act of 1982 (TEFRA), Congress established parity between corporate and noncorporate retirement plans. To this end, most of the special rules applicable to Keogh plans were eliminated. Maximum limits for a defined benefit or defined contribution Keogh plan were changed to be the same as those for corporate plans. And many of the provisions relating to owner-employees were repealed. By treating Keogh plans and corporate plans more equally, Congress intended to mitigate the tendency for professionals to incorporate simply to take advantage of the higher amounts that were tax deductible under prior law.

At the same time many of the rules applicable specifically to owner-employees in Keoghs were repealed, TEFRA added new "top-heavy" rules for *all* qualified plans. The rules took the owner-employee concept, expanded it to include officers and other types of company "owners," and applied stricter vesting and contribution limits to plans that benefited a certain proportion of "key employees." These rules are described in chapter 4.

The Tax Reform Act of 1986 made numerous changes in the rules governing all qualified retirement plans, which also affect Keoghs (see chapter 4).

Eligibility

The self-employed individual is treated as an employer as well as an employee for tax purposes in contributing to a Keogh plan. In addition, the self-employed individual must make contributions to the plan on behalf of his or her employees.

Keogh plans may be classified as either defined contribution or defined benefit plans. Defined contribution plans are those in which the contributions are defined, and the eventual benefit depends on the total amount of contributions and their investment performance. Defined benefit plans do not specify the amount of contribution, but instead define the future retirement benefit in terms of a monthly pension. (See chapter 5 for a discussion of the differences between defined benefit and defined contribution plans.)

Self-employed individuals are also eligible to contribute to an IRA but may only contribute to both an IRA and a Keogh plan if their taxable income is below the levels established for IRAs (see chapter 15).

Contributions and Benefits

Contributions made by self-employed individuals are not currently taxable to the self-employed individual, and the contributions by the self-employed individual on behalf of his or her employees are not currently taxable to employees. The contributions and any earnings accumulate tax free until distribution, when they are subject to normal income taxes. If distribution occurs prior to age 59½, a penalty tax may be assessed (discussed below).

Employee after-tax contributions are also permitted. These contributions, which are currently taxed, generate *nontaxable* earnings. After-tax contributions are limited by statute to 10 percent of compensation. However, special nondiscrimination rules for after-tax contributions may effectively reduce this limit for some employees (see below).

Keogh plans are subject to the same contribution and benefit limits as other corporate retirement plans under Internal Revenue Code section 415. For defined contribution plans, the maximum annual addition may not exceed the lesser of 25 percent of the employee's compensation (earned income)[2] or $30,000 per year. The maximum annual benefit to a participant under a defined benefit plan is $90,000 or 100 percent of the participant's average compensation for his or her three consecutive highest-earning years. The $90,000 is adjusted annually to reflect changes in the cost of living. The 1990 limit is $102,582. The limit on annual additions to defined contribution plans

---

[2]The Internal Revenue Service defines compensation of the self-employed as "net earnings from self-employment, *which take into account the deduction for employer contributions to qualified employee retirement plans (including Keogh plans)* [emphasis added]. Earned income can be calculated using the following formula: Gross profits minus business expenses equals net income. Net income minus retirement plan contributions equals *earned income.*

is frozen at the $30,000 level until it equals one-fourth of the defined benefit limit; from that point on, it will also be adjusted for inflation.

Distributions

Keogh plan distributions can be paid in the same manner as other plans, namely in a lump-sum payment (where the entire account balance is distributed in one sum) or in periodic distributions from accumulated reserves as an annuity. The annuity can be in the form of a *life* annuity—in which a monthly payment is made to a retiree for his or her remaining lifetime and ceases upon the retiree's death—or in the form of a joint and survivor annuity, in which the surviving spouse continues to receive monthly payments after the retiree's death. Plan distributions can also be paid out in regular installments for a fixed number of years (see chapter 4 for further discussion).

Taxation

At retirement, Keogh plan benefits are taxed as they are received. The tax treatment depends on the type of distribution—annuity or lump sum—and generally follows normal qualified plan rules (see chapter 4). An exception to these rules applies for lump-sum distributions. A self-employed individual is limited in the use of income averaging and capital gains treatment to the attainment of age 59½, death, or disability. Distributions from a Keogh plan, like other qualified plans, prior to age 59½ are penalized. Unless the distribution meets one of a limited number of exceptions, it is subject to a 10 percent excise tax in addition to regular income tax (see chapter 4 for more information).

Rollovers—Prior to the Deficit Reduction Act of 1984 (DEFRA), tax-free rollovers of lump-sum distributions could not be made by a self-employed individual from a Keogh plan to an employer-sponsored pension plan or another Keogh plan. DEFRA permitted a tax-free rollover from one qualified plan to another of a distribution attributable to contributions made on behalf of a participant while he or she was self-employed.

Tax-free rollovers of Keogh plan distributions can also be made to an IRA. If an amount otherwise eligible for the lump-sum tax treatment is rolled over into an IRA, however, the special income averaging tax treatment is *not* available upon subsequent distribution from the IRA.

Loans—Loans to participants in Keogh plans are permitted under the rules governing all qualified plans (see chapter 4). However, a

Keogh plan may not make loans to self-employed individuals who are owner-employees.

Nondiscrimination

Keogh plans must satisfy the same nondiscrimination requirements as other qualified retirement plans. These are designed to guarantee that highly compensated employees do not disproportionately benefit in terms of participation in the plan or in benefits provided. (Chapter 17 describes these requirements in detail.)

Conclusion

Over the past two decades, Congress has passed a number of laws designed to provide tax incentives for self-employed individuals to supplement retirement income in addition to their Social Security benefit. Despite these incentives, the unincorporated self-employed have not participated in Keogh plans at a very high rate, yet there is some evidence of growth. In 1987, 5.6 percent of some 10 million unincorporated self-employed contributed to a Keogh plan, compared with 4.8 percent of approximately 9 million self-employed in 1983.[3]

Bibliography

J.K. Lasser Tax Institute. *All You Should Know About IRA, Keogh, and Other Retirement Plans*, revised ed. New York: Prentice-Hall, Inc., 1987.

Piacentini, Joseph S. Employee Benefit Research Institute. "Pension Coverage and Benefit Entitlement: New Findings from 1988." *EBRI Issue Brief* no. 94 (September 1989).

Simone, Joesph R., and Fred R. Green. *The Pension Answer Book*, 5th ed. Greenvale, NY: Panel Publishers, 1990.

---

[3]These data are derived from the pension and employee benefit supplements to the Census Bureau's Current Population Surveys conducted in May 1983 and May 1988. The Employee Benefit Research Institute cosponsored each supplement along with the U.S. Department of Health and Human Services in 1983 and with the Social Security Administration, the U.S. Department of Labor, and other federal agencies in 1988. The 1988 survey question about Keoghs asked respondents about the prior year's participation (1987) while the 1983 survey asked about the current year (1983). For further information, see Piacentini, 1989.

14. Cash Balance Pension Plans

Introduction

Cash balance pension plans are new to the retirement plan area. First established in 1985, they have received widespread attention and now cover an estimated 500,000 employees.[1] However, they are still a novelty to most employers, and there are relatively few in operation.

A cash balance plan is a defined benefit plan that looks much like a money purchase defined contribution plan (see chapter 4). Each participant has an account that is credited with a dollar amount that resembles an employer contribution, generally determined as a percentage of pay. Each participant's account is also credited with interest. The plan provides benefits in the form of a lump-sum distribution or annuity. On termination of employment, the amount of the lump-sum distribution is equal to his or her vested account balance. If the employee instead elects to receive the benefit in the form of an annuity, the amount of the annuity is actuarially equivalent to the account balance.

Despite the similarities to a defined contribution plan, a cash balance plan is actually quite different because it defines future pension benefits, not employer contributions. Each account expresses the current lump-sum value of the participant's accrued benefit; in so doing, the account is merely a bookkeeping device and does not relate directly to plan assets. Similarly, employer contributions are based on actuarial valuations, so they may be more or less than the sum of the additions to participants' accounts. Finally, interest is credited at a rate specified in the plan and is unrelated to the investment earnings of the employer's pension trust.

Benefits

Credits to Accounts—The annual benefit accrual in a cash balance plan is expressed as a lump-sum amount, which is added to each participant's account balance. This cash balance credit is typically either a flat dollar amount or a percentage of the participant's pay.

---

[1] Estimate by Kwasha Lipton.

As with traditional pension benefit formulas, credits may increase with years of service or with pay.

Accounts are credited with an interest rate specified in the plan. The interest rate must be fixed, either as a specified rate or a rate related to some index, such as the consumer price index (CPI) or the rate on U.S. Treasury bills. Although there is no required minimum or maximum rate, the interest rate credited is often competitive with market rates.

Many cash balance plans provide a minimum annuity benefit, in which the benefit is defined to be the greater of the employee's account balance or a pension defined in the traditional manner.

Investment of Assets—Under a cash balance plan the risks and rewards of investment performance are borne by the employer, not the participants. The investment of assets under a cash balance plan can be considered from the same perspective as that of any other defined benefit plan. Total plan assets are not necessarily related to the sum of employee account balances. The trust may be invested in stocks, bonds, and/or other vehicles. As with other defined benefit plans, the employer seeks the highest long-term return consistent with appropriate levels of risk.

Generally, the goal is to achieve returns higher than the rate specified in the plan. However, some employers have invested cash balance plan assets with the goal of achieving an investment return that directly parallels the growth of participant accounts. A guaranteed investment contract (GIC) issued by an insurance company is a popular form of investment in this case.

Section 415 Limits—Cash balance plan benefits are limited by Internal Revenue Code (IRC) section 415 in the same manner as any other defined benefit plan (see chapter 4). These limits are applied to the annuity equivalent of the cash balance account, not—as in a defined contribution plan—to the annual addition to the account.

Minimum Standards

Cash balance plans are subject to the same Employee Retirement Income Security Act of 1974 (ERISA) requirements as other defined benefit plans, including minimum standards for eligibility, vesting, and funding; these are described in detail in chapter 3. The following discussion addresses areas specific to cash balance plans.

Vesting—Like other qualified retirement plans, a cash balance plan is required to meet ERISA's minimum vesting requirements of full vesting after five years (cliff) or graded vesting over years three through seven. Many cash balance plans provide earlier vesting than other defined benefit plans, which often only provide the minimum required vesting schedule. Usually cash balance plans provide cliff vesting rather than graded vesting.

Funding—Minimum funding requirements apply to cash balance plans in the same manner as for other defined benefit plans (that is, the normal cost plus amounts required to amortize any unfunded accrued liability over a period of years, subject to the full-funding limit). See chapter 4 for a detailed discussion of funding.

Distributions

Cash balance plans generally provide participants the option of receiving their vested account balances in the form of a lump-sum distribution or as an annuity at the time of retirement or employment termination. If the distribution is paid as an annuity, the amount paid will be the actuarial equivalent of the lump-sum distribution. Lump-sum distributions are popular with participants.

The usual joint and survivor and preretirement survivor requirements apply to cash balance plans (see chapter 4). Thus, in general, benefits for a participant with an eligible spouse must be paid in the form of a qualified joint and survivor annuity unless the participant and spouse elect otherwise. Some employers further encourage the selection of an annuity by using a high interest rate to convert accounts into annuities. In practice, however, terminating employees elect immediate payment of a lump-sum distribution.

The preretirement survivor annuity requirements apply to cash balance plans in the same manner as to other defined benefit plans. However, almost all cash balance plans go beyond the minimum requirements and pay the full account balance in the event of the employee's death.

Loans—Loans to participants are permitted under cash balance plans, but as a practical matter may be complex to administer—just as with other defined benefit plans. Under a defined contribution plan, when a distribution is made, the loan can be automatically paid off, but under a defined benefit plan, if the participant elects a monthly annuity, there is no way to assure repayment of the loan. Cash balance plans thus should not look to the account balance as collateral for the loan.

Integration with Social Security

Because the cash balance plan is a defined benefit plan, the integration rules for defined benefit plans apply to it. However, the proposed regulations and other Internal Revenue Service (IRS) regulatory guidance have shied away from addressing cash balance plans. Since cash balance plans favor younger employees, who are typically lower paid, they may be able to integrate more heavily than traditional defined benefit plans. At this writing, however, there is an absence of regulatory guidance.

Plan Termination Insurance

Like any defined benefit plan, a cash balance plan is subject to plan termination insurance and must pay annual premiums to the Pension Benefit Guaranty Corporation (PBGC). Also, as with other defined benefit plans, a cash balance plan may be terminated only if plan assets are sufficient to provide all benefit liabilities (that is, all accrued benefits), unless the employer is in "distress."

Upon termination of a cash balance plan, all participant accounts vest to the extent funded, and plan assets are allocated among plan participants. If the plan has residual assets, these may be used to provide additional benefits or may revert to the employer, whichever the plan provides.

Plan assets may be less than the sum of account balances, either because plan assets declined in value or because the employer contributed less than the sum of the additions to individual accounts. In this case, PBGC will pay the "guaranteed" portion of vested benefits. (See chapter 3 for more information about plan termination insurance.)

Comparison with Defined Contribution Plans

A cash balance plan is similar in many ways to a defined contribution plan, particularly a money-purchase plan or a profit-sharing plan, under which the employer contributes at a fixed rate.

An employer's cost under a cash balance plan is typically lower than the cost under a defined contribution money-purchase plan with the same level of additions to participant accounts, because the actuary may anticipate both forfeitures and investment earnings in excess of the rates to be credited to account balances. To the extent experience differs from the actuarial assumptions, future contributions to a cash balance plan will be adjusted, which may lead to more cost volatility. The employer's pension expense must be determined in accordance with the Financial Accounting Standards Board's accounting rules for all defined benefit plans. (See VanDerhei, 1988, for a detailed explanation of these rules.)

122

If a defined contribution plan is qualified as a profit-sharing plan, elective salary deferrals are permissible under Internal Revenue Code section 401(k), but this is not permitted under a cash balance plan.

A defined contribution plan is not subject to PBGC premiums and plan termination insurance provisions. Since all benefits are always fully funded under a defined contribution plan, plan termination insurance is not needed. Under a cash balance plan, as in a defined benefit plan, it is possible for participants to lose part of their accrued benefits upon plan termination in spite of the plan termination insurance.

A cash balance plan will generally be less difficult and expensive to administer than a defined contribution plan. Account recordkeeping is much simpler under a cash balance plan because there is no need to reconcile account balances with trust assets, and there are typically no employee contributions, loans, withdrawals, or fund transfers. However, an actuarial valuation is required.

Annuities can be paid directly from the trust of a cash balance plan and are generally greater than what the employee could obtain from an insurance company using his or her account balance. Under a defined contribution plan, an employee wishing an annuity must have his or her balance transferred to an insurance company.

Comparison with Defined Benefit Plans

Under a typical defined benefit plan, two employees with equal pay but differing ages will earn the same amount of retirement income for each year of service. Because the money invested for a younger employee can grow with interest for many more years than that invested for an employee close to retirement, the cost of funding the pension earned for a younger employee is less than that for an older employee. In addition, under a final average pay plan the benefits previously earned are increased each year as the average salary upon which they are to be based grows, further increasing the cost for older employees. For employees who terminate employment at younger ages, both the accrued benefits and the costs are low. The lower benefits are likely one of the reasons younger employees place low value on traditional defined benefit plans.

Traditional pension plan benefit formulas are oriented to the total retirement benefit, taking retirement age and length of service into account. In contrast, cash balance plans emphasize annual accumulations and may therefore not be as flexible as traditional plans in providing specified levels of retirement income.

123

Defined contribution plans and cash balance plans are attractive to younger, shorter-service employees, who generally find the accounts concept attractive and who may have little interest in retirement.

A cash balance plan may be more difficult and costly to administer than a traditional defined benefit plan. The actuarial valuation process is considerably simplified, but records of plan accounts must be kept. In practice, the cost may be more or less than a traditional defined benefit plan, depending on the number of employees, plan design, and data processing facilities.

Conclusion

Cash balance plans are still in their infancy. To employees they appear more like defined contribution plans, with individual accounts whose returns can be monitored regularly and with a benefit at employment termination directly related to the employee's account balance. To employers, a cash balance plan qualifies as a defined benefit plan and thus has both benefit design and funding flexibility. At the same time, it is subject to the related funding and accounting rules and plan termination insurance premiums. Additionally, as with a defined contribution plan, participant record-keeping is required.

Thus, cash balance plans are truly hybrid in their approach to providing retirement income. But the characteristics that make these plans appealing to employers and employees can make the design and administration more complex than that of either defined benefit or defined contribution plans. Whether one is an employer considering establishing a cash balance plan or an employee participating or about to participate in one, a thorough understanding of the design and goals of cash balance plans is needed.

Bibliography

Amoroso, Vincent, F.S.A. "Cash Balance Plans." *BNA Pension Reporter* (22 February 1988): 339–342.

Brennan, Lawrence T. "Cash Balance Pensions Will Increase in Popularity." *Business Insurance* (2 November 1987): 57, 66.

Grubbs, Donald S., Jr. "The Cash-Balance Plan—A Closer Look." *Journal of Pension Planning & Compliance* (Fall 1989): 263–276.

VanDerhei, Jack L. Employee Benefit Research Institute. "Employers' Accounting for Pensions and Other Post-Employment Benefits." *EBRI Issue Brief* no. 82 (October 1988).

15. Individual Retirement Accounts

Introduction

Through enactment of the Employee Retirement Income Security Act of 1974 (ERISA), Congress established individual retirement accounts (IRAs) to provide workers who did not have employer-sponsored pensions an opportunity to save for retirement on a tax-deferred basis. U.S. tax law has substantially changed the eligibility and deduction rules for IRAs since then. The Economic Recovery Tax Act of 1981 (ERTA) extended the availability of IRAs to all workers, including those with pension coverage. The Tax Reform Act of 1986 (TRA '86) retained tax-deductible IRAs for those not covered by an employer-sponsored pension but restricted the tax deduction among those with pension coverage to individuals with incomes below specified levels. In addition, TRA '86 added two new categories of IRA contributions: nondeductible contributions, which accumulate tax free until distributed, and partially deductible contributions, which are deductible up to a maximum amount less than the $2,000 maximum otherwise allowable.

While TRA '86 made IRAs less advantageous for some individuals, most individuals may contribute the maximum amount on a tax-deductible basis. For all individuals, IRAs remain a tax-effective way to save for retirement. However, like any other financial arrangement, IRAs require careful planning and monitoring. And because their ultimate purpose is to provide retirement income, investments need to be directed toward long-term return. This chapter offers an introduction to IRA eligibility rules, contribution limits, distributions, taxation, and investment options.

Eligibility

IRAs may be established under one or more of the following circumstances (summarized in table 15.1).

- *Individuals who are not "active participants" in an employer-sponsored retirement plan*—Regardless of income level, any part-time or full-time worker who is younger than age 70½ and not an "active participant" in an employer-sponsored plan may establish and contribute to a personal IRA. The Internal Revenue Service (IRS) defines "active partici-

125

TABLE 15.1
Current IRA Eligibility Test

Adjusted Gross Income Married, filing:			You or Spouse Covered by Pension Plan?	Type of Contribution ($2,000 maximum)
Jointly	Separately	Individual		
$40,000 or under	$0	$25,000 or under	Yes	Fully deductible
$40,000 or under	$0	$25,000 or under	No	Fully deductible
between $40,000 and $50,000	less than $10,000	between $25,000 and $35,000	Yes	Partially deductible
between $40,000 and $50,000	less than $10,000	between $25,000 and $35,000	No	Fully deductible
$50,000 or over	$10,000 or over	$35,000 or over	Yes	Nondeductible
$50,000 or over	$10,000 or over	$35,000 or over	No	Fully deductible

Source: Employee Benefit Research Institute.

pant" as a person who is "covered" by a retirement plan: that is, an employer or union has a retirement plan under which money is added to the individual's account or the individual is *eligible* to earn retirement credits. An individual is considered an active participant for a given year even if he or she is not yet vested in a retirement benefit. In certain plans, the individual may be considered an active participant even if he or she was only with the employer for part of the year.

IRA investors must have *earned* income, which can include: (a) wages, salaries, tips, professional fees, bonuses, and other amounts received for personal services; (b) commissions and income generated through self-employment; (c) payments from the sale or licensing of property created by authors, inventors, artists, and others; or (d) alimony. *Unearned* income derived from real estate rents, investments, interest, dividends, or capital gains cannot be used as the basis for IRA contributions.

- *Individuals who are active participants in an employer-sponsored plan and whose adjusted gross income (AGI) does not exceed $25,000 (single taxpayers) or $40,000 (married taxpayers filing jointly)*—These taxpayers may make a fully deductible IRA contribution. Again, contributions can only be made from earned income.

- *Individuals who are active participants in an employer-sponsored plan and whose AGI falls between $25,000 and $35,000 (single taxpayers) and between $40,000 and $50,000 (married taxpayers filing jointly)*—These taxpayers may make a fully deductible IRA contribution of less than $2,000 and a nondeductible IRA contribution for the balance, as follows. The $2,000 maximum deductible deduction is reduced by $1 for each $5 of income between the AGI limits. For example, a single taxpayer with AGI of $30,000 could make a $1,000 deductible IRA contribution and a $1,000 nondeductible contribution. Under a special rule, the deductible amount is not reduced below $200 if a taxpayer is eligible to make *any* deductible contributions. Again, contributions can only be made from earned income.

- *Individuals who are active participants in an employer-sponsored plan and whose AGI is at least $35,000 (single taxpayers) or at least $50,000 (married taxpayers filing jointly)*—These taxpayers may only make nondeductible IRA contributions of up to $2,000; earnings on the nondeductible contribution are tax deferred until distributed to the IRA holder. Again, contributions can only be made from earned income.

- *IRAs established as rollover vehicles for lump-sum distributions from employer-sponsored pension plans or other IRAs*—A worker who receives a distribution from his or her employer-sponsored retirement plan, an IRA, or a Keogh can generally place the distribution in a rollover IRA without tax penalty or current taxation, provided at least one-half of the distribution is rolled over (see "Rollovers").

Contribution Limits

Maximum Deductible Contributions—As stated earlier, IRA contributions may not exceed $2,000 per year. The amount that is tax deductible varies according to a worker's income tax filing status, AGI, and pension coverage status. Single workers may contribute up to $2,000 or 100 percent of earned income (whichever is lower) per year if they are not active participants in an employer-sponsored plan or if they are covered and have AGI of not more than $25,000. For those with AGI between $25,000 and $35,000, the deductible amount is prorated (see "Eligibility").

- *Two-Earner Couples*—Where a husband and wife both have earned income, each may contribute up to $2,000 or 100 percent of earned income (whichever is lower) per year. This means that a two-earner couple may then make a combined annual deductible contribution of up to $4,000. If a husband and wife file a joint tax return and *either* spouse is covered by an employer-sponsored plan, both are restricted in their eligibility to make deductible IRA contributions under the rules that apply to their combined AGI. Therefore, they are each allowed full $2,000 deductible contributions if their combined AGI does not exceed $40,000; a deductible IRA contribution of less than $2,000 and a nondeductible IRA contribution for the balance of the $2,000 if their combined AGI is between $40,000 and $50,000; and no deductible contribution if their AGI is $50,000 or above (a nondeductible IRA contribution of $2,000 *would* be allowed for each working spouse).

  If a married individual files a separate tax return, the spouse's active participation does not affect the individual's eligibility to make deductible IRA contributions. But if a married individual files separately, the phase-out of the $2,000 deduction begins with $0 of AGI and ends at $10,000. Therefore, for each $5 of AGI above $0, the maximum $2,000 IRA deduction is reduced by $1, or 20 percent of income. For example, if a married person is an active participant, has $3,000 of income, and files a separate return, the maximum allowable IRA deduction would be $1,400 (that is, $2,000 − $600 (0.20 × $3,000)). If the same individual had AGI of $10,000 or more, no deductible IRA contribution would be allowed.

- *One-Earner Couples*—A married worker with a nonworking spouse may contribute up to $2,250 or 100 percent of the employed spouse's earned income (whichever is lower) per year, provided the worker (a) is not an active participant in an employer-sponsored plan or (b) is an active participant but has AGI that does not exceed $40,000. A *spousal IRA* may also be established if a spouse has a small amount of earned income but elects to be treated as earning no income and makes no IRA contribution. A spousal IRA can be set up as a single IRA with a subaccount for the spouse, or as separate IRAs for each spouse. The dollar limit on deductible contributions to spousal IRAs is phased out for active pension plan participants in accordance with the same rules that apply to nonspousal IRAs (that is, a 20 percent reduction in the $2,000 IRA maximum deduction for each $1 between the AGI limits). The maximum amount that can be placed in either spouse's account is $2,000 (that is, the entire $2,250 cannot be placed in one spouse's account). Those contributing

$2,250 must file a joint tax return in the year the contribution is made. If the worker is covered by a pension plan, one-earner couples with AGI greater than $40,000 but less than $50,000 could make partial, deductible spousal IRA contributions and partial, nondeductible IRA contributions; one-earner couples with AGI of $50,000 and above could only make a nondeductible spousal IRA contribution.

- *Nonworking Divorced Persons*—All taxable alimony received by a divorced person is treated as income for purposes of the IRA deduction limit. The regular IRA eligibility rules apply.[1]

Minimum Contributions—No minimum IRA contributions are required, and contributions are not required to be made in every year. However, the deductible amount is not reduced below $200, even if the individual's deductible contribution is less.

Employer-Sponsored IRAs

An employer may contribute to an IRA that has been set up by the employee or may set up an IRA for employees. The employee's interest must be nonforfeitable, and separate records showing the employee's contributions and the employer's contributions must be maintained. Although regular IRA contribution limits apply, the employer is also permitted to pay reasonable administrative expenses associated with the IRA.

Employers may also offer employees IRAs through payroll deduction arrangements. Automatic deductions from employees' earnings would be deposited in IRAs that are set up by the company. Some employers permit employees to select among a variety of investment options. This arrangement should not be confused with an employer-sponsored retirement plan called a simplified employee pension (SEP), in which an employer establishes an IRA for each employee and makes contributions on their behalf. SEPs have different contribution limits than IRAs and are subject to some of the same rules as other qualified retirement plans (see chapter 12).

Distributions

IRA distributions must begin by April 1 of the calendar year following the calendar year in which the individual reaches age 70½.

---

[1]When the working spouse reaches age 70½, deductible contributions to spousal IRAs are no longer permitted—even if the nonworking spouse is younger. If the working spouse is younger, deductible contributions are not permitted for the nonworking spouse after he or she reaches age 70; the working spouse, however, may continue to make contributions to his or her own separate IRA.

129

If an individual elects a lump-sum payment, the full amount must be distributed. If a distribution in the form of an annuity is elected, a minimum amount must be distributed to ensure full payout over the individual's expected life. The minimum distribution basically is computed by dividing the opening balance at the beginning of the year by the life expectancy of the individual, determined as of the date the individual attained age 70 and reduced by one for each taxable year elapsed after age 70½. An individual who has multiple accounts may choose the account(s) from which he or she would like to take the required distribution, instead of taking distributions from each account (see "Penalties").

Distributions can be paid in the following ways:

- *Lump-Sum Payments*—The entire account balance is distributed in one sum.

- *Periodic Certain*—The account balance is paid in a predetermined number of fixed payments over a specified period of time.

- *Life Annuity*—Payments are made to retirees for their remaining lifetimes and to their beneficiaries or estates upon their death, usually on a monthly basis.

- *Joint and Survivor Annuity*—Payments are made for the IRA holder's remaining lifetime, usually on a monthly basis. After the IRA holder's death, the surviving spouse continues to receive lifetime payments. The survivor usually receives only a portion (for example, 50 percent) of the amount paid to the primary IRA holder. In addition, the monthly income to the primary holder will be lower than under an individual life annuity; this reflects the additional cost of insuring income over two lifetimes rather than one.

Rollovers

The law permits individuals to roll over account balances from one IRA to another and from a qualified retirement plan to an IRA. To avoid tax penalties, the transfer of assets from one account to another must be completed within 60 days.[2]

Rollovers between IRAs—Under this arrangement, the individual may roll over his or her account balance from one IRA to another, offering greater investment flexibility. This type of rollover can occur only once annually. A transfer of IRA funds from one trustee to another, either at the individual's request or at the trustee's request, is

---

[2]IRS has ruled that IRA funds may be used for short-term loans provided they are redeposited in the same or another IRA within 60 days of withdrawal. Only one such transaction is permitted per IRA in any 12 month period.

not a rollover—it is a transfer that is not affected by the one-year waiting period.

Rollovers between Employer Plans and IRAs—If employer retirement plans provide lump-sum distributions, the amounts corresponding to pretax employee and employer contributions may be transferred to a rollover IRA if the amount represents at least one-half of the distribution. "Rollover" IRAs were designed specifically to provide a savings vehicle for lump-sum distributions without imposing a tax penalty. Rollovers of lump-sum distributions may be made at any age. However, if the individual is aged 70½ or older, distributions must begin during the year in which the rollover is received. Lump-sum distributions from employer plans paid to a surviving spouse after an employee's death can also be rolled over into an IRA without penalty.

An individual may also roll over a distribution from one employer plan into an IRA and at a later time roll over those same assets, plus any earnings, into another employer plan. In this case, the IRA acts as a conduit for the funds from one employer to another. However, the funds must be kept in a separate account and not mixed with any other funds.

Taxation

IRA taxation rules reflect the basic purpose of an IRA (that is, to provide retirement income). Use of IRA savings for purposes other than retirement income, therefore, is discouraged through tax penalties. IRA distributions may begin as early as age 59½, and no later than April 1 of the calendar year following the calendar year in which the individual attains age 70½. Distributions in the case of death or disability and made in the form of an annuity can begin prior to age 59½ without penalty. Distributions are considered income in the year received and are subject to applicable marginal income tax rates.[3]

Income Taxes—Each year, tax-deductible contributions to new or existing IRAs must be made by the tax return filing date. Contributions can be made in one full payment or in installments throughout the year. Income taxes on these contributions are deferred until IRA savings are distributed. The distributions are taxed as ordinary income in the year received, except for the portion of the total IRA distribution that is attributable to *nondeductible* contributions, which

---

[3]The future tax treatment of IRA distributions is unclear in many state and local jurisdictions, although some have announced that they will follow federal tax law.

are excludable from gross income. All IRAs (including rollover IRAs) are treated as a single contract, and all distributions from such plans in any taxable year are treated as a single distribution. If an individual withdraws an amount from an IRA that includes both deductible and nondeductible contributions, the amount excludable from gross income is determined by multiplying the withdrawal by a fraction, where the numerator is the individual's total nondeductible contributions and the denominator is the total balance (at the close of the calendar year) of *all* the individual's IRAs. For example, if an individual held four IRA accounts with a total value of $10,000, and $2,000 was the amount of the nondeductible contributions, then a withdrawal of, for example, $4,000 would be considered to consist of $800 attributable to excludable, nondeductible contributions ($4,000 × 2,000/ $10,000 or 0.2) and $3,200 fully taxable as ordinary income.

IRA lump-sum distributions are not eligible for income averaging or capital gains treatment.

Estate Taxes—The entire value of a lump-sum distribution is included in the deceased participant's gross estate.

Penalties—Under certain circumstances, tax penalties apply, as follows.

- Contributions in excess of the maximum limits described above are subject to a 6 percent excise tax on any excess contribution for each year the amount remains in the account. If an individual contributes more than the permissible amount, he or she can avoid the 6 percent tax penalty by withdrawing the excess, called "unwanted contributions," plus any earnings by the tax return due date in the year the contribution is made.

- Distributions prior to age 59½ are subject to a 10 percent penalty tax, unless they are taken as part of a series of equal payments made for the life (or life expectancy) of the employee or the joint lives (or joint life expectancies) of such employee and his or her beneficiary, or the IRA owner dies or becomes disabled. Neither rollovers between IRAs nor the portion of an early withdrawal that is attributable to nondeductible contributions is subject to the tax.

- Distributions of the minimum amount required not made by April 1 of the calendar year following the year in which the individual turns age 70½ are subject to a 50 percent excise tax imposed on the excess in the IRA.

- If total distributions from an IRA and any qualified employer retirement plan exceed $128,228 in 1990 (indexed to the consumer price index annually), a 15 percent excise tax is imposed on the excess.

132

Investments

IRA savings can be invested in retirement accounts and retirement annuities. The institutions that offer IRA investment vehicles include banks, brokerage houses, insurance companies, savings and loan associations, credit unions, mutual fund companies, other investment management organizations, and the federal government. IRA contributions can be placed in more than one account, provided the total annual contribution limits are not exceeded. Collectibles such as art, antiques, rugs, stamps, wines, and coins—other than certain U.S.-minted gold or silver coins and state-issued coins circulated after November 10, 1988—are not permissible IRA investments.

An IRA investor should understand the risks and limitations of the various investment options. Financial institutions are required to explain how their IRAs work and their financial ramifications. Before choosing an IRA, some important questions should be considered and answered. For example:

- What are the investor's retirement income needs? Should he or she invest in low-risk choices, or can he or she afford to gamble on higher risks that may produce higher returns?

- What are the administrative fees or commissions charged on the type of IRA under consideration?

- Is there a minimum deposit requirement?

- What is the interest rate and how is it computed? Is it likely to fluctuate over the worker's lifetime?

- Can the investment be quickly converted into cash in an emergency? Is there a penalty charge for early withdrawal (separate from the income tax penalty)?

- Should IRA contributions be made early or late in the tax year? (If money is invested early, it accumulates interest longer. But if money is invested late, individuals have use of their money throughout the year and may have a better idea how much they can invest in an IRA.)

Conclusion

IRAs can be an important addition to retirement savings opportunities. They are particularly useful for persons who do not have employer pension coverage and for highly mobile workers with minimal or no pension benefits due to limited service in any one job. The amount of retirement income generated by an IRA will depend on a variety of factors, including contribution amounts, the participant's age when the IRA is established, the rate of investment return, and the participant's age at retirement.

Bibliography

Internal Revenue Service. *Individual Retirement Arrangements*. Pub. no. 590. Available by calling the IRS Tax Forms Publications number listed in local telephone directories under "U.S. Government."

Salisbury, Dallas L. Employee Benefit Research Institute. "Individual Saving for Retirement: The 401(k) and IRA Experiences." *EBRI Issue Brief* no. 95 (October 1989).

16. Integrating Pension Plans with Social Security

Introduction

Social Security taxes and benefits are a higher percentage of total compensation for lower-paid employees than for higher-paid employees. To allow employers to balance the benefit tilt toward lower-paid employees inherent in the Social Security system, a system of pension "integration" rules evolved, culminating in 1971 with the release of Revenue Ruling 71-446, which was in effect until the enactment of the Tax Reform Act of 1986 (TRA '86). In effect, integration allows the employer's pension to be combined with Social Security to result in an overall retirement scheme. While pre-TRA '86 integration rules no longer apply, it is useful to review their application as a basis for understanding the new rules.

Integration works differently for defined benefit and defined contribution plans. Under defined contribution plans, prior to TRA '86 an employer was allowed to make a total contribution (that is, to the pension plan plus Social Security, exclusive of Medicare) that resulted in a constant percentage of compensation for all employees.

Integration rules for defined benefit pension plans represented the same logic although the employer's contributions to Social Security had to first be translated into benefits for the employee. Recognizing that Social Security (exclusive of Medicare) represents more than just retirement benefits for the employee (for example, spousal benefits as well as death and disability benefits), a value of 162 percent of the employee's retirement benefit was placed on the package of benefits received. Acknowledging the argument that the employer pays 50 percent of the payroll tax assessed for these benefits, pension integration rules for defined benefit pension plans were based on the concept that employers should be able to receive credit for approximately one-half of 162 percent (or 81 percent) of the primary retirement benefit for the employee.

In actual practice, this figure was increased up to 83⅓ percent. Employers with defined benefit plans utilizing the *offset* approach to integrating their pension plans were allowed to subtract up to 83⅓ percent of the *initial* primary Social Security benefit from the *gross* pension benefit.[1] A very large percentage of the employers adopting this approach concluded that it would be too difficult to communicate the rationale for taking credit for more than one-half of the Social Security retirement benefit actually received by the employee and only chose to offset 50 percent of the employee's primary Social Security benefit. Plans were allowed to offset by 83⅓ percent of the entire Social Security benefit, even when most of the benefit had been earned working for other employers.

Many employers chose to accomplish the same objective through an *excess* approach in which an employee would receive less benefit accrual (or none at all) for compensation below a threshold known as an *integration level*. The pre-TRA '86 mechanics of this approach were relatively complex and are no longer relevant for current pension plans. But it is important to recognize that, although the integrated pension plans of the past were actuarially equivalent to the other approaches, much of the controversy surrounding those plans resulted from the use of *pure* excess pension plans in which employees with compensation below the integration level could put in an entire career with an employer and receive no pension benefit.

One of the primary objectives of TRA '86 was to narrow the permitted integration spread and eliminate plans based solely on pay in excess of Social Security wages. This was accomplished (in principle) through the expansion of Internal Revenue Code (IRC) section 401(l), which essentially provides an exception for integrated plans to the general nondiscrimination rules that prohibit plans from providing highly compensated employees benefits that are greater, as a percentage of pay, than benefits provided to nonhighly compensated employees.[2]

Although section 401(l) was the only specific exception available for integrated plans, regulations on general nondiscrimination (IRC section 401(a)(4)) provide additional rules that apply to integrated plans. (See chapter 17.)

Integration after the Tax Reform Act of 1986

Although Congress' general philosophy toward integrated plans was expressed during the gestation of TRA '86, plan sponsors had little

---

[1]As explained in chapter 2, Social Security benefits receive automatic cost-of-living adjustments. Employers adopting this approach were not allowed to increase the offset as the retiree's Social Security benefit increased.

[2]The terms "highly compensated employee" and "nonhighly compensated employee" have specific statutory definitions. See chapter 4 for more detail.

in the way of guidance on permitted procedures to comply with the new methods of integrating until the Internal Revenue Service (IRS) issued proposed regulations in November 1988—a month and a half before the TRA '86 compliance deadline for calendar year plans. Further guidance was provided in June 1989 through Notice 89-70. The following discussion is based on the proposed regulations and Notice 89-70.

IRC section 401(l) and its related regulations explicitly allow for three different approaches to integration: defined benefit offset, defined benefit excess, and defined contribution. Regardless of which of these approaches is chosen, the employer must take into account three key elements in the design of an integrated plan:

- *Integration Level*—This is a threshold based on compensation that determines which participants will receive benefit accruals or contributions in excess of the basic rate and the proportion of their compensation that will benefit from the higher rate.

- *Maximum Offset or Spread*—This refers to the so-called "permitted disparity" between benefit accruals (in a defined benefit plan) or contributions (in a defined contribution plan). It places a limit on the difference that can exist between the accruals or contributions of employees who earn more than the integration level and those who earn less.

- *Two-for-One*—This is a constraint not found in pre-TRA '86 legislation that implicitly prevents employers from integrating a plan to prevent lower-paid employees from receiving any pension benefits or contributions. For defined benefit *excess* and defined contribution plans, this is similar in concept to one of the nondiscrimination tests for 401(k) arrangements (see chapter 9). The two-for-one rule limits the maximum benefit or contribution for employees earning more than the integration level to twice the value (expressed as a percentage of compensation) below the integration level. Thus, if compensation below the integration level receives no benefit or contribution, no additional amount may be provided to compensation in excess of the threshold. For defined benefit *offset* plans, this rule is implemented (albeit in a complex manner) by limiting the dollar amount of the offset to one-half of the gross dollar benefit (before applying the offset).

Defined Contribution Plans

In general, an integrated defined contribution pension plan must be designed so that the maximum spread between the two contribution levels is 5.7 percent[3] and the contribution rate above the in-

---

[3]This figure may increase in the future with increases in the Old Age portion of the employer's Social Security tax rate.

tegration level is no more than twice the rate below. For example, a defined contribution plan providing 5 percent of compensation for amounts below the integration level may not provide more than 10 percent for compensation in excess of the integration level. Anything more than 10 percent would violate the two for one rule. However, if a defined contribution plan provided a 7 percent contribution for compensation less than the integration level for the year, the maximum contribution for compensation greater than the integration level would be 12.7 percent. Anything greater than 12.7 percent would violate the 5.7 percent constraint. The integration level typically used for defined contribution plans is the Social Security wage base at the *beginning* of the current year.

An employer with a defined contribution plan may integrate the plan at a lower dollar threshold. In such cases, there are two alternatives. Under the first, an employer may choose an integration level less than or equal to 20 percent of the wage base of the current year or $10,000, whichever is greater. In 1990 this option would result in a maximum uniform dollar amount for all participants of $10,260 (because 20 percent of $51,300 (the 1990 Social Security wage base) is $10,260, which exceeds $10,000). This option allows an employer to adopt an integration level lower than the wage base, but it also results in a threshold so low that the vast majority of participants will receive the higher contribution rate on at least a portion of their compensation.

A second alternative allows the employer to designate an integration level at a point between the full wage base and the amount determined under the first alternative. Realizing that using such an interim integration level increases the possibility of discrimination, IRS requires that the 5.7 percent constraint mentioned above must be reduced if the second alternative is used.[4]

Defined Benefit Plans

An integrated defined benefit plan must be based on *average annual compensation*, defined as an average of at least three consecutive years' pay,[5] compared to nonintegrated plans, which may use different formulas. The employer is allowed to choose the averaging period, but in an integrated plan the employer must use the years of an

---

[4]A proportional reduction is also required in the old age portion of the Social Security contribution rate. See footnote 3.

[5]If a participant has worked less than three years, compensation must be averaged over the entire period of service.

138

TABLE 16.1
1990 Covered Compensation for Integration Purposes, Selected Years

Year of Birth	1990 Covered Compensation
1910	$ 5,316
1920	12,276
1930	25,008
1940	39,180
1950	48,840
1957 or later	51,300

employee's career that produce the highest average. (Due to their systematic differences in benefit accruals, exceptions are granted for career average or unit benefit plans. These plans may determine each year's benefit using that year's compensation.) (See chapter 4 for a discussion of pension plan formulas.)

Integration Level—An important concept for determining the integration level used in defined benefit plans is the participant's *covered compensation*, defined as the average of the Social Security wage base for the 35 years up to *and including* the employee's Social Security retirement year. Although the Social Security normal retirement age is scheduled to increase in the future under a very detailed set of rules, for purposes of integration, the retirement age is determined as follows:

Year of Birth	Social Security Retirement Age
1937 and earlier	65
1938 through 1954	66
1955 and later	67

Covered compensation amounts for 1990 are provided for selected years of birth in table 16.1.

However, the actual integration level chosen for the plan must not exceed the wage base at the beginning of the year and may either be the covered compensation for each participant or one of the following four alternatives:

- *Each employee's covered compensation from a previous year (frozen covered compensation)*—Rather than change the integration level each year, em-

139

TABLE 16.2
Maximum Permitted Disparity for Different Integration Levels

Integration Level as a Percentage of Covered Compensation for Employees Reaching Social Security Retirement Age in 1990	Maximum Permitted Disparity
>100%–125%	0.69
>125%–150%	0.60
>150%–175%	0.53
>175%–200%	0.47
>200% to Wage Base	0.42

ployers may use the covered compensation table for a certain year for up to five years. However, the same table must be used for all participants.

- *A uniform dollar amount for all employees*—The plan may either automatically use the greater of $10,000 (to rise in 1992) or one-half of covered compensation for employees who reach Social Security retirement age in the current plan year or satisfy two complex demographic requirements described in the proposed regulations.

- *Uniform percentage of each employee's covered compensation*—Under this approach, the integration level may be a uniform percentage (greater than 100 percent) of each employee's covered compensation, provided that the permitted disparity (discussed below) is reduced.

- *Uniform dollar amount without demographic tests*—Under this approach, a plan may specify an integration level that is any uniform dollar amount (as described above) but does not exceed the wage base for the year. Although there are no demographic tests to be satisfied under the method, the proposed regulations require that the permitted disparity be reduced to a specified factor if the integration level exceeds covered compensation (table 16.2).[6]

Excess Defined Benefit Plans—Under an excess defined benefit plan, the percentage of compensation at which benefits accrue with respect to compensation above the integration level may not be greater than 0.75 percent of compensation per year of service.[7] Moreover, this rate

---

[6]The permitted disparity of 0.75 percent must be reduced to the lesser of the factor determined in accordance with table 16.2, or 80 percent of the otherwise applicable factor (generally, the 0.75 percent factor, unless further reductions are required for the early commencement of benefits).
[7]Only years of service during which benefits accrue may be counted.

may not be more than twice the rate applied to compensation below the integration level.

Offset Defined Benefit Plans[8]—The limits for an offset plan are based on *final average compensation*, defined as the average of a participant's annual compensation (excluding pay in any year above that year's wage base) for the three-consecutive-year period ending with the current plan year. (If a participant has worked less than three years, then his or her compensation is to be averaged over the entire period of service.) The maximum offset is equal to 0.75 percent of final average compensation (up to the integration level) per year of service. As in the other two types of integration, the two-for-one rule is in effect and in this case specifies that the offset cannot be more than one-half the benefit that should be provided, prior to the application of the offset, with respect to the participant's average annual compensation not in excess of final average compensation (up to the integration level).

The concept of an offset plan is probably best illustrated through an example of a plan that does *not* satisfy the requirements. Assume that a plan provides, for each year of service, 1 percent of average annual compensation, reduced by 0.75 percent of final average compensation (up to the integration level). If an employee with 20 years of service has average annual compensation of $40,000 and final average compensation (up to the integration level) of $26,000, the plan would provide an annual normal retirement benefit of $8,000 [1 percent × 20 years × $40,000] minus $3,900 [0.75 percent × 20 years × $26,000] or $4,100. Although this would satisfy the 0.75 percent requirement, it would violate the two-for-one rule since the offset of $3,900 is more than $2,600. The $2,600 figure is one-half of the benefit based on average annual compensation not in excess of final average compensation (up to the integration level) [½ × 1 percent × 20 years × $26,000].

Career Cap—Both the excess and offset approaches for defined benefit (but not defined contribution) plans are subject to an additional constraint for long-term employees. The annual permitted differential of 0.75 percent is capped at 35 years of service *with the current employer.*

Adjustments—The 0.75 percent factor mentioned above must be adjusted in the event of early retirement or integration levels that

---

[8]Prior to TRA '86, the allowable offset for an integrated defined benefit plan was based on the participant's *Social Security* benefit, but thereafter is based on his or her compensation and service.

TABLE 16.3
Maximum Permitted Disparity for Early Retirement

Age at Which Benefits Begin	Social Security Normal Retirement Age		
	65	**66**	**67**
67	0.750%	0.750%	0.750%
66	0.750	0.750	0.700
65	0.750	0.700	0.650
64	0.700	0.650	0.600
63	0.650	0.600	0.550
62	0.600	0.550	0.500
61	0.550	0.500	0.475
60	0.500	0.475	0.450
59	0.475	0.450	0.425
58	0.455	0.425	0.400
57	0.425	0.400	0.375
56	0.400	0.375	0.344
55	0.375	0.344	0.316

are outside specified boundaries. If benefits are paid before Social Security normal retirement age, the maximum 0.75 percent must be reduced in accordance with table 16.3 even if benefits under the pension plan are actuarially reduced for early retirement. Adjustments to the 0.75 percent factor may also be required for different integration levels. The maximum permitted disparity for integration levels that are higher than covered compensation is shown in table 16.2.

Effective Dates and Transition

On a purely technical level the new integration requirements take effect for plan years beginning in 1989, although certain exceptions are provided for collectively bargained plans.

An important question from a long-term perspective regards the impact on employees who have been accruing benefits under the old rules. Employers with plans that have pre-1989 benefit accruals may choose either of the following approaches as long as they are applied consistently to all participants.

- Each participant's accrued benefit is frozen as of the transition date and future benefits are accrued under the new rules.[9] Under an amendment

---

[9]For each employee, the number of years the accrued benefit has been integrated must

to the regulations issued on May 10, 1990, the accrued benefit as of the transition date under a final average pay plan may be adjusted for future increases in the employee's average annual compensation, provided the plan meets, or is amended to meet, the two-for-one rule with respect to the benefit for service prior to the transition date.

- Each participant's benefit is the greater of the benefit calculated under the new rule or the benefit accrued at the transition date.

---

be subtracted from the 35-year limit in the new rules. In other words, if a participant had completed five years of service before the 1989 plan year, then the cumulative maximum permitted disparity with respect to that participant's total benefits would be 22.5 percent [0.75 percent × (35 − 5)].

17. Nondiscrimination, Minimum Coverage, and Participation Requirements for Pension Plans

Introduction

Qualified pension plans have long been subject to statutory and regulatory requirements designed to ensure that the tax advantages would result in broad-based coverage of employees—as opposed to plans set up to benefit only the highly paid employees and/or managers of the firm. Although these requirements have met with various degrees of success, legislators sought to accelerate this progress and further broaden employee access to employer-sponsored pension plans through various provisions of the Tax Reform Act of 1986 (TRA '86).

This chapter deals with three specific criteria that must be simultaneously satisfied for a plan to have tax-qualified status: nondiscrimination, minimum coverage, and minimum participation requirements. The proposed regulations on the nondiscrimination rules, which provide a three-part test to ensure that contributions or benefits provided under the plan do not discriminate in favor of highly compensated employees,[1] are discussed first. This is followed by an examination of the proposed regulations on the minimum participation requirements and a discussion of the minimum coverage requirements that consider overall employee participation in pension plans. All of these regulations were recently proposed by the Internal Revenue Service (IRS) and may undergo modification before being finalized.

Nondiscrimination Rules

Overview

Section 401(a)(4) of the Internal Revenue Code (IRC) provides that a plan is qualified only if the contributions or benefits provided under the plan do not discriminate in favor of highly compensated employees. The proposed regulations for section 401(a)(4) set forth three requirements a plan must meet to satisfy this condition:

---

[1] See chapter 4 for a definition of highly compensated employees.

- either the contributions or the benefits provided under the plan must be nondiscriminatory in terms of their amount;

- the benefits, rights, and features provided under the plan must be available to employees in the plan in a nondiscriminatory manner; and

- the effect of the plan in certain special circumstances (e.g., plan amendments, grants of past service credit, and plan terminations) must be nondiscriminatory.

Each of these requirements will be explored in more detail below.

Nondiscrimination in Amount of Contributions or Benefits

Although separate rules are provided for determining whether contributions and benefits are nondiscriminatory, it is generally permissible for a pension plan to satisfy this requirement by showing that either the contributions or the benefits are nondiscriminatory. An exception to this general rule applies to employee stock ownership plans (see chapter 10) and plans subject to section 401(k) or 401(m) (see chapter 9). In these cases, the plan must prove that contributions are nondiscriminatory.[2]

Nondiscrimination in Amount of Contributions—The proposed regulations for section 401(a)(4) provide two safe harbor tests for defined contribution plans. The first applies to a defined contribution plan with a uniform allocation formula that provides employees with uniform allocation rates. Permitted disparity that is explicitly taken into account under the allocation formula may be taken into account in applying this test. The second permits a defined contribution plan with a uniform allocation formula weighted for age or service to satisfy the requirement if the average rate of allocation for highly compensated employees under the plan does not exceed the average rate of allocation for nonhighly compensated employees under the plan.

If a plan does not satisfy one of these safe harbor tests, then the requirement will be met if no highly compensated employee under the plan has an allocation rate exceeding that of any nonhighly com-

---

[2] A host of technical considerations also arise in this determination. Although they are beyond the scope of this book, readers should be aware that plans may satisfy these requirements on an aggregated or restructured basis (section 1.401(a)(4)-9); plans with multiple formulas may satisfy these requirements on the basis of each separate formula; most collectively bargained plans automatically satisfy the nondiscrimination rules (section 1.401(a)(4)-1(c)(6)); and certain safe harbor testing methods are provided for target benefit plans and defined benefit plans that are part of a floor-offset plan (section 1.401(a)(4)-8).

pensated employee under the plan. For purpose of this calculation, permitted disparity under section 401(l)—that is, differences in rates that occur due to integration with Social Security (see chapter 16)—may generally be taken into account by imputation. Also, considerable flexibility is provided to employers in applying this general test under the grouping and restructuring tests. Plans subject to section 401(k) or 401(m), however, must satisfy the special rules provided for them.

Nondiscrimination in Amount of Benefits—The proposed regulations contain four safe harbors under which a plan is considered nondiscriminatory with respect to the amount of benefits. All require that the plan have a uniform benefit formula, that any subsidized early retirement or joint and survivor benefit be provided on similar terms to substantially all covered employees, that the formula base benefits on a nondiscriminatory definition of compensation, and that the plan have a uniform retirement age for all employees.

Two safe harbors apply to unit credit plans that provide a benefit for each year of service based upon a fixed percentage of pay or a fixed dollar amount. The first is for plans that provide for the accrual of these benefits on a unit credit basis, and the second is for plans using the fractional accrual rule.[3] The other two apply to flat benefit plans that satisfy the fractional accrual rule.[4] An example of such a plan is one that provides a benefit of 50 percent of compensation accrued evenly over all years of service or participation. Such a plan satisfies the safe harbor only if the plan provides that the maximum flat benefit will be accrued over a period of at least 25 years.

Those plans that do not satisfy any of the safe harbors must satisfy the general test for nondiscrimination with respect to the amount of benefits. This is accomplished only if no highly compensated employee has an accrual rate greater than that of any nonhighly compensated employee. The disparity permitted under section 401(l) may be taken into account by imputation for this purpose. The employer is generally required to determine accrual rates with respect to both the normal form of benefit and the most valuable form of benefit.

---

[3]That is, the employee's accrued benefit is not less than the projected normal retirement benefit prorated for years of plan participation.

[4]The second safe harbor for flat benefit plans is a nondesign-based safe harbor that requires that the average accrual rate of nonhighly compensated employees as a group be at least 70 percent of the average accrual rate of highly compensated employees as a group.

Nondiscriminatory Availability of Benefits, Rights, and Features

Optional forms of benefits, ancillary benefits, and other rights and features provided under the plan must be nondiscriminatory. Special rules exist for acquisitions, mergers, and similar transactions. An optional form of benefit is a distribution alternative that is available under a plan, an early retirement benefit, or a retirement-type subsidy. Each optional form of benefit must be currently available and effectively available to a nondiscriminatory classification of employees. Current availability focuses on the availability of the option to employees, but assumes that certain conditions such as age or service under the terms of a plan are currently satisfied. Effective availability examines whether actual availability of the option, taking into account the ability of employees to satisfy age and service requirements, substantially favors highly compensated employees.

Ancillary benefits include certain Social Security supplements, disability benefits, ancillary life insurance and health insurance benefits, death benefits under a defined contribution plan, preretirement death benefits under a defined benefit plan, and shut-down benefits.

Other rights or features are defined as any right or feature applicable to employees under the plan, other than a right or feature taken into account as part of an optional form of benefit or ancillary benefit provided under the plan and other than a right or feature that cannot reasonably be expected to be of more than insignificant value to an employee. For example, the following are specifically included in this definition:

- plan loan provisions;
- the right to direct investments;
- the right to a particular form of investment;
- the right to a particular class or type of employer securities;
- the right to make a particular rate of before-tax, after-tax, or matching contribution;
- the right to purchase additional retirement or ancillary benefits under the plan; and
- the right to make rollover contributions and transfers to and from the plan.

Nondiscriminatory Effect of Plan in Special Circumstances

Plan amendments and grants of past service credit must not have the effect of discrimination in favor of highly compensated employees.

148

The proposed regulations contain a safe harbor under which a grant of up to five years of past service credit is deemed to be nondiscriminatory. Restrictions on distributions are also prescribed to place a limit on the annual distributions received by the top-paid 25 employees. However, the distribution restrictions do not apply if the plan's funding ratio is at least 110 percent (measured on a current liability basis) or if the benefit payable is less than 1 percent of the current liability.

Employee Contributions

Generally, benefits derived from employer contributions and benefits derived from employee contributions must separately satisfy the nondiscrimination requirements. The proposed regulations provide rules relating to the determination of the employer-derived benefit in a defined benefit plan that also includes employee contributions not allocated to separate accounts. It also provides rules for determining whether employee contributions under a defined benefit plan are nondiscriminatory.

Permitted Disparity

The proposed regulations allow the disparity permitted by section 401(l) to be taken into account in showing that the amount of contributions or benefits satisfies section 401(a)(4). In many cases, this merely requires inspection of the plan benefit or contribution formula, as where a plan is using one of the safe harbor rules for showing nondiscrimination in the amount of contributions or benefits. These safe harbors require that the plan formula satisfy 401(l) in form. Thus, for example, a single defined contribution plan that takes permitted disparity into account under a uniform formula satisfies section 401(a)(4) with respect to the amount of contributions if the disparity under the formula satisfies section 401(l) and the regulations thereunder. Similarly, a single defined benefit plan or target benefit plan that takes permitted disparity into account under a uniform formula satisfies section 401(a)(4) with respect to the amount of benefits if the disparity under the formula satisfies section 401(l) and the regulations thereunder.

If a plan does not use the safe harbor rules, or if two or more plans are combined for purposes of section 401(a)(4), permitted disparity is taken into account by using specified formulas that determine an adjusted allocation or accrual rate that reflects the amount of permitted disparity that may be taken into account.[5]

In the case of a defined contribution plan, the plan's allocation rates are adjusted to take into account permitted disparity. This adjusted rate is used to determine whether the amount of contributions under the plan is nondiscriminatory under the general test and to apply the average benefit percentage test of section 410(b) (described later in this chapter). If an employee's compensation does not exceed the taxable wage base in effect as of the beginning of the plan year, the employee's adjusted allocation rate equals the sum of the employee's accrual allocation rate and maximum allocation rate that the plan could have used under the permitted disparity rules. If an employee's compensation exceeds the taxable wage base in effect as of the beginning of the plan year, the employee's adjusted allocation rate is the lesser of two rates provided in section 1.401(a)(4)-7(b)(3).

The process for a defined benefit pension plan is similar, although covered compensation (defined in chapter 16) is used to dichotomize employees instead of the taxable wage base. In this case, if an employee's compensation does not exceed the employee's covered compensation as of the beginning of the plan year, the employee's adjusted benefit accrual rate is the sum of the employee's actual accrual rate and the maximum excess allowance under the permitted disparity rules described in chapter 16. If an employee's compensation exceeds the employee's covered compensation as of the beginning of the plan year, the employee's adjusted benefit accrual rate is the lesser of two rates provided in section 1.401(a)(4)-7(c)(3).

Minimum Participation Requirements

Overview

TRA '86 added IRC section 401(a)(26), which specifies that, on *each* day of the plan year, all plans must benefit 50 employees of the employer or 40 percent of all employees of the employer, whichever is less. This was designed to limit the extent to which a defined benefit plan may operate as an individual account for a small group of employees, and to limit the extent to which an employer is able to design

---

[5]The adjusted rates attempt to transform the allocations of accruals under the plan for each employee to determine the excess rate each employee would receive if the same dollar value of allocation or accrual had been achieved under a plan formula containing the maximum permitted disparity under section 401(l). The resulting excess rates are the allocation rates or accrual rates that are compared to determine whether the plan satisfies the general tests described previously.

different benefit formulas for different employees in order to maximize benefit disparities in favor of highly compensated employees.

Proposed regulations for section 401(a)(26), issued on May 10, 1990, focus on the first of these two objectives. The regulations take the view that the new 401(a)(4) rules (discussed earlier) should adequately address the second policy objective.

These regulations also provide a simplified testing method under which the plan is treated as satisfying 401(a)(26) if it satisfies the requirements on a single day during the plan year, as long as the day selected is reasonably representative of the employer's employees and the plan's coverage.

Employees Who Benefit under a Plan

An employee is treated as benefiting under a plan for a plan year only if he or she actually accrues a benefit for the plan year. An employee who is eligible under either a 401(k) or 401(m) plan for the plan year is treated as benefiting under the plan. This is the case without regard to whether the employee has a benefit under the plan and without regard to whether the employee makes elective contributions under the plan for the year.

Defined Contribution Plans

A defined contribution plan satisfies this requirement if it provides current benefits to the requisite number of employees of the employer and satisfies the requirement automatically if it does not currently benefit any employees or former employees.

Defined Benefit Plans

A defined benefit plan satisfies this requirement with respect to current accruals by providing a current benefit to the requisite number of employees and satisfies the requirement with respect to its prior benefit structure[6] if the requisite number of employees either have a meaningful accrued benefit or are currently receiving a meaningful benefit accrual. Former employees may be aggregated with employees in establishing that the requisite number of employees have a meaningful accrued benefit under the plan.[7]

---

[6]The prior benefit structure under defined benefit plans for a plan year includes all benefits accrued to date under the plan. Each defined benefit plan has only one prior benefit structure, and all accrued benefits under the plan as of the beginning of a plan year are included in the prior benefit structure for the year.

[7]Special rules exist for multiemployer defined benefit plans.

Whether the employer is providing (or has provided) a meaningful benefit is determined based on all of the facts and circumstances.

Plans Excepted from the Minimum Participation Requirements

Plans meeting one of the following four exceptions are treated as satisfying section 401(a)(26) without further testing of participation under the plan:

- plans not benefiting highly compensated employees;
- multiemployer plans that benefit only employees included in a unit of employees covered by a collective bargaining agreement;
- certain underfunded defined benefit plans; and
- plans involved in certain acquisitions and dispositions.

Testing Former Employees

If a defined benefit plan provides additional benefits to former employees during a plan year, the plan must satisfy section 401(a)(26) with respect to former employees. This is accomplished if the plan satisfies the minimum participation rule for former employees. Alternatively, it may be accomplished if the plan benefits at least five former employees, and it either

- benefits more than 95 percent of all former employees with accrued benefits under the plan or
- at least 60 percent of the former employees receiving an additional benefit are nonhighly compensated employees.

Minimum Coverage Requirements

General Rule

In general, a plan must satisfy one of two requirements under IRC section 410(b) for both active and former employees on one day in each quarter.[8]

Ratio Percentage Test—Under this test, the percentage of the employer's nonhighly compensated employees benefiting under the plan must equal at least 70 percent of the percentage of the employer's

---

[8]This requirement generally is effective with respect to plan years beginning after December 31, 1988. TRA '86 specified three tests but one was mathematically redundant and has been deleted under the proposed regulations.

highly compensated employees benefiting under the plan. For example, if a plan benefits 60 percent of the employer's highly compensated active employees and 35 percent of the employer's nonhighly compensated active employees, it fails this test because the plan's ratio percentage is less than 70 percent (35 percent/60 percent = 58⅓ percent).

Average Benefit Test—This test has two parts, both of which must be satisfied. Under the first, the nondiscriminatory classification test, the plan is required to benefit a classification of employees that does not discriminate in favor of highly compensated employees. Under the second, the average benefit percentage test, the average benefit percentage[9] of nonhighly compensated employees must equal at least 70 percent of the average benefit percentage of highly compensated employees.

Nondiscriminatory Classification Test

To satisfy the nondiscriminatory classification test under section 410(b), a plan must cover a classification of employees that is reasonable, reflecting a bona fide business classification such as salaried and hourly employees. Moreover, the plan must either

- benefit at least a safe harbor percentage of nonhighly compensated employees or
- pass a facts and circumstances test and benefit at least an unsafe harbor percentage of nonhighly compensated employees.

Safe Harbor/Unsafe Harbor Tests—Under these tests the plan's ratio percentage must be at least equal to the safe (or unsafe) harbor percentage. Mathematically, this is the same test as the ratio percentage test explained earlier, but it substitutes the safe (or unsafe) harbor percentage for 70 percent. The safe (or unsafe) harbor percentages are based on the concentration percentage[10] of all nonhighly compensated employees within the employer's work force. Table 17.1 illustrates the safe harbor and unsafe harbor percentages for specific concentrations of nonhighly compensated employees.

---

[9] The regulations provide detailed guidance concerning the calculation of the individual benefit percentages that are separately averaged for high- and low-paid employees. Benefit calculations are generally performed using the same actuarial techniques required by the nondiscrimination rules, with several important simplifications.

[10] The concentration percentage is defined as the ratio of the nonhighly compensated employees to the employer's total work force (minus any excludable employees), whether or not they are covered by the plan.

TABLE 17.1
Section 410(b) Nondiscriminatory Classification under the Safe Harbor/Unsafe Harbor Tests

Concentration Percentage	Safe Harbor Ratio Percentage	Unsafe Harbor Ratio Percentage
60.00% or less	50.00%	40.00%
62.00	48.50	38.50
64.00	47.00	37.00
66.00	45.50	35.50
68.00	44.00	34.00
70.00	42.50	32.50
72.00	41.00	31.00
74.00	39.50	29.50
76.00	38.00	28.00
78.00	36.50	26.50
80.00	35.00	25.00
82.00	33.50	23.50
84.00	32.00	22.00
86.00	30.50	20.50
88.00	29.00	20.00
90.00	27.50	20.00
92.00	26.00	20.00
94.00	24.50	20.00
96.00	23.00	20.00
98.00	21.50	20.00

This still leaves a gray area for a plan if it has neither passed the safe harbor test nor failed the unsafe harbor test. In this case, it may be considered nondiscriminatory based on a review of all "facts and circumstances."

Facts and Circumstances Test—The regulations indicate that the following factors, among others, may be considered in applying the "facts and circumstances" test:

- the employer's underlying business reasons for the classification;

- the percentage of the work force that benefits under the plan;

- whether the number of covered employees in each salary range is representative of the total number of employees in that salary range; and

- how close the classification comes to satisfying the safe harbor percentage.

154

Other Factors That Affect Testing

Plans Deemed to Pass—The following plans are deemed to satisfy the minimum coverage requirements:[11]

- frozen plans (that is, plans in which no employees are accruing additional benefits);
- plans of an employer that employs only highly compensated employees;
- plans that benefit only nonhighly compensated employees; and
- plans that benefit only union employees (unless more than a de minimis number of professionals are included).

Excludable Employees—In general, all active and former employees are taken into account in applying the minimum coverage tests except:[12]

- employees who have not satisfied the plan's minimum age and/or service requirements (see chapter 3);
- nonunion employees who do not benefit under a plan because of a collective bargaining agreement (when testing a plan that benefits union employees);[13]
- collective bargaining unit employees (when testing a noncollective bargaining unit plan);
- participants who fail to accrue a benefit or receive an allocation solely because of a minimum service requirement;[14] and
- nonresident aliens with no U.S. source of income.

Mandatory Disaggregation of Plans—Certain single plans must be disaggregated into two or more separate plans, each of which must satisfy section 410(b). The following are examples.

- *Collectively Bargained Units*—The portion of a plan that benefits employees under a collective bargaining agreement and the portion of the plan that benefits nonunion employees must be treated as separate plans.

---

[11]Special rules also apply to tax-credit employee stock ownership plans (ESOPs) and governmental and church plans.

[12]Although not available at the time of this writing, it is possible that future regulations will provide guidance on whether the employer may be treated as having two or more separate lines of business for purposes of the minimum coverage rules.

[13]Certain plans that benefit more than 2 percent of a firm's professional employees are not treated as collectively bargained plans.

[14]This exclusion will apply if there is a requirement that the employee be working on the last day of the plan year, or that an employee performs at least 500 hours of service.

- *Employee Stock Ownership Plans*—For plan years after 1989, a plan with an ESOP and a non-ESOP feature is treated as two plans.

- *Section 401(k) and 401(m) Arrangements*—The portion of a plan that includes (1) a section 401(k) cash or deferred arrangement or (2) matching or employee contributions subject to section 401(m) rules (see chapter 9) are treated as separate plans.

Aggregation of Plans—For purposes of applying the ratio percentage test and nondiscriminatory classification test, two or more separate plans are permitted to be treated as a single plan. However, the aggregate plan would have to satisfy the nondiscriminatory benefit and contributions test of IRC section 401(a)(4). Also, an employer may not permissively aggregate plans that have been disaggregated on a mandatory basis (e.g., ESOPs and non-ESOPs, union plans and nonunion plans).

Generally, for purposes of the average benefit percentage test, all qualified plans of an employer, including qualified cash or deferred arrangements and matching or employee contributions subject to section 401(m), must be aggregated and treated as a single plan. However, union plans are tested separately from nonunion plans.[15] Also, the new regulations permit separate testing of defined contribution and defined benefit plans.

Multiemployer/Multiple Employer Plans—Each separate employer's portion of a multiple employer plan that is maintained by more than one employer for nonbargained employees is tested separately. If one employer fails, the whole plan, for all employers, potentially could be disqualified. A multiemployer plan (a plan maintained by more than one employer for collectively bargained employees) is treated as one plan, and all participating employers are treated as one employer.

Former Employees—Former employees who "currently benefit" under the plan (e.g., are granted an ad hoc cost-of-living increase under a plan amendment) are tested separately from active employees. An employer may elect to disregard former employees who are not "currently benefiting" and who terminated prior to 1984 or more than 10 years before the year being tested.

Under a special rule, if at least 10 former employees are currently benefiting under the plan and at least 60 percent of the former employees who are currently benefiting under the plan are nonhighly

---

[15]At the time this chapter was written, the IRS was considering whether ESOPS should be tested along with non-ESOPs.

compensated, the plan will be deemed to pass with respect to former employees.

Compliance

A plan failing to meet the requirements of section 410(b) described above must be brought into retroactive compliance by the end of the applicable plan year. This may be accomplished either by extending coverage to a broader group of employees or modifying contribution allocations or benefit accruals.

18. Planning for Retirement

Introduction

Retirement is a relatively new phenomenon. Until a few decades ago, most men and many women worked throughout their lives. Those who were unable to continue working were sustained either by their family or by a public facility for destitute people. Since Social Security retirement benefits were first paid in 1940, it has been customary for workers to retire at age 65.[1] The growth of employer pension plans and increased life expectancy have also contributed to present retirement trends.

On average, individuals who reach age 65 today can expect to live to age 80. Expanded life expectancy brings with it a new awareness of the aging process. Retirement is increasingly an important part of one's total life. Unfortunately, many still view their retirement years as a time of crisis. Retirement is a challenging period that can bring rewards and new experiences. A happy and satisfying retirement, however, requires an adjustment period that is greatly aided by thoughtful, effective planning in earlier working years.

Ideally, one should begin planning for retirement between the ages of 30 and 40. Planning at a later time, however, is better than not planning at all. A survey of working Americans conducted for the International Association for Financial Planning in 1988 revealed that many Americans are insecure about their long-term future—40 percent of the respondents expressed fear that they would outlive their retirement dollars. Advance planning can minimize this risk and also alleviate some of the psychological problems that sometimes accompany retirement (Kiechel, 1988).

The first part of this chapter identifies some areas that need attention by those who are preparing for retirement. It is not intended to provide all the necessary information, but rather to highlight certain questions that need early consideration. The discussion focuses on financial planning, preventive health, health care costs, living arrangements, use of leisure time, interpersonal relationships, and es-

---

[1] The normal retirement age under Social Security will be increased gradually from age 65 to age 67, beginning in the year 2000. For more information on Social Security, see chapter 2.

159

tate planning. The second part of the chapter looks at the potential role of employers in helping employees to prepare for retirement.

Financial Planning

A difficult aspect of retirement planning is ensuring adequate household income. A common misconception is that financial planning is only necessary for wealthy people. Retirement income planning may be even more important for average- or low-income people. Workers should be saving and investing the largest amounts at the peak of their earning power. Additionally, they should understand that certain options existing at one point in time may not be available later.

Throughout their career years, workers should give careful consideration to the following questions: At what age should I retire? What kind of retirement lifestyle do I want? Where will I live? How much money will I need? What are my assets and liabilities now? What will they be at retirement? How can I cope with inflation? If I should die before my spouse, will my family be left with an adequate income?

Retirement income is generally derived from three sources: Social Security, pensions, and personal savings. In addition, retirees may have access to life insurance, home equity, welfare programs, or new forms of employment.

Social Security—Social Security provides a monthly benefit to retired, blind, or disabled workers who have contributed to the system during their working years. Various requirements must be met before benefits are payable. For those who qualify, benefits are paid to workers and their nonworking spouses, widows, widowers, divorcees, dependent children, and dependent parents. Under current law, Social Security benefits are adjusted annually for inflation.

Social Security replaces a portion of preretirement income. This amount is not designed to provide income sufficient to satisfy all retirement needs. It must be supplemented by private pensions, personal savings, and other investments.

Today, most workers qualify for reduced retirement benefits at age 62 and full benefits at age 65. Social Security has no minimum age or service criteria, thus all covered workers are also program participants. *Vesting* (that is, rights to benefits that cannot be revoked due to job termination) occurs when employees have at least one quarter of covered employment for every year between 1950 (or, if later, the year after reaching age 21) and the time they reach age 62. Individuals retiring at age 62 in 1990 or later need 40 quarters. Social Security vesting is relatively lenient; an overwhelming majority of the work force ultimately qualifies for benefits. Social Security payments are not automatically provided; workers must apply for full benefits three months before retirement (or two months if they retire early, that is, at age 62).

Workers should determine whether they will qualify for Social Security benefits. At least once every three years they should also obtain a Personal Earnings and Benefit Statement from the Social Security Administration. Answers to questions concerning Social Security can be obtained from local Social Security offices; the address and phone number are listed in the telephone book under "Social Security Administration." The administration also has a nationwide toll-free number: (800) 937-2000. (For more information on Social Security, see chapter 2.)

Private Pension Programs—The nation's private pension system covers more than 40.5 million individuals and provides benefits to more than 8.0 million beneficiaries aged 55 or older (Employee Benefit Research Institute, 1989). Some people, however, are not eligible for such pensions because they have short service with their employer, or they do not receive benefits because they do not stay long enough with the employer to vest. Generally, employees must become eligible to participate in a plan when they have worked for the employer for one year. Vesting must occur for employer contributions to private-sector, single-employer pension plans according to one of two schedules: 100 percent at the end of five years of service, or 20 percent after three years of service and an additional 20 percent after each subsequent year of service, reaching 100 percent at the end of seven years of service. (For a discussion of vesting under multiemployer plans, see chapter 6.)

Full pension benefits are usually offered at a specified age—frequently age 65. It is usually possible to retire early with reduced pension benefits. Pension payments from qualified plans received prior to age 59½ are generally subject to an additional 10 percent federal penalty tax. The 10 percent tax does not apply, however, to certain distributions: those made in the form of substantially equal payments over the life or life expectancy of the participant (or the joint lives or life expectancies of the participant and his or her beneficiary); those made after the participant has separated from service and is at least age 55 by the end of the year in which separation occurs; those used for payment of medical expenses to the extent deductible for federal income tax purposes (expenses that exceed 7½ percent of adjusted gross income); distributions received from an

161

employee stock ownership plan before January 1, 1990; and those made to or on behalf of an alternate payee pursuant to a qualified domestic relations order. If the pension payment is received in the form of a partial or total distribution, the 10 percent tax does not apply if the distribution is rolled over into an individual retirement account (IRA) within 60 days of receipt.

Most pension plans do not provide automatic cost-of-living adjustments, although some provide ad hoc pension supplementation on a discretionary basis. This is an important consideration in retirement planning, since inflation reduces the value of fixed pension income. Some pension plans permit employees to voluntarily contribute to the plan; these contributions result in higher retirement income.

Under the Employee Retirement Income Security Act of 1974 (ERISA), employer plans automatically provide benefits to surviving spouses of retired workers, unless an employee rejects this option in writing. The Retirement Equity Act of 1984 stipulates that an employee may reject a surviving spouse's benefits only with the written consent of the spouse.[2] Survivors' benefits are provided through a joint and survivor annuity. Before retirement, workers and their spouses should confirm the status of their survivor benefits. Other options provided by many plans include: single or straight life annuities, period certain annuities, and lump-sum distributions. Particular care is required when considering a lump-sum distribution from an employer's plan. Important considerations include the health of the employee and spouse, the ability and willingness to manage a significant amount of money, the availability of this money for nonretirement purposes, and the complex rules governing the tax treatment of lump sums (for example, 5 and 10 year averaging, capital gains, and IRA rollover rules).

Private pension plan participants should thoroughly understand their plans. By doing this, they can develop reasonable estimates of future pension benefits. ERISA sets minimum funding, participation, and vesting standards for private pension plans. ERISA also requires reporting and disclosure of pension plan financial and operations information to plan participants and beneficiaries. Reports to participants must be written in a manner calculated to be understood

---

[2]The Employee Retirement Income Security Act of 1974, as modified by the Retirement Equity Act of 1984, also provides that vested employees must be given the option to take a survivor benefit through their plan. For more information on survivor benefits under Social Security and employer-sponsored plans, see chapters 2, 4, and 28.

by the average participant or beneficiary. (For further discussion of ERISA requirements, see chapter 3.)

Federal Pensions—Civil service employees are covered by their own retirement income program. Full civil service pension benefits are generally provided to retirees who satisfy one of several possible age and service criteria: aged 55 with 30 years of service, aged 60 with 20 years of service, or aged 62 with five years of service. Pension benefits are automatically adjusted for inflation.

Changes in the federal pension program were implemented as a result of the 1983 Social Security Amendments. Effective January 1, 1984, Social Security participation became mandatory for all newly hired federal employees. Before the 1983 amendments, federal employees generally did not participate in Social Security.

These recent federal hires are also covered by a new pension system. Full benefits are payable at age 57 with 30 years of service; benefits paid after age 62 arc indexed to inflation, and participants who work beyond age 62 continue to accrue benefits. Workers also have the option of taking part in a capital accumulation plan, to which they and the government contribute. For more information on civil service pensions, see chapters 38 and 39; also contact the U.S. Office of Personnel Management, 1900 E Street, NW, Washington, DC 20415.

Military Plans—The Military Retirement System has traditionally provided high lifetime benefits. For active duty military personnel with 20 years of service, the system offers very early retirement with an immediate and continuing lifetime benefit. Military personnel do not contribute to their pension plans. Their retirement benefits are automatically adjusted with inflation. Military plans, however, do not provide vesting of nondisability retirement benefits for those with fewer than 20 years of service. Military retirees who are aged 62 or older are also entitled to Social Security benefits.

The Military Retirement Reform Act of 1986 implemented a new pension plan for persons entering the armed forces after August 1, 1986. Under the old system, military personnel who retired after 20 years of service received annual benefits of one-half their base pay for the three highest-earning years. Benefits rose 2.5 percent for every additional year of service up to 30, when benefits peaked at 75 percent. Persons entering the military after August 1, 1986, and retiring with 20 years of service will receive 40 percent of their base pay for the three highest years; those retiring with 30 years of service will receive 75 percent. Benefits for early retirees are adjusted for each year of service less than 30 years.

Veterans' Pensions—Veterans may be considered for pensions from the Veterans Administration if they have wartime service. To receive benefits, veterans must be totally and permanently disabled or aged 65 or older and have income below a specified amount. More information can be obtained by contacting a local Veterans Administration office.

Keogh Plans and IRAs—Keogh plans for the self-employed and IRAs are voluntarily established by employers and individuals. Keoghs and IRAs offer tax savings on individual contributions and their investment earnings. Each year, those eligible for IRA participation may contribute up to $2,000 ($2,250 for those with nonworking spouses) or 100 percent of earned income (whichever is lower). Persons eligible to deduct IRA contributions may claim the deduction for the tax year in which contributions are made. The deductibility of IRA contributions for taxpayers who are covered by an employer-sponsored retirement plan and have income above specified levels is restricted. Distributions from IRAs are taxed in the year they are received. A 10 percent penalty is imposed on most distributions received before age 59½. (For more information on IRAs and Keoghs, see chapters 13 and 15, respectively.)

The self-employed and employees of unincorporated businesses can save for retirement through Keogh plans. The maximum annual contribution for a defined benefit plan is the lesser of the amount needed to fund a $90,000 annual benefit or 100 percent of the employee's average compensation for the highest three years. For a defined contribution plan, the annual contribution maximum is $30,000 or 25 percent of compensation, whichever is less. (These limits are identical to those found in corporate plans.) Distributions from Keoghs are taxed in the year they are received, with a 10 percent penalty imposed on those who take a distribution before age 59½, unless the distribution meets one of the statutory exceptions.

Personal Savings—Personal savings are an important part of retirement income, supplementing pensions and Social Security benefits. In determining how much money you will need from savings to maintain your standard of living throughout your retirement years, it is important to factor in the effect of inflation on purchasing power. Table 18.1 provides a series of calculations that can be used to determine how much a worker must save each year to accumulate a specific amount of money for retirement.

Access to Home Equity—Most individuals accumulate their largest share of personal wealth in home equity. More than 60 percent of the elderly own their own homes, and 49 percent own them free of any

How Much Do You Have to Save?

Column A	Forms of Payment	
	Column B	Column C
years of saving	one lump-sum payment	15 annual payments
5	0.216	2.79
10	0.112	1.45
15	0.077	1.00
20	0.060	0.77
25	0.049	0.63
30	0.041	0.53
35	0.035	0.46

You can use this chart to determine how much you must save at the end of each year to accumulate a specific amount of money (adjusted for inflation). These calculations assume a 6 percent annual rate of return on savings and a 4 percent annual rate of inflation.

Step 1: Decide how much money you want to receive and choose the form of payment desired: one lump-sum payment (Column B) or 15 equal annual payments (Column C). Write the amount you want to receive here _____.

Step 2: Look under Column A and find the number of years you plan to save. Then find the corresponding number under Column B or Column C (depending on the form of payment you chose) and write the number here _____.

Step 3: Multiply the number you get resulting from Step 2 by the amount of money you want to receive (Step 1). This will give you the amount you must save at the end of each year to reach your target amount (adjusted for inflation) _____.

Example 1: To determine how much you must save at the end of each year to accumulate one lump-sum payment of $50,000 (adjusted for inflation) after 10 years, multiply $50,000 by 0.112. You will need to save $5,600 at the end of each year. (The actual sums accumulated will vary because the target of $50,000 is calculated in terms of today's values. Therefore, these numbers show what you will have to save to accumulate, in the future, the equivalent of $50,000 in today's dollars. At the assumed 4 percent annual rate of inflation, your actual lump-sum payment in 10 years would be $74,012 in nominal dollars.)

Example 2: To determine how much you must save at the end of each year to finance 15 annual payments of $20,000 each (adjusted for inflation) starting after 25 years, multiply $20,000 by 0.63. You will need to save $12,600 at the end of each year. (The actual sums accumulated will vary because the target amount is calculated in terms of today's values. Therefore, these numbers show what you will have to save to finance the target amount in today's dollars. At the assumed 4 percent annual rate of inflation, your actual first payment in 25 years would be $55,449 in nominal dollars, and the last payment would be $96,020 in nominal dollars. The total amount accumulated would be $691,293 in nominal dollars.)

Source: Employee Benefit Research Institute.

debt. At retirement, these homeowners can convert their home value into income-generating assets, or they can continue living in their home and enjoy the financial and personal advantages of owning residential property.

Two basic types of home equity conversion are reverse mortgages and sale leasebacks.

Reverse mortgages provide a stream of monthly loan advances to the homeowner, who retains title to the property. Repayment of these advances is deferred until the homeowner moves or dies. Appreciation in the home's value during the loan period typically belongs to the homeowner or his or her estate. Some reverse mortgages, however, allow the loan grantor to increase payments to the homeowner in exchange for a share of the appreciation. Reverse mortgages are not yet widely available in every state. Careful review of the reverse mortgage documents by a qualified independent advisor is critical prior to entering an arrangement.

In a *sale leaseback* plan the home is sold to an investor; the former homeowner retains the right to rent the home for life. Each month the investor pays the former owner and in exchange receives a rent payment. Upon the former homeowner's death or change of residence, all rights associated with the house belong to the investor. Appreciation during this rental period also belongs to the investor, as does responsibility for maintenance and taxes. As with reverse mortgage arrangements, consulting with a tax and legal advisor prior to entering a sale leaseback plan is important. For more information on home equity conversion, contact a savings and loan institution or the National Center for Home Equity Conversion, 110 East Main Street, Madison, WI 53703, or the Home Equity Information Center, American Association of Retired Persons, 1900 K Steet, NW, Washington, DC 20049.

Life Insurance—One major purpose of life insurance is to produce an immediate income for surviving dependents when working spouses or pensioners die. As a source of retirement income, life insurance assures that benefits will be paid to surviving beneficiaries according to the policy's stated conditions. The rate of return on savings invested in some policies, however, is relatively low.

Workers may purchase individual life insurance and pay premiums out of personal income. Sometimes, employers pay group life insurance premiums for active as well as retired employees. Workers should inquire whether employer plans will continue to provide coverage after retirement and, if so, to what extent the death benefit amount may be reduced.

Other Savings Alternatives—There are many other types of investment instruments that produce retirement income (for example, stocks,
bonds, mutual funds, and savings accounts). Workers should understand their alternatives and weigh the advantages and disadvantages
of each against their individual needs.

Employment—Many older persons who are eligible for retirement
continue working, at least part time. Aside from the financial advantages, employment provides a productive and structured activity.
Currently, a Social Security earnings test limits the amount that can
be earned before Social Security benefits are partially or fully reduced. In 1990, retirees aged 65 through 69 can earn up to $9,360
without a reduction in Social Security benefits. Those who retire
before age 65 are permitted to earn up to $6,840. One benefit dollar
will be withheld for every three dollars in earnings above the limit;
beginning at age 70, however, there is no limit on the amount that
can be earned without penalty. Some employment agencies now spe-
cialize in placing older workers, and some employers sponsor job
search seminars for retiring workers.

Public Welfare Programs—For those who reach retirement age without adequate income, public welfare programs are available. These
assistance programs offer economic support based on demonstrated
need.

Supplemental Security Income (SSI) is a federally administered program that provides cash assistance to low-income aged, blind, and
disabled adults who have assets below specified limits. Benefits are
indexed to cost-of-living increases. Additionally, many states supplement the basic federal benefit. Income from other sources reduces
available SSI benefits; however, the benefit calculation disregards
the first $20 of unearned monthly income (regardless of source), plus
the first $65 of earned income, as well as one-half of earnings above
$65. For more information, contact your local Social Security Ad-
ministration office.

Benefits available through the federal Food Stamp Program vary
with household size and income and are inflation adjusted. For more
information on food stamps, contact your local or county social services offices.

Preventive Health Care—Many of the problems associated with old
age are not necessarily caused by the aging process but are the consequence of years of neglect, according to geriatrics experts. Coronary
heart disease, high blood pressure, stroke, adult-onset diabetes, os-
teoporosis, certain respiratory problems, and various types of cancer
become more prevalent as we age. Yet individuals can control these

167

problems by avoiding damaging health behaviors such as smoking, overeating, unbalanced eating patterns, and the abuse of alcohol and drugs. In addition, a sedentary life is increasingly seen as a threat to good health. Although the positive effect of sustained exercise on cardiovascular health has been known for some time, it has recently been reported that regular exercise also reduces the incidence of death from heart and lung disease, cancer, natural causes, and trauma.

A number of special programs have been developed to encourage good health habits at affordable prices. Programs that provide low-cost nutritional meals to older people can be located by contacting an area senior center. To encourage exercise, the YMCA, YWCA, and other athletic facilities offer reduced membership rates for people over age 65.

Financing Health Care Costs

Health care costs have risen dramatically during the past decade. It has become imperative to plan ahead for potential large costs associated with unexpected illness during retirement.

Medicare—Medicare is the federal health insurance program under Social Security. It consists of two parts: Part A (Hospital Insurance) helps pay for inpatient hospital care and certain follow-up care; Part B (Supplementary Medical Insurance) helps pay for doctors' services, outpatient hospital services, and other medical supplies and services not covered by Part A. Medicare offers public health insurance protection to all persons aged 65 or older who are entitled to receive Social Security (as well as the severely disabled under age 65), whether or not they actually receive benefits.

Medicare coverage is not automatic. Application must be made three months before reaching age 65. Those who are enrolled in Part A are automatically enrolled in Part B, unless they choose not to be. There is an additional monthly charge for Part B. Those who are not covered by Social Security may pay to participate in parts A and B or Part B alone.

Workers should ascertain whether their group health coverage will continue after retirement beyond the 18 month period required by law. (For more information on health insurance coverage, see chapter 19.) Since Medicare does not cover all expenses, many retirees purchase additional health insurance coverage on their own. Employer group plans sometimes can be converted to individual policies. If this option is not available, some policies (known as Medicare supplement, or "Medigap," policies) are designed specifically to fill in the gaps not covered by Medicare. To assure that major medical expenses will be covered, retirees must understand their private insurance coverage and how it coordinates with Medicare.

Health Maintenance Organizations—Participants in a health maintenance organization (HMO) make fixed monthly payments to the HMO. In turn, the HMO provides most or all of the needed health care services. Such fixed-price arrangements permit retirees to estimate future health care costs more accurately. Many Medicare beneficiaries receive all Medicare-covered health services through enrollment in HMOs. (For more information on HMOs, see chapter 24.)

Medicaid—Medicaid offers health assistance to people with low incomes. It is jointly financed by federal and state governments. Each state may elect to participate and administers its own program. Medicaid reimburses health care providers for specified services rendered to older and disabled persons, as well as members of families with dependent children who satisfy income tests. Covered services and the amount of deductibles (that is, an amount an individual is required to pay before receiving any Medicaid payments) differ from state to state, but medical services are free to most SSI recipients.

Long-Term Care—Many chronically ill and functionally impaired older persons require ongoing health and social services known as long-term care. There are about 8 million elderly persons in the United States who have some degree of chronic dependency requiring long-term care and about 1.5 million who are in nursing homes (Friedland, 1988, 1990). Care for debilitating chronic conditions is expensive and can rapidly deplete a lifetime's savings, yet is not covered by Medicare or most supplemental insurance policies. Some private long-term care policies are available and some companies are now offering this coverage as an employee benefit, but it is expensive and premiums increase based on the age of the applicant at the time of purchase. Research and test marketing efforts undertaken by the public and private sectors may in the future lead to better options for financing and delivering long-term care.

Even as they approach their own retirement, many persons are confronted with the prospect of providing financial, emotional, and often physical support to their parents and other older relatives. This added responsibility, sometimes referred to as elder care, can make it difficult to plan for retirement effectively. Some individuals may be forced to delay their retirement or to postpone travel or relocation plans.

Independent Living Arrangements

Choosing an appropriate living environment after retirement requires careful thought and planning. Many options are available and should be considered before making a decision. For example, an elderly family may choose to stay in their present home or move into an apartment, smaller house, mobile home, or continuing care community. They may buy or rent a home. They may stay in the same geographic area or move, possibly to an area with a more comfortable climate. Many older people choose to share homes with others as an alternative to living alone. These decisions should be based upon financial considerations as well as physical and social needs and desires. It is important to begin exploring and evaluating the possibilities well in advance of retirement.

Financial Considerations—The exclusion of capital gains on the sale of a home that has been a principal residence is available as a once-in-a-lifetime federal income tax break for older homeowners. If a homeowner is aged 55 or over, and if the home has been owned and occupied as his or her principal residence for at least three of the five years prior to the date of sale, he or she may sell the home and enjoy a one-time exemption from federal income taxes on profits of up to $125,000. Many states have similar tax breaks, although the conditions and amounts of excluded gains may differ from federal provisions.

Property taxes should also be considered when choosing a retirement home, as states vary widely in the amount of this tax and the rate at which it can be expected to increase. Some states offer deferral programs that let older homeowners put off payment of their property taxes until they sell the property or die. Others offer credits or homestead exemptions that reduce property taxes outright. Residents of other states can get either a tax deferral or a credit, depending on the amount of their income and assets. For more information, contact local Internal Revenue Service offices.

Housing Assistance—Under the 1937 Housing Act and subsequent amendments, several programs have been developed to provide direct and indirect housing assistance to older people. Such assistance can be separated into four basic categories: homeownership, rental, rental subsidy, and nursing home/intermediate care facility programs. There are often long waiting periods for housing assistance, so inquire and apply early. These programs are subject to change, and interested parties should keep abreast of new developments. Many of these programs are limited to older people with low incomes. More information can be obtained through local housing authorities or social services offices.

Physical and Social Considerations—Before moving to a new home, consider issues such as the accessibility of public transportation. A time may come when driving a car is not possible. Older persons should be in close proximity to grocery stores, doctors, and other frequently visited places. Isolation and loneliness are common concerns for older people; they should locate where it is easy to establish contact with others.

Life-Care Community Centers—Life-care communities, or continuing-care retirement communities, offer an alternative to living independently. They combine the financing and delivery of housing and long-term care. At once, these facilities can offer long-term care insurance, long-term care, and a home. Estimates of the number of life-care communities in the United States vary due to discrepancies in definitions, but the American Association of Homes for the Aging esimates that there are 700. Nearly all of these facilities are operated by nonprofit organizations and most are affiliated with religious organizations. The community is typically situated in a campus-like setting that includes apartments or townhouses, a central eating and recreation facility, and a nursing facility. The structure enables individuals to live independently in their own apartments. If cooking becomes too difficult, residents can have meals in a central facility; home health aides are available to deliver meals, and full-time nursing care is provided in the nursing home. Social activities are included, and the centers often have a medium for self-governance.

Generally life-care communities are financed by a substantial entrance fee (which may be refundable to the resident's estate at death) and a monthly fee, which together guarantee housing, social services, nursing services, and access to a nursing home bed. In about one-third of the communities this basic commitment is modified to include a charge of 80 percent or more of the per diem nursing facility. In these modified contracts, the amount of financial risk residents face varies inversely with the number of days covered under the contract. As few as 5 days a year to more than 180 days are covered, depending on the community.

The remaining one-third, called fee-for-service communities, have available all of the services included in the all-inclusive plans, but the monthly fee covers only a portion of these services. The services not included—in particular, nursing home care—must be paid for as used. While these communities guarantee access to a nursing home bed, the individual is still at risk for the financial consequences of using that bed. The life-care community is not at risk, and therefore this arrangement is not an insurance plan.

Among the 365 life-care communities listed in the *National Continuing Care Directory*, 37.8 percent, or 31,750 dwelling units, are all inclusive. Entrance fees for a single person range from a low of $35,000 in Indiana to a high of $128,000 in Massachusetts, with the average fee being $60,700. Monthly fees are $1,205 in Massachusetts and $653 in Indiana, and average $891 for all communities (Friedland, 1988).

Use of Leisure Time

One of the greatest challenges to workers facing retirement is the satisfactory use of a dramatic increase in leisure time. Discovering positive ways to use free time requires energy and imagination. People who develop outside interests and commitments in their working years are more likely to adjust well in retirement. It is solely the responsibility of a retiree to structure his or her time and to invest it in satisfying activities. Retirement frequently provides an opportunity for more active involvement in community, travel, avocation, and/or further education.

A newly retired person can begin by exploring community resources. Public libraries can be a good source of information about community programs. Free adult education courses are offered by many community colleges. Recreational activities are sponsored by various organizations (for example, area senior centers, the YMCA and YWCA, and local recreation departments). Opportunities for volunteer work may be available.

Interpersonal Relationships

Friends—Work provides an environment for meeting people and sharing common interests; thus, retirement can result in less interaction with people. Finding new ways to meet people and develop friendships is important. Again, those who develop strong friendships and family relationships in earlier years usually have a happier, more productive retirement.

Spouses—Adjustments are also necessary in spousal relationships. Developing friendships and outside interests before retirement reduces the strain of retirement on a marriage. Another area that needs attention concerns the problems associated with the death of one's spouse. Early discussion of coping methods that can be used after a spouse dies may reduce present and future anxieties. Psychological and financial adjustments must be considered.

Estate Planning—A decedent's estate is made up of assets minus liabilities at death. Many people put off estate planning because they do not want to face the unpleasant thought of death. Lack of qualified legal assistance in estate planning can cause unnecessary hardship and expense for a decedent's surviving family and friends. The assets of those who die without a legal will are distributed according to state law, unless distribution is made by alternatives to a will (for example, jointly owned property with survivorship, beneficiary designations, and living trusts).

Wills should be prepared with legal asistance. To ensure validity, they must be properly witnessed and signed. Handwritten or spoken wills are often not valid. States have differing probate laws; therefore, it is advisable to have all important documents reviewed by a lawyer when relocating to another state. If there is a major change in family circumstances, such as a death, divorce, or marriage, the will should again be reviewed by a lawyer.

Considerations for the Employer

This chapter has stressed the worker's responsibilities in planning for retirement. Employers can also play an important role in helping employees prepare for retirement. The number of companies that are taking steps to assist employees in this way is increasing steadily. The remainder of this chapter will focus on employer-sponsored retirement planning programs.

Retirement planning programs have varied widely. Some employers have offered programs since the 1960s. Since the enactment of ERISA, more employers have begun to provide retirement planning assistance to retiring employees. The more assistance employees receive in preparing for retirement, the more likely it is that they will adapt successfully.

Interest in Retirement Planning Programs—Interest in retirement counseling programs is incrcasing for a number of reasons. The elderly are living longer, and they represent the fastest growing segment of our population. There is a growing appreciation of their problems. The 1978 amendments to the Age Discrimination in Employment Act have heightened awareness of the importance of the decision to retire.

ERISA has resulted in greater dissemination of information about benefit plans. As more information becomes available, interest in retirement planning programs is growing. Concerns about high rates of inflation have contributed to employees' uneasiness about their financial security during retirement. They have been forced to recognize the problems of living on relatively fixed incomes.

Employees nearing retirement age often experience feelings of insecurity and anxiety; this can lead to a reduction in productivity. By offering retirement counseling, employers have learned that they can alleviate anxieties and reduce the decline in productivity. Research shows that employees who believe their employers care about them tend to produce better work. Studies also show that employees who receive employer retirement counseling adapt better to retirement. By providing retirement counseling, employers invest in their employees' goodwill and create a positive public image. Loyal employees have helped organizations succeed, and most employers want to help them prepare for a satisfying retirement.

Program Content—Retirement planning programs generally include information on some or all of the following areas: financial planning (coping with inflation, investment options, estate planning, insurance, and the roles of Social Security, pensions, and taxes); health (the importance of nutrition, exercise, health maintenance, and health care); interpersonal relationships (interaction with friends and family); living arrangements (the importance of financial and geographical considerations in choosing a new home); leisure time (the need for recreational activities, hobbies, community involvement, and education); and new careers (the types of opportunities available for employment and volunteer work and guidance in brushing up on job-hunting skills).

Program Design—Individual counseling is a popular way of providing benefit information to employees. Some organizations, however, combine individual interviews with group sessions, or they conduct only group meetings. Much of the retirement planning information is similar for all employees, and group meetings can be efficient. Although attendance is encouraged, participation is usually voluntary.

Employers can purchase custom-tailored or prepackaged programs from firms with retirement planning expertise. Some employers use a combined approach, starting with a purchased packaged program and conforming it in-house to their employees' needs. Other methods of retirement planning include the use of expert speakers, printed materials, and audio/visual aids. The majority of retirement planning seminars enlist the assistance of outside professionals to conduct sessions on topics such as taxes, investments, health care, Social Security, estate planning, and psychological adjustment.

174

Timing and Length of Counseling Sessions—Topics can be covered in separate weekly sessions; however, a session of two to three consecutive days may be preferable. Some firms hold sessions during nonworking hours. Others hold sessions during work time to reinforce the firm's commitment to retirement planning. Participants should be encouraged to devote sole attention to the retirement counseling session; the session should not be interrupted by work. If a weekly format is adopted, two-hour sessions are generally advisable. Usually, in this period of time, one retirement topic can be discussed with a question and answer period.

Group Size—Because the success of a counseling program depends on attendee participation in group discussions, it is wise to limit attendance at each meeting to no more than 40 participants. Assuming that most employees bring a spouse or friend, 20 to 25 employees should be invited.

Who Should Attend—Employees, their spouses, and other close family members or friends generally attend retirement planning meetings. Inclusion of spouses and friends helps to alleviate an employee's anxieties about retirement. Additionally, it provides the employee with access to other informed persons. These persons can discuss future problems with the employee when they occur.

Participants' Ages—Generally, employees who are aged 55 or over are invited to participate in retirement planning programs. The 10 year period before normal retirement age is an appropriate time for an employee's financial and attitudinal preparation. Some employers encourage participation at even younger ages, particularly where the firm's pension plan permits early retirement with immediate receipt of a pension at age 55 or younger.

Bibliography

Alberding, Russell J. "Is That All I Get?—Helping Employees Evaluate How Ready They Are to Retire." *Employee Benefits Journal* (September 1986).

American Association of Retired Persons. *How to Plan Your Successful Retirement*. Washington, DC: American Association of Retired Persons, 1988.

Andrews, Emily S. Employee Benefit Research Institute. "Economic Incentives for Retirement in the Public and Private Sectors." *EBRI Issue Brief* no. 57 (August 1986).

Arnone, William J. "Preretirement Planning Comes of Age." *Pension World* (July 1989): 26–27.

Employee Benefit Research Institute. *What Is the Future for Defined Benefit Pension Plans?* Washington, DC: Employee Benefit Research Institute, 1989.

Friedland, Robert B. Employee Benefit Research Institute. "Shifts in the Tide: The Impact of Changing Demographics on Employers, Employees, and Retirees." *EBRI Issue Brief* no. 77 (April 1988).

———. *Facing the Costs of Long-Term Care.* Washington, DC: Employee Benefit Research Institute, 1990.

Kiechel, Walter, III. "Lifelong Retirement Planning." In *Lifelong Retirement Planning for Local Government Employees.* Washington, DC: International City Management Association, 1988.

McConnell, Stephen R. "The Emerging Politics of Catastrophic and Long-Term Care Policy." In *Where Coverage Ends: Catastrophic Illness and Long-Term Health Care Costs.* Washington, DC: Employee Benefit Research Institute, 1988.

Seibert, Eugene H., and Joanne Seibert. "Retirement: Crisis or Opportunity?" *Personnel Administrator* (August 1986): 43–49.

Siegel, Sidney R. "Preretirement Programs in the '80s." *Personnel Administrator* (February 1986): 77–83.

U.S. Congress. House. Select Committee on Aging. Subcommittee on Housing and Consumer Interests. And Senate. Special Committee on Aging. *Home Equity Conversion: Issues and Options for the Elderly Homeowner.* Washington DC: U.S. Government Printing Office, 1985.

Walsh, Patricia. *Lifelong Retirement Planning for Local Government Employees.* Washington, DC: International City Management Association in Cooperation with ICMA Retirement Corporation, 1988.

176

19. Health Insurance

Introduction

As the cost of health care continues to climb, health insurance is becoming an increasingly valuable employee benefit. Employers view it as an integral component of the overall compensation packages that allow them to attract and retain workers. In addition to health protection for themselves and their family members, health insurance is viewed by many employees as a sometimes substantial source of income protection. Depending on the nature of an illness and the benefits provided, an employee's financial well-being could be jeopardized by unanticipated medical expenses.

Nearly three in four workers in the United States are covered by an employer-sponsored health insurance plan. Coverage is more common among medium-sized and large employers than among small employers. Among the 32 million persons working full time in medium-sized and large establishments in 1989, 92 percent had medical care benefits that were fully or partially financed by their employer (U.S. Department of Labor, 1990). Among small employers, 63 percent sponsored a group health plan in 1989 (National Federation of Independent Business, forthcoming).

There are two primary types of health plans that may be offered by an employer: prepaid plans, such as those provided through health maintenance organizations (see chapter 24), and traditional fee-for-service plans offered by insurance companies and many self-insured employers. This chapter describes fee-for-service plans, including basic medical and major medical insurance.

Employee Participation

Many employers cover all eligible employees under a single health plan, although different employee groups may have different plans (for example, union members and nonunion members may have separate plans). Most employees are covered at the time they are hired or after they satisfy a waiting or service period (for example, three months).

Most plans cover employees and their dependents. All or part of the cost of the coverage for an employee or for his or her dependents may be paid by the employer. In some plans, the employer contribution for employee coverage may differ from the employer contribution for dependents' coverage. Employee costs for coverage are paid through payroll deduction.

Plan Operators

Employer-sponsored health benefits may use any of a variety of plan operators: commercial insurance plans, Blue Cross and Blue Shield plans, or self-funded plans.

Commercial Insurance Plans—Insurance companies are a major source of health insurance. Generally, the premium for such insurance protection is calculated to cover the benefits that will be paid, administrative costs, insurance sales commissions, state premium taxes, and surplus (that is, profit). Generally, for employee groups of 50 or more, the insurer maintains separate claims records for the group and periodically adjusts the premium to reflect the group's claims experience; these are called experience-rated plans.

Blue Cross and Blue Shield Plans—These plans are also a major source of health insurance coverage. Blue Cross plans cover hospital services; Blue Shield plans cover medical and surgical services. Participating physicians and hospitals agree to accept a predetermined fee from Blue Cross and Blue Shield as payment in full for each service (most physicians and hospitals are participating members). If a plan member visits a nonparticipating physician or hospital, and if the charge is above the scheduled Blue Cross and Blue Shield fee, the patient is responsible for paying any difference. Most Blue Cross and Blue Shield plans pay the health care service provider directly, rather than reimbursing the patient for charges.

Although many plans operate under the Blue Cross and Blue Shield name, each plan is independent; each generally operates in a specific geographic area. The various plans may offer different benefit structures.

Blue Cross and Blue Shield plans must comply with the following standards established by the Blue Cross and Blue Shield Association: they must enroll all applicants regardless of health, operate as nonprofit organizations, and offer conversion privileges to terminating employees.

Self-Insured Plans—Many larger employers self insure. These employers may administer their own medical plans or purchase *administrative services contracts* to take care of their administrative needs. Some self-insured employers also purchase *stop-loss cover-*

178

age from insurance companies to cover catastrophic health expenses above a maximum and, thus, limit the self-insured plan's liability.

Employers that self-insure do so for a number of reasons:

- Self-insured plans are not subject to state insurance premium taxes that otherwise would be reflected in their insurance premiums.

- Self-insured plans are exempt from state mandated benefit laws, which specify certain types and levels of coverage that group policies must include. As a result, a self-insured employer may offer a single plan to employees in different states, superseding differences in state-mandated benefits.

- The employer retains control of the plan's reserves.

- The employer can attempt to manage health care costs more directly.

Health Insurance Benefits

Insurance plans calculate fee-for-service payments to providers in different ways: based on usual, customary, and reasonable (UCR)[1] charges; a fixed schedule of fees; or a combination of the two.

The UCR approach recognizes all usual, customary, and reasonable charges for covered services. Plans that use fixed schedules recognize charges for covered services only up to a fixed dollar limit. This limit can take many forms; for example, a plan may limit hospital benefits to a fixed dollar amount per day and reimburse surgical charges according to a schedule of payment by procedure.

Some plans combine elements of UCR and fixed payment. An example would be a hospital plan that recognizes the UCR amount for room and board and a scheduled amount for surgical procedures. Most fee-for-service plans use UCR to determine payments for covered services.

Prepaid Plans—Whereas fee-for-service plans reimburse insured persons for covered charges they incur, prepaid plans promise to deliver needed health care and require that care be obtained from a prepaid plan provider. Because care is paid for before, rather than after, it is provided, there are no UCR or fixed dollar limitations. Refer to chapter 24 for a discussion of prepaid plans.

---

[1] Usual, customary, and reasonable means that the charge is the provider's *usual* fee for the service, does not exceed the *customary* fee in that geographic area, and is *reasonable* based on the circumstances. A fee may be considered reasonable when special circumstances require extensive or complex treatment, even though it does not meet the standard UCR criteria.

Deductibles, Coinsurance, and Maximum Coverage Limits

Major medical plans typically include deductible and coinsurance provisions, as well as coverage limits. These plan features are intended to reduce plan costs, encourage employees to be cost conscious, and reduce administrative expenses.

A *deductible* is a specified amount of initial medical costs that would otherwise be treated as covered expenses under the plan, which each participant must pay before any expenses are reimbursed by the plan. Deductibles typically range from $100 to $500. Under a plan with a $200 individual deductible, for example, a participant must pay the first $200 in recognized expenses for covered health care services. The plan then pays for additional health care expenses according to plan provisions.

The deductible must be satisfied periodically (generally every calendar year) by each participant, sometimes with a maximum of two or three deductibles per family. However, some plans contain a three month carry-over provision. If so, any portion of the deductible that is satisfied during the last three months of the year can be applied toward satisfaction of the following year's deductible.

Coinsurance provisions require the plan participant to pay a portion of recognized medical expenses; the plan pays the remaining portion. Commonly, the employee pays 20 percent, with the plan paying the remaining 80 percent of recognized charges. Most major medical plans include both deductibles and coinsurance provisions. Thus, once the plan participant pays the deductible (for example, the first $200 in medical expenses), the plan pays 80 percent of all other covered charges. Some services may have special copayment provisions (for example, 50 percent coinsurance).

Because 20 percent of a large medical claim may pose a significant financial burden for many individuals and families, most plans limit participants' out-of-pocket expenditures for covered services. In this case, once a participant has reached the out-of-pocket maximum, covered expenses are reimbursed in full for the remainder of the year. The out-of-pocket limit may be renewed at the start of the calendar year for each individual participant.

Most major medical plans impose a maximum dollar limit on the amount of health insurance coverage provided. Plans that impose limits may do so on an episode basis, such as per hospital admission or per disability. Or plans may impose an annual or lifetime maximum on payments for all covered services. Individual lifetime maximums are set usually at very high levels, such as $250,000 or $1

180

million. Separate lifetime maximums may be set for specific coverages such as psychiatric care.

Preexisting Conditions

Many insurance plans limit coverage for health conditions that were known to exist at the time the employee joined the plan. Some plans may cover these conditions after a waiting period of six months to a year has elapsed. Other plans may permanently exclude preexisting conditions from coverage.

Basic Health Insurance Plans

Basic health insurance plans primarily cover health care services associated with an episode of hospital care, including hospitalization, in-hospital physician care, and surgery, and generally also cover outpatient surgery. Basic health insurance plans typically pay for hospital room and board, physician care, and surgery on a UCR basis, but may pay other charges in full.

Hospitalization—Hospitalization coverage pays for inpatient hospital charges, such as room and board, intensive care, necessary medical supplies, general nursing services, and inpatient drugs. Some outpatient services (such as preadmission testing or emergency treatment as a result of an accident) may also be covered. The plan may have separate limits for certain types of care (for example, room and board benefits may be limited to a maximum number of days and total hospital benefits may be limited on a per admission basis).

Professional Care—Professional care coverage primarily includes in-hospital visits by physicians. Benefit limits typically apply, such as a dollar amount per visit or a limited number of visits per calendar year.

Surgical—Surgical coverage pays for surgical procedures performed by licensed physicians in hospitals, outpatient facilities, or physicians' offices. Services provided by assistant surgeons, anesthesiologists, and anesthetists may also be covered. Reimbursement typically is based on a fee schedule.

Major Medical Insurance

Major medical insurance plans are of two types—*supplemental* and *comprehensive*. Supplemental major medical plans cover some services that are excluded under basic plans and may also cover the same services but with higher coverage limits. Comprehensive major medical plans provide the combined coverage of a basic plan and a supplemental plan. Unlike basic medical plans, major medical plans cover a broad range of health care services and are designed to protect against large medical expenses.

Supplemental Plans—Supplemental major medical plans cover most medically necessary services excluded under basic plans, as well as charges that exceed the basic plan limit. Covered services typically include inpatient and outpatient hospital care, special nursing care, outpatient prescription drugs, medical appliances, durable medical equipment, and outpatient psychiatric care. These plans include deductible and coinsurance provisions and may limit total plan benefits.

Comprehensive Plans—Comprehensive major medical plans provide coverage for the same types of services covered under combined basic/supplemental plans and have replaced many combination plans. Comprehensive plans also include deductible and coinsurance requirements but may provide first dollar coverage for emergency accident benefits or waive out-of-pocket expenses for certain types of benefits altogether.

Other Health Care Plans

Medical plans generally exclude services that are predictable or not considered medically necessary, including most types of dental, vision, and hearing care. As a result, stand-alone plans providing these benefits are growing in popularity. Because of their highly elective nature, various limits are placed on the benefits provided. For information about dental care and vision care plans, refer to chapters 20 and 22, respectively.

Retiree Health Insurance

While employer-sponsored health coverage for retirees remains common, it has become less so in recent years. In 1988, 54 percent of full-time participants in health plans sponsored by medium-sized and large establishments had partially or wholly employer-paid coverage continued after retirement before age 65—a 17 percent decrease from 1986; 45 percent had coverage continued after retirement at age 65—a drop of nearly 30 percent (U.S. Department of Labor, 1989). Retirees also have the option of continuing in an employer-sponsored plan for a period of time, and/or converting to an individual policy, at their own expense (see "Continuation of Coverage").

Employer plans that continue health coverage for retired workers typically maintain benefits at preretirement levels, although coverage for Medicare-eligible retirees usually is secondary to that provided under Medicare (that is, benefits covered by the employer plan are reduced by the amount Medicare pays). Retired workers also may be required to contribute more toward the cost of coverage or begin contributing if they did not do so as active workers.

The trend toward reduced or terminated coverage for retirees may continue as a result of proposed accounting requirements that would require employers to identify the costs of future retiree medical benefits as a liability on their balance sheets (Barber and Horkitz, 1990).

Continuation of Coverage

The Consolidated Omnibus Budget Reconciliation Act of 1985 (COBRA), as amended in subsequent legislation, requires employers with health insurance plans to offer continued access to group health insurance to qualified beneficiaries if they lose coverage under the plan as the result of a qualifying event. COBRA requires continued access for 18 months (or 29 months if the qualified beneficiary is disabled) for:

- covered employees, spouses, and dependent children who lose coverage when a covered employee terminates employement (for reasons other than gross misconduct) or there is a reduction in his or her hours of employment; and

for 36 months for:

- surviving spouses and dependent children who lose coverage as a result of a covered employee's death,
- spouses and dependent children who lose coverage as a result of a covered employee's divorce or legal separation from his or her spouse,
- spouses and dependent children who lose coverage as a result of a covered employee's becoming entitled to receive Medicare benefits,
- dependent children who lose coverage as a result of their own ineligibility for benefits under the plan, and
- spouses and dependent children of a retired covered employee who loses coverage as a result of the bankruptcy of the retired covered employee's employer (retired covered employees or their widow(er)s are eligible for lifetime continuation).

Prior to enactment of the Omnibus Budget Reconciliation Act of 1989 (OBRA '89), coverage could be terminated prior to the end of the maximum required period if the qualified beneficiary became covered under another group health plan. OBRA '89 provides that COBRA may not terminate before the maximum period, however, if the qualified beneficiary becomes covered under another group health plan that excludes or limits a preexisting condition.

The coverage offered must be identical to that available prior to the change in the worker's employment status. The qualifying employee or dependent may be required to pay up to 102 percent of the premium (disabled qualified beneficiaries may be required to pay up to 150 percent of the premium for months 19 through 29). At the end of the coverage period, the employer must offer conversion to an individual policy if the group plan includes a conversion privilege (an option required in some states).

Employers that violate COBRA must pay a penalty tax of up to $100 per day per affected qualified beneficiary (limited to $200 per day for affected family units) for the duration of the noncompliance period.

Group health plans for public and private employers with fewer than 20 employees are excluded from these provisions, as are plans sponsored by churches (as defined in section 414(e) of the Internal Revenue Code); the District of Columbia; or any territory, possession, or agency of the United States.

Conclusion

For many decades, health insurance plans have played a significant role in employee benefit planning. As the costs of health care and individual health insurance policies continue to rise, employer-sponsored programs have an ever greater value for employees and their families.

The development of health maintenance organizations; preferred provider arrangements (discussed in chapter 25); and dental care, prescription drug, vision care, and hearing care plans attests to the dynamic nature of this employee benefit area, as does the development of health promotion and employee assistance programs (discussed in chapter 26). The need for effective health care cost management will continue to guide future innovation in plan design, as will new government regulations related to health insurance benefits.[2]

---

[2]Many aspects of employer-provided health insurance plans are affected by government regulations such as the Employee Retirement Income Security Act of 1974 (ERISA). For more information on ERISA's impact on medical care plans, see chapter 3.

Bibliography

Barber, Jean, and Karen Horkitz. Employee Benefit Research Institute. "Features of Employer-Sponsored Health Plans." *EBRI Issue Brief* no. 100 (March 1990).

Chollet, Deborah J. *Employer-Provided Health Benefits: Coverage, Provisions and Policy Issues*. Washington, DC: Employee Benefit Research Institute, 1984.

Custer, William S. *Employer Health Care Plan Design, Plan Costs, and Health Care Delivery*. EBRI Special Report. Washington, DC: Employee Benefit Research Institute, 1989.

_____. Employee Benefit Research Institute. "Issues in Mental Health Care." *EBRI Issue Brief* no. 99 (February 1990).

_____. *Health Insurance Coverage for the Near Elderly*. EBRI Special Report. Washington, DC: Employee Benefit Research Institute, forthcoming.

Employee Benefit Research Institute. *Retiree Health Benefits: What Is the Promise?* Washington, DC: Employee Benefit Research Institute, 1989.

National Federation of Independent Business. *Small Business Employee Benefits, 1989*. Washington, DC: National Federation of Independent Business, forthcoming.

Piacentini, Joseph S., and Timothy J. Cerino. *EBRI Databook on Employee Benefits*. Washington, DC: Employee Benefit Research Institute, 1990.

U.S. Department of Labor. Bureau of Labor Statistics. "Employee Benefits Focus on Family Concerns in 1989." USDL news release 90-160, 30 March 1990.

_____. *Employee Benefits in Medium and Large Firms, 1988*. Washington, DC: U.S. Government Printing Office, 1989.

Additional Information

Health Insurance Association of America
1025 Connecticut Ave., NW, Suite 1200
Washington, DC 20036
(202) 223-7780

Health Research Institute
1600 S. Main Plaza, Suite 170
Walnut Creek, CA 94596
(415) 676-2320

Self-Insurance Institute of America, Inc.
P.O. Box 15466
Santa Ana, CA 92705
(714) 261-2553

20. Dental Care Plans

Introduction

Health authorities agree that many Americans' dental care could be improved substantially. Among the deterrents to better care are the public's perception that dental care costs are high and the fact that correction of many dental problems is often postponed for long periods. In 1989, 66 percent of employees in medium-sized and large establishments had employer-sponsored coverage for dental care (U.S. Department of Labor, 1990).

A 1988 survey of 1,600 private-sector employers indicated that 79 percent offered dental coverage to employees (A. Foster Higgins & Co., Inc., 1988). Employee sharing of dental costs has also increased, with 63 percent of plans requiring employee contributions in 1988, compared with 54 percent in 1984, according to another recent survey (Hewitt Associates, 1989).

A sound dental insurance plan has two primary objectives: to help pay for dental care costs and to encourage people to receive regular dental attention, which can prevent potentially serious problems.

When dental coverage is provided to employees and their eligible dependents, the plan sponsor (that is, the employer, union, or joint fund) usually pays the employee's entire dental insurance premium and may make some contribution to the dependents' premiums. In some cases, the employee and the plan sponsor share the cost.

Among the organizations that offer dental care plans are insurance companies, dental service corporations, Blue Cross and Blue Shield plan administrators, health maintenance organizations, and *closed-panel* groups of dental care providers. In addition, some employers self-fund and self-administer their plans. Managed-care dental programs currently represent about 10 percent of the market, and estimates put this figure at 25 percent by 1995.

Services

A dental insurance plan should specify the types of services that are and are not covered. Covered services include:

- diagnostic procedures (oral examinations, regular checkups, and x-rays);
- preventive procedures (fluoride treatment and cleaning, polishing, and scaling teeth);

187

- restorative procedures (repairing teeth, including fillings and crown work);

- oral surgery (operations performed in the mouth);

- endodontics (root canal therapy—treating teeth that have diseased roots);

- periodontics (treating gum diseases);

- prosthodontics (replacing missing teeth with fixed or removable prostheses, including bridgework, partial removable dentures, and full dentures); and

- orthodontics (correcting malpositioned teeth).

Services that are usually not covered include:

- hospitalization due to necessary dental treatment;[1]

- cosmetic dental work (for example, closing a gap between two front teeth);

- cleaning and examinations performed more often than twice a year; and

- services covered by workers' compensation or other insurance programs.

Payment of Benefits

Several types of dental plans are common.

Nonscheduled Plans—Typically, these plans cover dental costs based on *usual*, *customary*, and *reasonable* charges. These charges are defined as the usual fee charged by the dentist, the customary or prevailing fee charged by other dentists in the same geographic area for the same treatment, and a reasonable amount based on the circumstances involved.

Scheduled Plans—These plans use a schedule of benefits that provides a flat-dollar amount for each service. If a dentist charges more than the scheduled amount, the participant is responsible for the difference.

Combination Plans—Some dental plans combine the usual, customary, and reasonable payment method with the schedule-of-benefits

---

[1]Hospitalization for dental treatment as well as other dental services may be covered under standard health insurance plans. For more information on health insurance, see chapter 19.

payment method. For instance, a plan may pay for diagnostic and preventive services under the usual, customary, and reasonable method but pay for other services under the schedule-of-benefits method.

Closed-Panel Plans—In a closed-panel arrangement, a designated group of dentists (that is, a closed panel) provides services to an employee group. The full cost of services is paid when employees go to providers specified by the plan. Employers pay a premium for such services; premiums are used to pay dentists' salaries, or they cover a fixed cost per beneficiary. If employees go to providers who are not in the closed panel, the plan will pay only a specified amount; the employee must pay any excess.

Dental insurance plans may also require payment of a *deductible* (that is, an amount a participant must pay before receiving any insurance payments).

Dental plans—either in the form of one or more of the types discussed above or as part of reimbursement accounts—are increasingly included in flexible compensation plans. (For more information on flexible compensation plans, see chapter 33.)

Other Dental Plan Features

Predetermination of Benefits—Before beginning dental treatment, a plan participant may want to know how much he or she will be charged for the treatment and how much the plan will pay. A plan may require the participant's dentist to fill out a predetermination-of-benefits form describing the proposed treatment and its cost. The participant would then send the form to the claims office, which would, in turn, advise the participant and the dentist of the amount the plan would pay. Some plans require this procedure when anticipated charges exceed a stated amount (for example, $100).

Alternative Benefits—Dental problems can often be successfully treated in more than one way. When this situation occurs, many dental plans base payments on the least expensive treatment that is customarily used for the condition in question. For example, a decayed tooth may often be satisfactorily repaired with either a crown or a filling. In this case, a dental plan bases its payment on the filling, which is the less expensive treatment. The participant and the dentist may proceed with the more expensive crown only if the participant agrees to pay the difference.

Cost Sharing—Most dental plans are designed with cost-sharing features that require the participant to pay some portion and the plan to pay the remaining portion of the charges for dental services. Two common cost-sharing features are deductibles and copayments.

As noted earlier, a deductible is an amount a participant must pay before receiving any insurance payments. Depending on a plan's design, deductibles must be satisfied once annually or once in a lifetime. Consider a hypothetical example in which a participant's first dental bill for the year is $75; the bill covers the filling of several cavities. The yearly deductible under this plan is $50. Thus, the participant pays the first $50. The remaining $25 is covered, either partially or fully, by the plan. No other deductible is required in this year. The participant will have to pay another $50 deductible in the following year, however.

If a plan has a coinsurance feature, the plan and the participant share the costs of each covered dental service. The plan pays a specified percentage of covered services (for example, 80 percent) and the participant pays the balance (in this case, 20 percent). Additionally, a plan may offer a number of coinsurance schedules, depending on the treatment. For example, a plan may pay 80 percent of a dentist's bill for filling a cavity but only 50 percent of a bill for orthodontic work.

In some plans, coinsurance is used in conjunction with a deductible. Under such a plan, after the yearly deductible (for example, $50) has been paid by the participant, the plan will pay some stated percentage (for example, 80 percent) of additional dental expenses.

Some plans require a deductible and/or coinsurance for some types of treatment but not for preventive care services. These features are intended to encourage regular dental visits and preventive care.

Benefit Limits—Most dental plans set maximum limits on the amount they will pay for each participant (for example, $1,000 per person per calendar year). Separate maximum limits may apply for different treatments (for example, an annual maximum of $1,000 per person for all dental services other than orthodontics, with orthodontics limited to a $750 lifetime maximum).

Claims Payment—Payment of claims under a group dental plan generally follows the same procedure as payment of claims under a group medical plan. The participant and the dentist fill out and submit claim forms. Payment for covered services may be sent to the dentist or to the participant. Dental insurance plans usually experience heavy claims the first year because of a backlog of unmet dental needs in a newly covered employee group.

Effective and economical use of a group dental plan requires close interaction among the employee, the employer, and the service provider. It requires that all parties work together to achieve the plan's goal of maintaining good dental health at a reasonable cost.

Continuation of Coverage—The Consolidated Omnibus Budget Reconciliation Act of 1985 (COBRA) requires employers with dental plans to offer continued access to group dental insurance for former employees and their dependents. For an explanation of these rules, see chapter 19.

Bibliography

A. Foster Higgins & Co., Inc. *A. Foster Higgins Health Care Benefits Survey, 1988*. Princeton, NJ: A. Foster Higgins & Co., Inc., 1988.

Hewitt Associates. *Salaried Employee Benefits Provided by Major U.S. Employers: A Comparison Study, 1984 through 1988*. Lincolnshire, IL: Hewitt Associates, 1989.

Sutton, Harry L., Jr. "Prescription Drug and Dental Programs." *Employee Benefits Journal* (June 1986): 20–26.

U.S. Department of Labor. Bureau of Labor Statistics. "Employee Benefits Focus on Family Concerns in 1989." USDL news release 90-160, 30 March 1990.

———. *Employee Benefits in Medium and Large Firms, 1988*. Washington, DC: U.S. Government Printing Office, 1989.

21. Prescription Drug Plans

Introduction

Prescription drug plans were first introduced in 1964. Coverage for prescription drugs encourages beneficiaries to complete prescribed drug therapy in order to avoid more costly medical complications later. The average price of prescription drugs has risen nearly 40 percent since 1980. In 1988, drug costs accounted for 10 percent to 12 percent of most employers' total health care expenditures, up from 4 percent in the early 1970s. Although most major medical plans cover prescription drugs, some employers and joint funds prefer to provide separate drug plans for the following reasons:

- Employees may not otherwise know that their medical plans cover the cost of prescription drugs.

- Participants covered under health care insurance plans that require payment of large or separate deductibles may not submit prescription claims.

- Employees may be confused by the paperwork required by typical medical plans (for example, saving drug store receipts and filing claims).

- The influx of prescription drug claims at the end of a medical plan year can cause problems for plan administrators.

Employers may cover employees under prescription drug plans after a brief waiting period and pay part or all of the employees' premiums. In addition, some plans cover employees' dependents. As is the case with health insurance, some employers pay the full cost of dependent coverage, while others require payroll deductions to cover part or all of the cost.

A variety of organizations offer prescription drug plans: commercial insurance companies, Blue Cross and Blue Shield plans, health maintenance organizations, labor unions, and independent prescription drug services. In addition, some employers self fund their plans. Drug plans also are available through such organizations as the American Association of Retired Persons, often on a mail order basis (see discussion of mail order arrangements under "Payment of Benefits").

Services

Prescription drug plans provide coverage for out-of-hospital prescription drugs. They usually cover *legend* drugs, which—under federal law—cannot be dispensed without a prescription (Rosenbloom and Hallman, 1981).

Generally, prescription drug plans do not cover proprietary medicines, medical appliances or devices, nonprescription drugs, in-hospital drugs, blood and blood plasma, immunization agents, and any drugs or medicines lawfully obtained without prescription (with the exception of insulin). Plans may also specifically exclude contraceptive drugs.

Many plans place limits on the quantity of a drug that may be dispensed at any one time. A typical limitation is a 34 day supply or 100 doses, whichever is greater. A higher limitation usually applies to maintenance drugs. Most plans do not place a maximum on the overall covered quantity of a drug. Some plans may, however, limit the total dollar cost of prescription drugs that will be reimbursed.

Prescription drug plans typically require only a small copayment, such as $1 to $5 per prescription, from the covered person for drugs provided under the plan. Thus, the relatively large deductible (the amount a participant is required to pay before receiving any insurance payments), the coinsurance percentage, and the reasonable and customary charges provision of traditional major medical plans do not apply in the case of basic prescription drug plans (Rosenbloom and Hallman, 1981).

Payment of Benefits

The most common types of plans include *open panel plans*, *closed panel plans*, *mail order plans*, and *nationwide panel plans*.

Open panel plans permit employees to choose the pharmacies they use. Participants pay for prescriptions and send the receipts, with claim forms, to the plan administrator for reimbursement. If a plan has a deductible, receipts are usually accumulated until the deductable is satisfied and then are submitted to a claims office at one time.

Closed panel plans generally employ a number of pharmacies, ranging from a few to several thousand. These pharmacies dispense drugs to plan members at prices agreed upon by the plan provider and the pharmacy. Sometimes the price is the pharmacy's cost plus a dispensing fee. The plan administrator pays the panel pharmacies directly. Plan members pay only the applicable deductible and are not required to submit claim forms. If plan participants use a nonpanel

194

pharmacy (for example, in an emergency situation), they must submit a claim form as though they were in an open panel plan.

In mail order plans, employees send their prescriptions to specified mail order firms. Because of volume, mail order pharmacies frequently offer prescriptions at lower prices than other pharmacies. Approximately 60 percent to 70 percent of prescription drugs are for maintenance or long-term medication; the other 30 percent to 40 percent are for emergencies. Costs can be reduced by 20 percent to 40 percent under mail order arrangements because all claims are processed at one location; thus, the use of a claim form is eliminated most of the time. Their "door-to-door" service also makes these plans attractive. However, they are not designed for drugs that are needed immediately.

Nationwide panel plans, also known as prescription card service plans, are popular. They use a network of pharmacies, usually through a *prepaid drug plan administrator* (that is, a firm administering plans for insurance companies, employers, joint funds, and others) and negotiate price discounts. Also, nationwide panel plans provide participating employees with a credit card that is used to purchase prescription drugs. Sometimes a nationwide panel plan includes a mail order option; this approach achieves savings on maintenance drugs while maintaining access to a community pharmacy for emergency situations.

In addition to these plans, many pharmacy chains negotiate discounts with employers in a type of preferred provider arrangement.

Conclusion

After more than 20 years, prescription drug plans are now mature and have grown in number. Coverage may be decreasing, however, as plan deductibles are increased in an attempt to contain overall health plan costs. A few plans have encountered problems, especially at the start. For example, under certain plans, credit card misuse has been a problem. Also, since prescription drugs do not have stated *reasonable and customary charges*,[1] some pharmacists may have charged inflated prices because a third party paid the bill. In fact, charges for prescription drugs have risen faster than those for hospital care in recent years. Despite the limited incidence of these problems, pre-

---

[1]Reasonable and customary charges are those that are considered reasonable based on the circumstances and those that are customarily charged for drugs in a particular geographic area.

scription drug plans now work reasonably well and appear to be popular.

Bibliography

Rosenbloom, Jerry S., ed. *The Handbook of Employee Benefits*, 2nd ed. Homewood, IL: Dow Jones-Irwin, 1988.

Rosenbloom, Jerry S., and G. Victor Hallman. *Employee Benefit Planning.* Englewood Cliffs, NJ: Prentice-Hall, Inc., 1981.

Sutton, Harry L., Jr. "Prescription Drug and Dental Programs." *Employee Benefits Journal* (June 1986): 20–26.

22. Vision Care Plans

Introduction

Vision problems are common in the United States; more than one-half of the population requires optometric care. Approximately 12 percent of 6 year olds require vision care services, while 96 percent of 70 year olds do. The need for eye care becomes pronounced at about age 40. Vision problems are often chronic and require regular attention.

Except for medical or surgical treatment and, in some cases, contact lenses after cataract surgery, traditional health insurance plans have provided little or no vision care coverage. Employer-sponsored vision care plans are designed to insure vision care services.

Similar to most medical plans, vision care benefits are usually available to a group of covered employees after a nominal waiting period; the employer often pays the cost for employee coverage. In addition, most plans provide for coverage of employees' dependents; this coverage can be extended in a number of ways: the employer may pay for dependent protection, the employee may pay, or the employer and the employee may share the cost.

A variety of organizations offer vision care plans to employee groups. These include jointly managed funds, health maintenance organizations, administrators of Blue Cross and Blue Shield plans, vision care corporations, optometric associations, closed-panel groups of vision care providers, and insurance companies. In addition, some employers self-fund and self-administer their plans.

The principal providers of vision care are:

- *Ophthalmologists*—Medical doctors specializing in eye examination, treatment, and surgery. Some ophthalmologists dispense eyeglasses and contact lenses.

- *Optometrists*—Health care professionals who are specifically educated and licensed at the state level to examine, diagnose, and treat conditions of the vision system. Optometrists may not operate on the eye and, in most states, may not administer therapeutic drugs. Most optometrists dispense eyeglasses and contact lenses.

- *Opticians*—Persons who make and/or sell lenses and eyeglasses.

197

Extent of Coverage

Vision plans may cover eye exams, eyeglasses, contact lenses, and orthoptics (exercises for the eye muscles). In 1989, among employees in medium-sized and large private establishments who participated in medical plans, 35 percent had vision care benefits. Nearly 100 percent of these plans covered eye exams, 68 percent had eyeglass coverage, and 66 percent had contact lens coverage (U.S. Department of Labor, 1990).

Services

The typical vision care plan covers eye examinations, lenses, frames, and the fitting of eyeglasses. Eye examinations provide the information needed for lens prescriptions and may reveal eye diseases such as glaucoma or cataracts. (They may also reveal evidence of diabetes or high blood pressure.) Many plans cover some portion of the cost for contact lenses; however, some plans only cover contact lenses if vision cannot be corrected to a stated level with conventional lenses (for example, following cataract surgery).

Nearly all vision care plans impose limitations on the frequency of covered services and glasses. Typically, they limit participants to one eye examination within a 12 month period, one set of lenses within a 12 month period, and one set of frames within a 2 year period. Most plans do not cover the additional cost of oversized, photosensitive, or plastic lenses, nor do they cover prescription sunglasses.

Payment of Benefits

Similar to other types of health insurance, vision care plans cover services in a variety of ways. For example:

- Some plans pay the full cost of services, provided it satisfies the *usual, customary, and reasonable* cost criteria. In other words, the covered amount is the provider's usual fee for the service, the customary or prevailing fee for the service or product in that geographic area, and a reasonable amount based on the circumstances involved. A fee may be considered reasonable when circumstances necessitate extensive or complex treatment, even though it does not meet the usual, customary, and reasonable criteria.

- Sometimes vision care plan participants are required to pay *deductibles*. The deductible is a specified amount of vision care costs that the participant must pay before any costs are paid by the plan. Under a plan with a $50 individual deductible, for example, a participant must pay his or her first $50 in vision care expenses. The plan then pays for additional vision care expenses in accordance with other plan provisions.

- Plans may have a *coinsurance* arrangement in which the plan participant pays some portion of the vision care expenses and the plan pays the remainder. The plan participant, for instance, may pay 20 percent and the plan may pay 80 percent.

- Other plans specify a covered dollar amount for each service. Under the *schedule-of-benefits* approach, the plan participant pays any amount over the scheduled dollar limit. The schedule is usually adjusted at intervals to keep it consistent with changes in the cost of care.

- Plans may also use a *closed-panel arrangement*, in which a designated group (that is, a closed panel) of vision care professionals provides services to an employee group. The full cost of services is paid when plan participants go to providers specified by the plan. Employers pay a premium for such services, which may cover a fixed cost per beneficiary. The providers are reimbursed for their cost of materials plus a dispensing fee. If participants go to providers who are not in the closed panel, the plan pays only a specified amount; the participant must pay any excess.

- Plans commonly use a combination of the approaches described above. A plan that covers services based on usual, customary, and reasonable charges may also require payment of a deductible or coinsurance. Coinsurance may also be included in a schedule-of-benefits approach.

When considering the cost of a vision care plan, a potential plan sponsor should be aware that such plans have a high incidence of claims in the first year because there may be a backlog of unmet needs in a newly covered employee group. An employer-sponsored vision care plan should include a program to increase employee awareness and understanding of vision care and the plan; effective communication among all involved parties (that is, employee, employer, and service providers); and an efficient claims filing and payment system.

Continuation of Coverage

The Consolidated Omnibus Budget Reconciliation Act of 1985 (COBRA) requires employers with vision and other health care plans to offer continued access to group health insurance for former employees and their dependents. For an explanation of these rules, refer to chapter 19.

Bibliography

Jain, Rita S. "Employer-Sponsored Vision Care Brought into Focus." *Monthly Labor Review* (September 1988): 19–23.

Rosenbloom, Jerry S., ed. *The Handbook of Employee Benefits*. Homewood, IL: Dow Jones-Irwin, 1988.

U.S. Department of Labor. Bureau of Labor Statistics. "Employee Benefits Focus on Family Concerns in 1989." USDL news release 90-160. 30 March 1990.

23. Managing Health Care Costs

Introduction

Health care spending in the United States has grown rapidly, reaching nearly $540 billion, or 11.1 percent of Gross National Product, in 1988 (U.S. Department of Health and Human Services, 1990). This growth has occurred largely as a result of advances in medical technology, population growth, increased life expectancy, lower infant mortality, and general price inflation.

In the United States, about 65 percent of the civilian population under age 65 receives health insurance coverage through employer-sponsored plans. Health care costs incurred by employers on behalf of employees and their insured family members have risen dramatically, reaching nearly $133 billion (4.6 percent of compensation) in 1988, up from $12 billion (2.0 percent of compensation) in 1970. Benefit payments from employer-sponsored health programs rose to nearly $146 billion in 1988, up from nearly $15 billion in 1970.

Although cost management strategies have not been as widely adopted by employers as is generally assumed (Custer, 1989), in recent years virtually all employers offering health insurance coverage to their employees have taken at least some steps to manage costs. While such measures are designed to contain individual employer spending, they may also serve the broader goal of managing the increase in overall health care costs.

The variety of plan design changes that have been adopted by employers can be grouped into three categories:

- Changes that increase employee incentives to use health care more economically, including the imposition of higher deductibles and coinsurance levels for all or for some services covered by a plan and the expansion of covered services to include less expensive alternatives to inpatient hospital care.

- Changes that specifically restrict the inappropriate use of services, such as requiring a formal review of hospital utilization, case management, second opinions, and same-day surgery.

- Changes that restructure the delivery of health care services within a plan, including incentives for employees to select prepaid health plans (health maintenance organizations, or HMOs) and the establishment of preferred provider organization (PPO) arrangements, which encourage employees to seek services covered by conventional health insurance plans from less costly providers.

Changes most commonly initiated by employers include imposing or increasing cost-sharing requirements, requiring that tests be performed prior to hospital admission, and covering ambulatory surgical care, treatment in extended care facilities, and second surgical opinions. Other changes, although somewhat less common, include coverage of home health and hospice care, case management and utilization review programs, annual physical examinations, wellness or health promotion programs, and coverage through HMOs or PPO arrangements (Friedland, 1987). (For more information on health insurance, HMOs, PPOs, and health promotion programs, see chapters 19, 24, 25, and 26, respectively.)

A 1988 survey of 2,271 firms found that 89 percent covered care provided in ambulatory surgical facilities, 84 percent required preadmission testing, 77 percent covered home health care, 81 percent had provisions for either optional or mandatory second surgical opinions, and 52 percent had wellness programs. Sixty-five percent and 26 percent, respectively, offered an HMO or PPO option (The Wyatt Company, 1988). The prevalence of selected features over time is shown in table 23.1.

In addition to these changes within the framework of existing employer health insurance plans, some employers have initiated a much more sweeping reorganization of their health insurance benefits. In some cases, this reorganization involves simply offering more than one health insurance plan option to employees while contributing the same amount under each plan option. Other employers have more fundamentally reorganized their plans within the framework of flexible benefit or "cafeteria" plans. Most employers adopting flexible benefit plans do so to try to induce employees to share more of, and take greater responsibility for controlling, their health care costs.

Improving Incentives for Economic Health Care Use

Plan design changes that encourage employees to use health care services more economically include increasing employee cost sharing and redesigning service coverage under the plan. Increased cost sharing required by a plan involves the portion of the cost—called the

TABLE 23.1

Percentage of Employer Health Plans with Selected Cost Management Provisions, Selected Years, 1984–1988

Provision	1984	1986	1988
Preadmission Testing	87%	83%	84%
Precertification of Length of Stay	17	31	61
Second Surgical Opinion[a]	54	83	81
Home Health Care	68	70	77
Hospice Care	39	52	66
Wellness Programs	15	28	52
Annual Physical	18	41	36
Ambulatory Surgical Facilities	81	89	89

Source: The Wyatt Company, *1988 Group Benefits Survey* (Washington, DC: The Wyatt Company, 1989).

[a]Either optional or mandatory.

copayment or coinsurance[1]—paid by the employee for services actually used. Cost sharing under employer group plans may be increased by raising deductibles and coinsurance levels for all or some services covered by a plan or by raising employee premiums for their own or for their dependents' coverage.

Because changes in the level of cost sharing, and sometimes the range of covered services, reduce real compensation levels by raising employees' out-of-pocket health care costs, they have generally been resisted by employees, particularly by those with collectively bargained health plans. It is important, therefore, for employers to effectively communicate to employees the reasons that changes are being made in their health plans and for employees to fully understand their role in the health care partnership—that of being *efficient* consumers of health care. This may be accomplished through in-house newsletters and other literature, audio-visual presentations, meetings, telephone hotlines, and benefit summaries that identify the health coverage component of an employee's annual compensation.

Despite some employee resistance to greater cost sharing, many employers report having raised the deductible or copayment provisions of their group health plans in recent years. As a result, "first dollar" coverage for inpatient hospital expenses has become much less common. First dollar coverage pays initial expenses (a specified

---

[1]Copayment refers to a flat payment (for example, $10 per office visit). Coinsurance refers to a percentage of payment (for example, 20 percent of total covered expenses).

amount, depending on the plan) for hospital care, with no deductible or coinsurance provision on the "first dollar" of care delivered.

Changes in the range of services covered by a plan may redirect patient use of health services toward less expensive substitutes for inpatient hospital care. For example, employers have expanded the range of group health plans to include coverage of home health care services, hospice services, and outpatient hospital care, including preadmission testing, outpatient surgery, or surgery performed in free-standing surgical centers. Coverage of these services is aimed at discouraging the unnecessary use of inpatient hospital care or prolonged hospital stays.

Restricting Inappropriate Use of Benefits

Another technique for managing employer health care costs is to restrict the inappropriate use of certain benefits under the plan. For example, coverage for inpatient hospital care by plan participants may depend on complying with a case management or hospital utilization review program or obtaining a second confirming surgeon's opinion before undergoing elective surgery.

Hospital utilization review assesses the appropriateness of hospital admission, inpatient hospital services, and hospital discharge. Individual employers or insurers may conduct their own programs or contract with peer review organizations to evaluate hospital use. Hospital utilization review may be conducted prospectively (before admission), concurrently (during the hospital stay), or retrospectively (after discharge).

The use of prospective, or preadmission, review is increasing rapidly. Insurers may conduct such reviews themselves or instead may subcontract with an organization in each locality that conducts reviews for a number of third-party payers. Some of the prospective review programs also provide concurrent monitoring and require reauthorization for hospital stays that exceed the originally agreed-upon duration.

Plans that require or pay for a second or third medical opinion before elective surgery are common. Second-opinion surgery provisions are often enforced either by refusing payment or by imposing greater cost sharing for expenses related to surgery performed without a second opinion.

Same-day surgery provisions eliminate unnecessarily early hospital admissions and higher hospital room and board costs. Plans that do not require same-day surgery may not cover hospital room and board charges for nonemergency weekend admissions unless surgery is scheduled for the following morning.

Restructuring Service Delivery

The emergence of PPO arrangements is an important development. A PPO is a contractual arrangement between providers and buyers of health care services. Under the arrangement, providers may agree to grant discount rates to those paying (for example, insurers and employers) in return for faster payment, a patient base, or both. In addition, the PPO provider may cooperate in utilization review to monitor and control the growth of health service use and plan costs. As an incentive for the insured to use the PPO benefit plan, coverage is usually greater for services received from PPO providers than for those delivered by other providers. Greater coverage for services obtained through the PPO arrangement might be achieved by waiving the deductible or decreasing the employee's coinsurance requirement.

The number of PPO arrangements has consistently grown over the last several years. (For more about this type of arrangement, see chapter 25.)

Adopting Flexible Benefit Plans

A flexible benefit or "cafeteria" plan is an employee benefit plan that gives employees some choice among cash or nontaxable benefits provided by an employer.

Flexible benefit plans typically include two or more health plans. They may also include, for example, dental coverage, group life insurance, dependent care benefits, and a cash account—sometimes called a reimbursement account—from which employees may reimburse themselves on a pretax basis for out-of-pocket health care or dependent care expenditures.

Employer goals in establishing a flexible benefit program are complex. They often include:

- managing the cost of group health benefits by inducing employees to share more of the health care costs covered by the plan;

- offering employees new, specialized benefits tailored to the needs of individuals in a demographically changing work force, without substantially raising total benefit costs;

- enhancing employee perceptions of the value of employer-provided benefits; and

- limiting employer contributions to a defined dollar amount.

A cash reimbursement account in a flexible benefit plan may be helpful in reducing health care costs paid by both employers and employees under the plan. Employees may be more willing to "trade down" to a less generous health insurance plan option if they can pay out-of-pocket expenses with pretax dollars. Reimbursement accounts offer employees this opportunity. Employees must decide at the beginning of the plan year how much they wish to contribute to the reimbursement account. Any unused balances are forfeited by employees at the end of the plan year.

Despite restrictions on the use of reimbursement accounts, flexible benefit plans still offer employers an opportunity to reduce their benefit *costs*—and reduce their overall *expenditures* for health coverage and other benefit programs. Employers are able to fix their contribution to health insurance benefits—either absolutely or as a percentage of a lower-cost health insurance option—rather than automatically raise their contribution as plan costs rise. With or without a reimbursement account, a flexible benefit plan gives employees an incentive to opt for lower-cost health coverage: choosing a more generous, and more costly, health plan reduces an employee's ability to elect alternative benefits (including pretax savings) or higher cash earnings.

Adjusting the price of alternative health insurance plans offered in a flexible benefit program is important to the plan's success in managing health insurance costs. Employers providing more than one health plan anticipate "adverse selection" on the part of employees. That is, employees who foresee few medical needs during the year are most likely to choose a low-cost, less generous health insurance plan. Employees remaining in the most generous—and most costly—health insurance plan are likely to have higher health care costs, on average, than employees who choose a less generous health plan. The average cost of the most generous plan is likely to rise much faster than the average cost of the least generous plan. Employers would, therefore, like to adjust or "reprice" their plans to reflect the cost history subsequent to the initial offering of the alternative plans. (For more information on flexible compensation plans, see chapter 33.)

Effectiveness of Plan Redesign

Evidence of the effectiveness of plan design changes has started to become available as employers analyze utilization data, audit insurance claims for overcharges, and compare the costs associated with inpatient care with that for outpatient care.

According to the Spring 1988 *Annual ClaimFacts Survey* by Erisco, employers rated preadmission testing, outpatient surgery, home health care, and wellness programs as among the most effective techniques for managing health care costs. The strategy rated most effective was changing the health plan for retirees, who have higher average health care costs than active workers.

A 1986 survey by Hewitt Associates of companies offering flexible benefit plans indicates that when employees are given a choice from among a variety of medical coverage options, overall health care costs are reduced over time.

Prospective Medicare Pricing

Since the passage of the Social Security Amendments of 1983 (P.L. 98-21), Medicare payments to hospitals have been based on prospective pricing, a specific allowance for each patient based on 477 diagnosis-related groups (DRGs).

"Prospective pricing" for hospital care is intended to encourage more cost-effective use of hospital services. If the cost of care exceeds the Medicare payment, the hospital is responsible for the remaining cost. On the other hand, if the Medicare payment exceeds the cost of care, the hospital still receives the full payment. Before the DRG system, hospitals had few incentives to cut the cost of serving Medicare patients, since they were paid based on their actual cost of providing services.

Conclusion

Recent changes in employer group health plan design have received considerable publicity. Although no nationally representative data document the impact of these changes, private industry surveys suggest that some employer initiatives are effective in managing health care costs.

Strategies used by employers to control the cost of their health insurance plans often rely on making employees more aware of the costs associated with their utilization of health care. Many who would reform the nation's health care delivery system see the lack of consumer awareness of health care costs as a major source of cost inflation. Health care cost inflation itself has forced employers to consider major changes in their health benefit programs. These changes may offer promising ways to manage the rising cost of health care for all payers.

Bibliography

A. Foster Higgins & Co., Inc. *Foster Higgins Health Care Benefits Survey 1988*. New York: A. Foster Higgins & Co., Inc., 1988.

Barber, Jean, and Karen Horkitz. Employee Benefit Research Institute. "Features of Employer-Sponsored Health Plans." *EBRI Issue Brief* no. 100 (March 1990).

Custer, William S. Employee Benefit Research Institute. "Managing Health Care Costs and Quality." *EBRI Issue Brief* no. 87 (February 1989).

Friedland, Robert B. "Private Initiatives to Control Health Care Expenditures." In Frank B. McArdle, ed. *The Changing Health Care Market*. Washington, DC: Employee Benefit Research Institute, 1987.

Hicks, Laurence J. *Health Care Cost Management: Solutions for Employers*. Chicago: Illinois State Chamber of Commerce, 1986.

The Wyatt Company. *Medical Benefits for Active and Retired Employees*. Washington, DC: The Wyatt Company, 1988.

U.S. Department of Health and Human Services. News release, 3 May 1990.

Additional Information

Health Research Institute
49 Quail Court, Suite 200
Walnut Creek, CA 94596
(415) 676-2320

National Association of Employers on Health Care Action
304 Key Executive Building
104 Crandon Blvd.
Key Biscayne, FL 33149
(304) 361-2810

24. Health Maintenance Organizations

Introduction

Critics of traditional fee-for-service payment for health care claim that it is a major contributor to health care cost inflation. They assert that this payment method offers little incentive for controlling costs. Health maintenance organization (HMO) advocates believe HMOs offer greater potential for controlling health care costs while maintaining quality medical care.

HMOs provide a wide range of services to subscribers and their dependents on a prepaid basis. Subscribers purchase HMO coverage for a contract period by paying a fixed periodic fee. HMOs generally emphasize preventive care and early intervention. Because HMOs are contractually obligated to provide all covered medical services for a fixed dollar amount, they have an incentive to provide care early, before illnesses become more serious. At the same time, HMO members tend to have lower rates of hospitalization than persons covered by traditional fee-for-service insurance plans.

The first HMO was established in 1929. The number of HMOs has risen dramatically since then. As of July 1, 1989, there were an estimated 590 HMOs covering 32.5 million people (InterStudy, 1989). In 1989, 17 percent of participants in employer-sponsored health care plans in medium-sized and large establishments were in HMOs (U.S. Department of Labor, 1990). More than 1 million older Americans were enrolled in HMOs through Medicare in October 1988.

How HMOs Work

HMOs both finance and deliver health care services. Instead of paying a health care provider each time a service is delivered, HMO subscribers agree to pay periodic fees. In turn, HMOs provide for virtually all of their subscribers' health care needs. (Subscribers may be required to make a modest copayment for some HMO services.) Each HMO develops its own rates and benefits, although certain HMOs that are regulated by federal law must provide at least the basic health services required by law. HMOs accept the risk of providing covered health care services at a cost that does not exceed subscribers' premiums. Thus, they have an economic incentive for monitoring utilization and costs.

HMOs' basic functions are to provide comprehensive health care services to subscribers; to contract with or employ physicians and other health care professionals who will provide the covered medical services; and to contract with one or more hospitals to provide covered hospital care (a few HMOs own and operate hospitals).

The role of an HMO is different from that of a commercial insurer or Blue Cross and Blue Shield plan. HMOs both finance *and* provide health care services. Conventional insurance plans simply reimburse health care providers—whom the patient has to locate—usually under a fee-for-service arrangement, although commercial insurers, self-insured employers, and Blue Cross and Blue Shield plans increasingly are using preferred provider organization (PPO) arrangements and other managed care arrangements to encourage employee use of certain designated health care providers.

Types of HMOs

There are three primary types of HMOs: *group model plans* (sometimes called *prepaid group practice plans*), *staff model plans*, and *individual practice associations* (IPAs).

Group model HMOs contract with physician groups to provide services to HMO subscribers. They usually reimburse physicians on a capitation basis (that is, at a fixed rate per HMO patient). Group model HMO physicians spend most of their professional time serving HMO subscribers; the rest of their time may be spent in their private practices. Group model HMOs may contract with multiple specialty physician groups as well as with general practitioners or other primary care physicians. Group model HMOs may own one or more hospitals or may contract with local hospitals to provide services to subscribers.

Staff model HMOs are similar to group model plans. Under a staff model plan, however, physicians and other health care professionals are directly employed by the HMO (that is, they are members of the HMO's staff).

IPAs are groups of physicians in private practice who provide some services to HMO subscribers but primarily provide services to patients who are not subscribers. These physicians do not operate from a central facility. However, the HMO monitors the appropriateness and quality of care provided to subscribers as well as utilization of services. Typically, the IPA physician shares in the financial loss when the cost of providing covered health services to HMO subscribers exceeds total subscription fees. IPAs have grown faster than other types of HMOs. As of January 1, 1989, there were 387 IPAs with a total enrollment of approximately 13.5 million people.

Health Maintenance Organization Act of 1973

The Health Maintenance Organization Act of 1973 was intended to encourage the growth of HMOs. In addition, it established requirements for an entity seeking designation as a federally qualified HMO. Under these requirements, HMOs must offer certain benefits and satisfy federal regulations for administrative, financial, and contractual arrangements. The U.S. Department of Health and Human Services administers the act and oversees HMO qualification.

Some HMOs are not federally qualified because they do not meet the act's requirements or because they have not applied for qualification. All HMOs must, however, be state certified.

As of January 1, 1989, 317 HMOs were federally qualified; these HMOs provided health care services to 80 percent of all HMO subscribers.

HMOs generally provide more comprehensive services than are covered by commercial insurance plans or Blue Cross and Blue Shield plans. For example, federally qualified HMOs must provide routine examinations, and they also limit copayments.

Services that federally qualified HMOs must provide include primary and specialty physician care, inpatient and outpatient hospital care, emergency care, short-term outpatient mental health care, medical treatment and referral for alcohol/drug abuse and addiction, diagnostic laboratory services, diagnostic and therapeutic radiology services, home health care, and preventive health care.

At its discretion, a federally qualified HMO may also provide a broad range of supplemental health care services, such as intermediate and long-term care (for example, institutional or home health care), adult vision care, dental care, long-term or inpatient mental health care, long-term physical therapy and rehabilitation services, and prescription drugs. These supplemental services can be offered on a fee-for-service basis. (For more information about dental care, prescription drug, and vision care plans, see chapters 20, 21, and 22, respectively.)

The federal HMO law and regulations also include the following provisions.

- The HMO solicitation must be in writing; it must be directed to a managing official at the solicited location. The written request must be extended at least 180 days before renewal or expiration of the employer's regular health benefit contract or collective bargaining agreement. Additionally, the HMO must satisfy other requirements before it will be considered as an optional employer plan (for example, information must be available on the HMO's ownership and control, facilities, operation hours, service areas, and rates). In actual practice, most employers who offer HMOs do so voluntarily (that is, not as a result of the formal solicitation process). See "Dual Choice Requirement."

- Employers who offer HMOs must provide for annual group enrollment periods, during which employees can choose either the HMO or the regular health insurance plan without waiting periods, exclusions, or restrictions due to health status.

Health Maintenance Organization Act Amendments of 1988

Responding to employer concerns about selection bias and HMO pricing, Congress enacted the 1988 amendments to the HMO act (P.L. 100-517) on October 24, 1988. The new law relaxed some regulations applying to federally qualified HMOs, allowing employers to negotiate HMO rates and coverage more easily.

Dual Choice Requirement—One of the major components of the 1973 HMO act required most employers to offer their employees a qualified HMO in addition to a traditional health plan, if requested to do so by such an HMO. The 1988 amendments repeal the dual choice requirement, effective October 24, 1995.

Equal Contribution Requirement—Regulations provided under the original act had interpreted the dual choice provision to require that mandated employers contribute the same dollar amount to federally qualified HMOs as they contribute to their highest-cost non-HMO health plan. The 1988 law eases this requirement and states that any contribution made by a mandated employer to a qualified HMO must be in an amount that does not "financially discriminate" against an employee enrolled in the qualified HMO. A contribution is considered not financially discriminatory "if the employer's method of determining the contributions on behalf of all employees is reasonable and is designed to assure all employees a fair choice among health benefit plans."

Community Rating Requirement—The original HMO act required that federally qualified HMOs *community rate* their services. A community rating system determines rates based on the HMO's total membership experience rather than on the experience of each subscriber group. The 1988 amendments allow employers to negotiate group rates on the basis of an estimate of how much it is likely to cost to provide services to the employee group. This type of pricing is similar to the "experience rating" used in fee-for-service insurance plans, except that HMOs are not permitted to adjust premiums retroactively if the estimates prove inaccurate. Employers with fewer than 100 employees can be charged no more than 110 percent of the community rate.

Conclusion

Since the passage of the 1973 HMO act, some observers have indicated that HMOs have been an important influence in restructuring our health care system and slowing rising health care costs. However, the growth of HMOs was relatively slow during the 1970s for a number of reasons, including physician reluctance to leave fee-for-service medical practice and beneficiary reluctance to accept restrictions on freedom of provider choice. Additionally, there was some initial confusion over the 1973 act. The act has been amended several times; the 1988 amendments are expected to promote competition among HMOs for employers' business which, in turn, could lower employers' cost of providing health coverage to employees.

Some changes are occurring. Sustained growth in HMO membership since 1980 suggests increasing employer and consumer interest in these arrangements. Employers, unions, and insurance companies have been more involved as direct sponsors and organizers of HMOs. Involvement of business and labor leaders has brought needed management skills. Also, hospital managers and private practice physicians have become more interested in HMOs as well as other types of alternative health care delivery systems. However, HMO growth has recently slowed again. HMOs posted a 5.4 percent growth rate as of January 1, 1989, the second lowest annual rate of increase in recorded HMO history.

An indication of the importance that federal health authorities attach to HMO competition in the health care marketplace is the program enacted as part of the Tax Equity and Fiscal Responsibility Act of 1982 (TEFRA). The program is intended to encourage HMO participation in Medicare by paying HMOs in a manner consistent with their cost efficiency. (HMOs can separately rate public employees and Medicare or Medicaid subscriber groups.) Medicare is currently authorized to pay HMOs in advance at a preset rate per enrollee, regardless of the amount or type of services rendered. Previously, Medicare would retrospectively pay HMOs, based on the "reasonable" cost of providing specific services to beneficiaries. Under final regulations issued by the U.S. Department of Health and Human Services in January 1985, financial incentives may lead to increased savings and enable more HMOs to offer expanded benefits, such as dental care, eyeglasses, and prescription drugs to Medicare beneficiaries.

TEFRA also defined competitive medical plans (CMPs) and authorized them to enter into contracts with the federal government to provide Part A and Part B services to Medicare beneficiaries. CMPs may be hospitals, large group practices, PPOs, nonfederally qualified HMOs, or any other organized group that has met certain financial solvency requirements. As of May 1, 1989, there were 37 CMPs in the United States.

Despite HMOs' growth, some observers question their ability to stem rising health care costs. Employers may achieve at least a one-time saving for each employee joining an HMO, but it is less apparent that costs will subsequently increase any more slowly than those for conventional fee-for-service health insurance coverage. Analysts hypothesize that because HMOs compete with fee-for-service plans, they must offer the same cost-increasing technology used in the fee-for-service sector. As a greater variety of providers and insurers compete for a share of the health care market, the future role of HMOs in the market becomes difficult to predict.

Bibliography

Hewitt Associates. *HMOs: An Employer's Guide to Complying With the Federal HMO Act*. Lincolnshire, IL: Hewitt Associates, 1986.
InterStudy. *InterStudy Edge* (1989, vol. 2).
U.S. Department of Labor. Bureau of Labor Statistics. "Employee Benefits Focus on Family Concerns in 1989." USDL news release 90-160. 30 March 1990.

Additional Information

American Managed Care and Review Association
1227 25th Street NW, Suite 610
Washington, DC 20037
(202) 728-0506

Group Health Association of America
1129 20th Street NW, Suite 600
Washington, DC 20036
(202) 778-3200

InterStudy
5715 Christmas Lake Road
P.O. Box 458
Excelsior, MN 55331-0458
(612) 474-1176

National Association of Employers on Health Care Action
304 Key Executive Building
104 Crandon Blvd.
Key Biscayne, FL 33149
(304) 361-2810

25. Preferred Provider Organizations

Introduction

Preferred provider organizations (PPOs) are not actually *organizations* at all but are contractual *arrangements*, generally between health care providers and an employer or insurance company to provide fee-for-service health care, usually at a discount. The term *PPO* covers a variety of arrangements and agreements among employers, insurers, providers, and entrepreneurial organizations.

Providers (for example, physicians and hospitals) agree to rates that they have prenegotiated with those who contract for their services (for example, employers and insurance companies) in return for an increased pool of patients, faster claims processing, or both. Some arrangements are based on a percentage of charges, on a specific cost per day, or on the cost to treat specific diagnostic groups. PPOs are sometimes used for a specific type of medical care, such as mental health, vision, or dental services.

In most cases, employees covered by a PPO benefit plan (subscribers) are free to choose any physician or hospital they wish but are given financial incentives to use the services of *preferred* providers. These incentives may include expanded benefits and lower costs for certain services. Employers may offer a PPO benefit plan instead of, or in addition to, a traditional indemnity plan and/or health maintenance organization (HMO).

Financial incentives for employees might include no deductible and only minimal copayments, while employees who choose nonparticipating physicians may be required to pay a deductible and larger copayments. For example, subscribers who use a preferred provider might have no deductible and a copayment of only $5 or $10 per office visit, plus extra services such as well-baby care and diabetes testing. Those who use nonparticipating physicians might be subject to a $200 or $500 deductible, 20 percent coinsurance, and no extra coverages.

PPO arrangements have been developed in response to employer concern over rising health care costs and to provider concern about growing competition from alternative health delivery systems, such as HMOs, that promise lower-cost services. PPO arrangements not only offer reduced prices for health care services but their proponents contend that PPOs can reduce costs by selecting cost efficient providers and implementing utilization review and control. Savings of at least 15 percent reportedly are typical.

The National Association of Employers on Health Care Action's 1988/89 directory lists 655 operational PPOs, the majority of which have been formed since 1983. The number of employees who are offered a PPO option continues to rise as more employers seek to manage their health care costs in this way. Results of a 1988 survey by the employee benefit consulting firm TPF&C indicate that one-fourth of 163 companies surveyed offered their employees a PPO option, while another 22 percent said they were considering doing so.

Types of PPO Arrangements

There are three primary types of PPO arrangements: provider based, entrepreneur based, and purchaser based. They differ according to their types of sponsorship.

- Provider-based PPO sponsors include hospitals, physician groups, joint hospital/physician arrangements, dentists, podiatrists, and other health professionals.
- Entrepreneur-based PPO sponsors include private investors, third-party administrators, and utilization review organizations.
- Purchaser-based PPO sponsors include Blue Cross and Blue Shield plans, commercial insurers, employers, and community groups.

One type of PPO benefit plan is an exclusive provider organization (EPO) benefit plan, established by self-insured (self-funded) employers. In an EPO benefit plan, employees *must* use EPO providers to receive coverage; PPO benefit plans merely offer a financial incentive for employees to do so. PPO benefit plans are subject to state insurance regulations, unless established or purchased by self-insured employers (see the discussion of self-insured group plans in chapter 23). Such employers consequently can establish EPO benefit plans, agreeing to reimburse only for services of the "exclusive" providers.

Sometimes employer-sponsored PPO benefit plans are known as negotiated provider agreements (NPAs) because they allow an employer to negotiate pricing and determine how health care utilization will be monitored.

Most existing PPO benefit plans were formed by hospitals, physicians, and investors, but those sponsored by Blue Cross and Blue Shield plans and commercial insurers represent the largest share of PPO enrollment.

218

Relatively few employers have organized their own PPO benefit plans, although some employers have created associations that sponsor plans within geographic areas. Employers sometimes use insurance carriers as intermediaries in a PPO arrangement, but more often they purchase a PPO benefit product developed by a Blue Cross and Blue Shield plan or other insurer.

Physicians who provide services through PPOs may have their own practices, be in small groups that belong to independent practice associations (IPAs), or belong to multispecialty group practices. A PPO may contract with a combination of these physician practice arrangements and offer subscribers a choice among groups.

PPO arrangements usually include both primary care physicians and specialists. In a large metropolitan area, a PPO may have agreements with as many as 10 or 15 hospitals and thousands of physicians.

Differences between HMOs and PPOs

Although HMOs existed 50 years ago, the rapid growth of both HMOs and PPO arrangements has occurred relatively recently. It is important to understand the major differences between them.

- HMOs are *organizations* that are responsible for the delivery of care, while PPO arrangements are *contractual relationships* between the purchasers and the providers of care.

- HMOs are prepaid systems, while PPO providers operate on a fee-for-service basis.

- HMO members must use the services of HMO physicians and affiliated hospitals to be covered, while PPO benefit plan subscribers generally are not restricted to preferred providers (with the exception of EPOs).

- HMOs must bear the financial risk for their operations, while in most PPOs the purchaser (the insurer, the employer, etc.), rather than the health care provider, bears the risk.

As new variations of PPO arrangements emerge, however, many are assuming characteristics of HMOs. For example, risk sharing between provider and purchaser is taking place in some PPOs. Also, some have begun to require primary care physicians to refer patients only to specific hospitals or specialists.

Managing Costs

PPO arrangements can be effective in managing costs only through medical practices that carefully use health care resources. This means that physicians and hospitals are expected to avoid unnecessary tests, x-ray examinations, and other procedures; to consider alternatives to hospitalization; and in general to practice efficient medicine.

Utilization review with feedback to the provider is a critical component of a PPO's cost management strategy. PPO sponsors may monitor claims, require prior authorization for certain types of treatment, and examine physician case records. Effective utilization review may also incorporate quality assurance measures.

Utilization review is often handled by the PPO health care providers, as is the case with many PPOs sponsored by hospitals, or by using an outside professional peer review organization. Hospitals or physician groups that conduct their own internal reviews are susceptible to the criticism that it is difficult for an organization to police its own behavior.

Employers who set up their own PPO arrangements, as well as Blue Cross and Blue Shield plans and insurance carriers that offer PPO benefit products, often set up their own utilization review systems to ascertain whether they are receiving cost-efficient services from the providers with whom they contract.

Self-insured employers or insurers who want to reduce their risk for large losses are in many cases able to negotiate risk-sharing agreements with providers. Risk sharing includes splitting costs in catastrophic cases, paying bonuses to health care specialists for keeping costs under certain dollar limits, and setting fees for certain procedures. If the procedure turns out to be more costly, the hospital absorbs the difference.

In provider-based PPOs that accept responsibility for a share of financial risk, expenditure targets might be set. If expenditures fall below the target, the savings might go to the physicians or be shared by the physicians and the employer. If expenditures exceed the target, the losses might be shared by the PPO and the employee or by the PPO, but only up to certain limits.

Legal Issues

More than 30 states regulate PPO benefit plans to varying degrees in such areas as provider selection, rate differentials, provision of emergency care, and reporting and disclosure requirements.

Questions as to the legal status of PPOs have impeded their development in some states. Some forms of provider-sponsored PPO arrangements have been found to be in violation of antitrust laws as horizontal price fixing arrangements (*Arizona v. Maricopa County Medical Society*, 1982) or as arrangements with the potential to restrain trade (*Group Life and Health Insurance Company v. Royal Drug Company*, 1979).

Although PPO arrangements in general are open to legal review, their dramatic growth is expected to continue. State laws may, however, restrict this growth somewhat. At least 12 states require that nonpreferred providers be paid a minimum percentage of the levels set for preferred providers, ranging from 70 percent to 80 percent.

Conclusion

Changes in health care delivery systems present employers with new possibilities for cost management. The rapid growth of PPO arrangements during the last decade suggests that they are finding acceptance with employers and insurers that are searching for alternatives to traditional indemnity plans in an effort to control rising health care costs.

PPOs are seen as having the potential to bring about price competition among providers. But they also hold out the promise that they can provide more than discounted prices. To ensure both cost-effective and quality care, however, PPO sponsors must be energetic in searching out efficient and competent providers and vigilant in discouraging excessive or inappropriate treatment by those providers.

Few scientific studies exist to support contentions that PPO arrangements help hold down health care costs. Many PPOs have been in existence too short a time for conclusive data to be available. Some trends, however, favor PPOs' continued growth, including the increasing surplus of physicians and hospital beds.

PPO benefit plans may also find greater acceptance by employees because they permit a broader choice of physicians than HMOs and other managed care plans. Some PPOs, however, are moving closer to the HMO model by using a primary care physician as a so-called "gatekeeper" who controls referral to specialists and hospitals.

In today's changing medical marketplace, different types of PPO arrangements continue to emerge in response to competition and the search for successful cost management strategies. If studies show that the PPO is a successful strategy for limiting increases in health care costs, its use is likely to continue to grow.

Bibliography

American Association of Preferred Provider Organizations. *Preferred Provider Organizations: Productive Partnerships for Cost-Effective, Quality Health Care*. Chicago: AAPPO, 1988.

Helitzer, Jack B. "State Developments in Employee Benefits: State Regulation of Preferred Provider Organizations." *Benefits Law Journal* (Winter 1988/89): 109–117.

National Association of Employers on Health Care Action. *NAEHCA Blue Book: A Digest of PPOs*, fourth annual ed. 1988/89. Key Biscayne, FL: NAEHCA, 1988.

Additional Information

American Association of Preferred Provider Organizations
111 E. Wacker Drive, Suite 600
Chicago, IL 60601
(312) 644-6610

National Association of Employers on Health Care Action
304 Key Executive Building
104 Crandon Blvd.
Key Biscayne, FL 33149
(305) 361-2810

26. Employee Assistance and Health Promotion Programs

Introduction

Employee assistance and health promotion programs are increasingly being used by employers as health care cost management measures and as tools for improving employee productivity, morale, and job satisfaction; reducing absenteeism and turnover; and improving the corporate image. While the two types of programs often have similar goals, their structures and components are quite dissimilar.

Employee assistance programs (EAPs) are generally counseling services directed toward acute problems that affect job performance, such as drug and alcohol abuse and emotional and financial problems. Health promotion programs, on the other hand, emphasize prevention of physical and emotional illness through healthier lifestyles. Many health promotion programs are called "wellness" or "fitness" programs.

Today, more and more employers are offering both types of programs. In showing concern for employees' physical and mental health, employers may offer in-house or outside counseling services; provide information on such problems as substance abuse, smoking, and stress through seminars, classes, or written materials; and start programs to assist employees in changing patterns of behavior that can lead to poor health.

Employers often provide coverage in their company medical plans for the treatment of substance abuse and mental health problems in addition to offering EAPs and health promotion programs.

Employee assistance and health promotion programs are being developed and offered by employers to address three basic issues: rising health care costs, increasing concern about how employees' personal problems affect job productivity, and growing awareness of the benefits of good health and fitness.

Since both types of programs are relatively new employer-sponsored benefits, there is not yet conclusive evidence of the programs' long-term effectiveness in reducing health care costs. However, if properly structured and communicated to employees, the programs demonstrate employer concern and commitment to employees' well-being.

EAPs offer employees, and in most cases their families, the opportunity to receive confidential professional counseling and assistance. Generally there is little, if any, cost to the employee. Health promotion programs, on the other hand, provide extra benefit options to employees through activities at the work place or at easily accessed facilities. Depending on the program's design, employees may pay a fee for participation in certain activities.

Employee Assistance Programs

Types—Some employers contract with specialists such as psychologists, social workers, or alcoholism counselors to provide services for employees who are referred through an EAP, while other employers offer direct assistance through their own staff counselors. An employer may also contract with a community agency to provide services to employees.

The problem areas generally covered in an EAP include alcoholism and drug abuse, emotional problems and stress, marital and family relations, and legal or financial issues. The most prevalent problem covered in EAPs is substance abuse.

The incidence of alcohol and drug abuse problems continues to increase. In a 1989 survey, 22 percent of respondents said that substance abuse was "significant" in the organization in which they worked (William M. Mercer Meidinger Hansen, 1989). The total cost to society of substance abuse and mental illness, including lost productivity and property damage, is estimated to have been as high as $237 billion in 1984.

Setting up a Program—If employees are to seek out the services of an EAP, the program must be structured to guarantee confidentiality and trust. Communication with employees about the program needs to emphasize the EAP's role in assisting those who need help.

The program generally begins with an assessment of all employees' needs. This can be done by reviewing claims for mental health treatment, absenteeism rates, accident rates, and employee interest in programs that deal with issues such as stress and caring for elderly relatives. Initial steps in setting up a program also involve deciding whether to develop an in-house program or contract out for services.

Supervisors and managers must be formally trained to refer employees to the EAP for problems that are affecting their job performance. Supervisors who label employees as alcoholics or drug abusers and who try to force or coerce them into treatment programs could cause legal problems for the employer.

Confidentiality of records makes the collection of information for evaluation difficult. However, employers will need to know how many employees use the EAP, the program's effects on job performance, and how employees feel about the program.

Advantages for Employers—EAPs may help employees deal with serious problems that could be interfering with their work performance and costing employers several billion dollars in productivity each year. American business spends between $204 million and $798 million each year on employee assistance programs, but it is estimated that they recover $3 to $5 for every $1 they spend.

Program costs are minimal for employers that mainly rely on referral to outside agencies. Employers that hire professional counselors or contract with outside providers will incur somewhat higher costs, but their EAPs will be more comprehensive.

Health Promotion Programs

Types—Health promotion programs range from modest efforts (for example, the distribution of pamphlets on health issues or the provision of showers or changing facilities for employees who exercise) to major initiatives such as elaborate, well-equipped gymnasiums and a full package of physical fitness activities.

One type of health promotion program—health risk screening—directly relates to health care by providing testing for high blood pressure, breast cancer, diabetes, and high cholesterol levels. Screening is sometimes followed by education on how to reduce identified risks. Other programs involve classes and seminars on such topics as good nutrition and ways to stop smoking, lose weight, and manage stress.

Some companies have their own exercise facilities for employees (and sometimes for family members as well), with swimming pools, jogging tracks, saunas, racquetball/handball courts, and workout rooms. If they do not have their own facilities, employers sometimes pay a share of employees' health club memberships.

Many companies and unions have initiated one or more of these wellness programs. A 1989 survey of 1,000 employers showed that a large majority (80 percent) sponsored at least one type of wellness program for their workers (Hewitt Associates, 1990). The most common programs were smoking cessation (63 percent), weight loss (48 percent), and stress management (44 percent). Other programs addressed disease prevention, lifestyle, and safety.

Setting up a Program—Careful planning helps to ensure high levels of employee participation. This planning should include:

- involving employees at all levels in the planning process;

- tailoring the program to the company and its work force;

- communicating the company's commitment to the program and belief in its importance;

- providing a variety of options and developing incentives for employee participation;

- conducting periodic health assessments for employees to measure progress in achieving goals; and

- evaluation of the program.

Employers have adopted a variety of incentives to encourage employee participation. Some employers pay a portion of the cost for employees to attend outside clinics to stop smoking or pay a higher percentage of medical expenses for employees who do not smoke or who regularly participate in an exercise program. Others set up competitions among employees, with prizes awarded to winners, or offer bonuses to employees who complete a specified number of hours of exercise.

Advantages for Employers—Companies with health promotion programs generally report lower absenteeism rates, lower health care costs, and more productive and satisfied employees. Some companies evaluate their programs by comparing the fitness of exercise program participants with that of a control group, in terms of such factors as weight control, smoking cessation, elevated blood pressure, and the number of sick days used. In many cases, however, data have not been collected over a long period of time. Some studies suggest that younger employees who are already fit, and who exercised regulary before joining a company program, are the ones most likely to join and remain in employer-sponsored fitness programs.

To make a health promotion program cost effective, an employer must communicate the program to employees, encourage broad participation, and regularly assess the program's effectiveness. Dropout rates can be high unless employers are innovative in their choice of programs and in the incentives they offer employees to participate.

Health promotion programs can be valuable in providing early detection of health problems and offering employees the means to reduce the risks from such problems. As employers modify and tailor programs to their employees' needs and desires, the programs' potential to improve productivity and reduce health care costs may increase.

Conclusion

It is estimated that employers spent more than $2,600 on health care costs per employee in 1989 (A. Foster Higgins & Co., Inc., 1989). Many employers believe they have achieved significant cost savings through the initiation of employee assistance and health promotion programs. Moreover, they point to employee satisfaction with such programs.

To establish whether EAPs and health promotion programs can be credited with health care cost savings, employers and researchers must track a large number of employees over a long period of time. Regardless of the results, many employers believe that the existence of these programs demonstrates employers' concerns for their employees and the value they place on employees' well-being and good health.

Bibliography

A. Foster Higgins & Co., Inc. *A. Foster Higgins Health Care Benefits Survey 1989*. Princeton, NJ: A. Foster Higgins & Co., Inc., 1989.

Bureau of National Affairs. *Employee Assistance Programs: Focusing on the Family*. Washington, DC: Bureau of National Affairs, 1988.

Custer, William S. Employee Benefit Research Institute. "Issues in Mental Health Care." *EBRI Issue Brief* no. 99 (February 1990).

Hewitt Associates. "Keeping Employees Healthy: A New Approach to Managing Health Care Costs." News release, 16 February 1990.

William M. Mercer Meidinger Hansen, Inc. "Substance Abuse in the Workplace." *The Bulletin* (March 1989).

Additional Information

Association for Fitness in Business
310 North Alabama, Suite A-100
Indianapolis, IN 46204
(317) 636-6621

Center for Corporate Health Promotion
1850 Centennial Park Drive, Suite 520
Reston, VA 22091
(703) 391-1900

EAP Digest
2145 Crooks Road, Suite 103
Troy, MI 48084
(313) 643-9580

Employee Assistance Professionals Association, Inc.
4601 N. Fairfax Drive, Suite 1001
Arlington, VA 22203
(703) 522-6272

Employee Assistance Society of North America
P.O. Box 3909
Oak Park, IL 60303
(708) 383-6668

Health Research Institute
1600 S. Main Plaza, Suite 170
Walnut Creek, CA 94596
(415) 676-2320

International Health Network
1701 K Street, NW, Suite 600
Washington, DC 20006
(202) 331-0378

27. Group Life Insurance Plans

Introduction

Many employers provide death benefits for survivors of deceased employees. There are two types of plans designed specifically for this purpose: *group life insurance plans*, which normally make lump-sum payments to a designated beneficiary or beneficiaries, and *survivor income plans*, which make regular (usually monthly) payments to survivors. Additionally, benefits may be paid to survivors from other employee benefit plans (for example, profit-sharing, thrift, and pension plans). Survivor benefits are also available through the Social Security program (see chapter 2).

The concept of *individual* life insurance was developed centuries ago, but *group* life insurance is a relatively recent innovation. In 1911, the first known group life insurance contract was created at the Pantasote Leather Company in Passaic, New Jersey. The contract was called the *yearly renewable term employees' policy* and included many features that are standard in today's group term life policies. By the end of 1912, there were 12 group contracts in existence, providing total coverage of $13 million; by 1940, there were 8,800 contracts, providing total coverage of $15 billion; and by 1945, there were 11,500 contracts, providing total coverage of $22 billion.

In the years after World War II, the wage freeze spurred a boom in group life insurance. Employees, knowing they could not get wage increases, requested additional benefits. Employer-sponsored life insurance coverage was one of the most often demanded benefits. As a result, in 1950, there were approximately 19,000 group contracts, providing total coverage of $48 billion.

Employer-sponsored life insurance has continued to grow. At the end of 1987, approximately 672,000 master policy group contracts were providing $3 trillion of coverage to Americans—most of it employer sponsored. This *group* coverage accounted for 40.8 percent of *all* life insurance coverage in the United States in 1987 (American Council of Life Insurance, 1989). Among full-time employees in medium-sized and large establishments in the United States, 94 percent had employer-provided life insurance coverage in 1989 (U.S. Department of Labor, 1990).

The Insurance Contract

The contract between the insurance company and the employer is usually for *group term* life insurance. Many associations and multiple employer plans also provide group term life benefits.[1] The word *term* means that the coverage is bought for a specific time period (usually one year), with a renewable provision, and remains in effect only as long as premiums are paid. It may be referred to as *yearly* or *annual renewable* term. Term insurance has no savings features and no buildup of cash value. It is pure insurance protection, paying a benefit only at death.

The cost of providing group life coverage varies depending on the insurer and the covered group. For small groups, charges are usually taken from a *standard rates table*. Monthly premiums typically range from 10 cents per $1,000 of coverage for employees in their early twenties to $2.50 per $1,000 of coverage for employees in their sixties. For large groups, the initial premium may also be taken from a standard rates table, but in the second and subsequent years of coverage the premium may vary according to the group's claims experience. After the first year, the net premium for a large group is essentially the sum of claims incurred plus the insurer's administrative costs and an amount to provide for profit and risk.

Plan Provisions

Eligibility—While some group life insurance plans cover all of a company's employees, others cover limited groups, such as hourly paid employees, salaried employees, members of a specific union, or employees at a certain plant location.

Amounts of Insurance—Employers provide varying levels of coverage. The amount of coverage can be based on one or more factors (for example, occupation and/or salary). The most common coverage is expressed as a flat dollar amount or as a percentage of salary. This approach is one of the most popular and is becoming even more so among insurers, employers, and employees. Some plans provide the same amount of coverage for all employees. Life insurance is frequently intended to replace a portion of the deceased employee's earnings for a period of time. In 1989, for 68 percent of covered workers in medium-sized and large establish-

---

[1]Other major types of group life insurance include *paid-up* and *ordinary* life insurance. Since term insurance is the most popular group coverage, this chapter focuses primarily on group term insurance.

ments, the amount of life insurance was based on earnings, typically one or two times annual pay. Most of the remaining participants were provided flat dollar amounts of coverage. (U.S. Department of Labor, 1990). Supplemental plans are often used to provide additional coverage.

Employee Cost—According to the Bureau of Labor Statistics, in 1989, 87 percent of employers paid the total premium for basic group life insurance (U.S. Department of Labor, 1990). In other plans, employees paid part or all of the cost; their contribution typically was a flat amount (for example, 25 cents or 50 cents per $1,000 of coverage per month) for each covered employee, regardless of age. In supplemental plans, the cost is often paid entirely by the employee, and the monthly premium per $1,000 of coverage increases with age.

Dependent Life Insurance—As part of the group life insurance plan, some employers offer insurance to employees or their dependents. The cost of dependent coverage is usually paid by employees who elect such protection.

Dependent life insurance usually provides a fixed amount of coverage for a worker's spouse and a smaller fixed amount of coverage for other eligible dependents. Generally, the other eligible dependents are unmarried children between the ages of 14 days and 19 years. However, some contracts cover children from birth, and some set the upper age limit as high as 25 if the dependent is a full-time student. Dependent coverage may continue indefinitely if the dependent is physically or mentally disabled and unable to be self-supporting.

The level of dependent coverage is usually less—sometimes much less—than employee coverage. (In some states the amount of dependent coverage is limited by law.) For example, a plan that provides two times pay for an employee may specify a flat $2,000 or $5,000 coverage amount for the employee's spouse and a flat $1,000 coverage amount for dependent children over the age of six months (and less for newborns).

Accidental Death and Dismemberment Insurance—Frequently, group life insurance plans include accidental death and dismemberment insurance. Thus, if death is the result of an accident, the plan may pay additional benefits. It may also pay benefits—usually stated fractions of the policy's face amount—for the accidental loss of a hand, a foot, or eyesight.

In 1989, 71 percent of employees of medium-sized and large establishments who were covered by life insurance received accidental death and dismemberment insurance, which provides additional benefits in the event of death or disability caused by an accident (U.S. Department of Labor, 1990). For 91 percent of workers with accidental death and dismemberment protection, benefits equaled basic life insurance benefits. The remainder had flat dollar benefit amounts.

Beneficiary Provisions—Under a typical group plan, employees may designate and change their beneficiaries. At death, the stipulated benefit is paid directly to the named beneficiary. If a beneficiary is not named, proceeds generally go to the deceased employee's estate. In the case of dependent insurance, unless someone is specifically named as beneficiary, the employee is considered the beneficiary.

Benefits for Retired Persons and Older Workers—Most group life policies are designed to cover active employees. Coverage for active older employees (age 65 is common) can be reduced to reflect the increase in the cost of life insurance as a result of age. At retirement, coverage is often reduced to a smaller amount or may be canceled.

In 1989, 52 percent of life insurance participants in medium-sized and large establishments were in plans that reduced benefits for older employees, normally beginning at ages 65 or 70. Life insurance coverage, typically reduced, continued after retirement for 42 percent of participants (U.S. Department of Labor, 1990).

Conversion Privileges—When an employee's insurance expires because he or she terminates employment with the company, the employee may usually convert his or her group coverage to an individual permanent life insurance plan. In some states a conversion privilege is mandated by law. Application must be made and a premium paid within one month after terminating from group coverage. (If the individual dies during the one-month period, the group protection is usually extended and benefits are paid.) The amount of converted coverage cannot exceed the amount of insurance previously provided under the group plan. Also, the premium will reflect the insurance company's standard rate for individual policies, based on the person's age and risk classification. When the amount of an employee's insurance is reduced because of age or retirement, conversion of the amount of the reduction is often allowed.

Disability Benefits—Group plans generally continue to provide some life insurance protection for a covered employee who becomes totally and permanently disabled. Although there are several methods in use, the most popular is a *waiver-of-premium* provision. Under such a provision, coverage is continued at no cost to the disabled employee, providing:

- the employee is under a specified age (usually 60) at the onset of disability;[2]
- the employee is covered under the plan at the onset of disability;
- disability continues until death; or
- proof of total and continuous disability is provided annually.

Optional Forms of Payment—The standard payment method for group life insurance claims is a lump-sum distribution. However, virtually all insurers permit other settlement arrangements at the insured employee's option (or the beneficiary's option, if the employee did not make an election before death). Alternative payment arrangements include installment payments and life income annuities.

Taxation

Group term life insurance is a tax-efficient benefit for the employer and the employee. The employer's premiums are tax deductible as a business expense, and the benefits paid to beneficiaries are exempt from federal income taxation. The proceeds, however, generally are subject to estate taxes.

Employees may receive up to $50,000 in employer-provided life insurance coverage without paying income tax on the amount. On coverage beyond $50,000, the employee is taxed on the cost of the balance. In cases where an employee contributes toward the cost of the insurance, that part of the contribution is credited to any coverage in excess of $50,000. Additionally, the $50,000 maximum does not apply if the employee is totally and permanently disabled or if the employee has legally specified that the policy proceeds go to a charitable organization.

FICA Tax—The Omnibus Budget Reconciliation Act of 1987 extended Social Security (FICA) taxes to any employer-paid portion of the cost of employee group term life insurance in excess of $50,000, effective January 1, 1988. Accordingly, employers must include the imputed amount in the gross wages they enter in box 10 of the applicable W-2 forms. The law includes an exception from the FICA rule for individuals who separated from service before 1989.

Extension of Imputed Income Rates—The Internal Revenue Service "table 1 rates" are the basis for valuing employees' imputed income for group term life insurance. Before the Technical and Miscellaneous

---

[2]Although this is a common provision, there are legal opinions that hold that it may violate the Age Discrimination in Employment Act.

Revenue Act of 1988 (TAMRA), the table rates stopped at age 64, and employees over age 64 were charged imputed income on the value of insurance for employees aged 60 to 64 ($1.17 per $1,000 of coverage per month). TAMRA extended the table rate schedule to ages beyond age 64, effective in 1989.

Group Universal Life Programs

Employers have begun offering group universal life insurance—a relatively new and fast-growing type of coverage that is paid for by the employee but usually offers lower premiums than similar insurance purchased on an individual basis. In addition, coverage is usually provided up to a limit without evidence of insurability (such as a medical examination).

Group universal life programs (also known by the acronym GULP) allow policyholders to vary the timing and amount of premiums in addition to the amount of the death benefit and the extent to which it increases. Premiums, minus mortality charges and expenses, create policy cash values. Such plans also provide competitive interest rates and allow buyers to accumulate tax-deferred savings.

Group universal life programs do not always offer spouse and child coverage, however. In addition, if a master group universal life contract is terminated or altered, terminated employees or retired employees may find the original costs and form of their insurance substantially revised. Finally, introduction of a GULP could entail a major communication effort on the part of the employer to inform employees about their choices and answer questions about the coverage and enrollment procedures.

Employee contributions to GULP premiums are made with after-tax dollars, often via payroll deduction. If the policy is surrendered early, there may be a penalty. Corporate benefits departments should be consulted before selections are made in order to better understand the policy's implications.

Conclusion

The death of a worker can be financially devastating to his or her family. Employer-sponsored life insurance benefits can ease the ensuing financial difficulties. The number of employer-sponsored life insurance plans continues to grow, attesting to their importance. To design effective programs, employers should consider how these plans fit in with other potential private and public sources of life insurance, survivor benefits, and death benefits.

Bibliography

American Council of Life Insurance. *1989 Life Insurance Fact Book Update.* Washington, DC: ACLI, 1989.

Curry, Tim, and Mark Warsrawky. "Life Insurance Companies in a Changing Environment." *Federal Reserve Bulletin* (July 1986): 449–460.

Jones, Ward E. "GULPs Are Not What They're Cracked Up to Be." *Benefits News Analysis* (January 1987): 28.

U.S. Department of Labor. Bureau of Labor Statistics. "Employee Benefits Focus on Family Concerns in 1989." USDL news release 90-160, 30 March 1990.

Additional Information

American Council of Life Insurance
1001 Pennsylvania Ave., NW
Washington, DC 20004-2599
(202) 624-2000

28. Survivor Benefits

Introduction

Most employers offer survivor or death benefits to their employees. Originally, these benefits were provided through group term life insurance, which paid a lump sum to a designated beneficiary or beneficiaries. (For more information on life insurance plans, see chapter 27.) Since 1937, benefits to the survivors of deceased employees have also been paid through other sources, including Social Security, employer-sponsored survivor income plans, and employer-sponsored pension plans. This chapter offers an overview of these three survivor benefit sources.

Social Security Survivor Benefits

Social Security benefits for *widows* and *widowers* are payable at age 60 providing the deceased spouse had attained Social Security's *fully insured* status[1] and the couple had been married for at least nine months. A widow or widower generally loses the right to benefits on the deceased worker's record when she or he remarries, unless the marriage takes place after age 60. *Survivor* benefits may also be paid to a spouse under age 60 (including a divorced spouse) who is caring for an entitled *dependent* child under age 16 if the deceased worker was either currently or fully insured.[2] The benefit rate for widows and widowers who began receiving benefits at age 65 can be as high as 100 percent of the deceased worker's primary insurance amount (PIA) plus any *delayed retirement credits* earned by the deceased worker.[3] The benefit for a surviving spouse caring for the former worker's child is 75 percent of the worker's PIA.

---

[1]Generally, to satisfy the fully insured requirement, a person must have earned at least one quarter of Social Security coverage for each year after 1950 (or, if later, the year when he or she reaches age 21) and before the year of death, disability, or his or her 62nd birthday, whichever occurs first.

[2]Requirements to determine whether a child is dependent vary according to whether the worker is a natural parent, legally adopting parent, stepparent, or grandparent. For more information, see U.S. Department of Health and Human Services, 1988.

[3]Currently, the delayed retirement credit is 3 percent for each year between ages 65 and 70 that a worker does not receive retirement benefits, either because the worker did not claim benefits or because of the worker's earnings. Between 1990 and 2008, the credit will increase to 8 percent annually.

If the widow or widower is disabled, benefits are payable at age 50. For a disabled widow(er) to receive benefits, certain conditions must be satisfied: the disability must be so severe that it prevents the individual from engaging in gainful activity, and generally it must have occurred prior to the seventh anniversary of the spouse's death. A disabled widow(er) may remarry after age 50 without affecting benefits. The current benefit rate for disabled widows and widowers who are aged 50 to 60 is 71.5 percent of the deceased worker's primary insurance amount.

A divorced person who was married to a fully insured worker for 10 or more years may also be entitled to survivor benefits.

Benefits for children and surviving spouses caring for entitled children, as well as lump-sum benefits, are payable if the deceased worker had attained fully insured or *currently insured* status.[4] Unmarried children under age 18 (or under age 19 if full-time high school students) are entitled to receive benefits. The child benefit rate is 75 percent of the deceased worker's primary insurance amount. (However, the combined spouse's and children's benefits cannot exceed a family maximum.) Dependent parents aged 62 or older may also be eligible to receive survivor benefits, providing specific conditions are satisfied. (See chapter 2 for more about Social Security.)

Survivor Income Plans

Survivor income plans typically pay benefits to *specified dependents* rather than to *designated beneficiaries* (who may or may not be dependents) of deceased employees. These benefits are generally paid in equal monthly installments. They are related to survivors' needs and are intended to provide continuing income support. Advocates of survivor income plans believe this need is greatest when the employee is young and has young children rather than when the employee has reached his or her peak earning years and probably has substantial life insurance protection.

When designing survivor income plans, employers should consider the income level necessary to maintain the survivors' living standard and additional benefit sources that survivors may receive (that is,

---

[4]To satisfy the currently insured requirement, a person must have earned six quarters of coverage in the 13 quarter period ending with the quarter in which death occurs. A lump-sum death benefit of $255, which is intended to help the worker's family pay the costs associated with the worker's last illness and death, is paid under specified circumstances to a deceased worker's surviving spouse or children.

other employer-provided death benefits and Social Security benefits). Some plans are designed to provide income for specified lengths of time; these plans enable survivors to make financial adjustments during a transition period. They may pay benefits for periods as short as two years or as long as 20 years.

Insurance companies are commonly used as providers of survivor income coverage. However, employers may also self insure this coverage. Survivor income plans may be entirely employer paid or they may be contributory. Employee contributions are generally made through payroll deductions.

Employee Eligibility—Survivor income plans may cover employees immediately upon employment or after a specified waiting period.

Survivor Eligibility—The definition of "qualified survivor" varies among plans. Typically, qualified survivors include an employee's spouse and any unmarried dependent children under age 18 (or age 19 if they are still in high school). Less frequently, eligible survivors include parents or other relatives. In some instances, coverage depends on whether or not the survivors are truly dependent on the employee for support.

Benefits—Survivor income plans are generally designed to supplement Social Security survivor benefits. Usually, survivor income plans base benefits on the employee's salary at the time of death. The spousal benefit is typically 20 percent to 30 percent, and children's benefits 10 percent to 20 percent, of an employee's salary before death. However, the family's combined benefit may be limited to an overall maximum (for example, 40 percent).

The amount of a survivor's monthly benefit can also be a fixed dollar amount (specified for all employees) or an amount designated according to an employee's position.

Duration of Benefits—Some plans are designed to pay benefits for time periods related to survivors' ages. Other plans pay benefits for survivors' remaining lifetimes. Generally, children's benefits stop once they reach the plan's age limit or if they marry before reaching the limit. Spouses' benefits may continue until age 60, when a widow(er) becomes eligible for Social Security survivor benefits. Other plans continue widow(er) benefits until the date when the deceased employee would have reached normal retirement age.

Spousal benefits may cease when the widow(er) remarries. However, some plans continue benefits for a specified period regardless of whether the widow(er) remarries. Other plans pay a *dowry* benefit—that is, a lump-sum benefit payable upon remarriage to encourage reporting of the marriage (Rosenbloom, 1988).

239

Taxation—The cost of survivor income benefit plans is tax deductible to the employer. Employer contributions to these plans are generally tax free to employees. If the employer provides the employee with coverage that exceeds $50,000 in life insurance value, the employee may be required to pay taxes on the *cost* of the insurance coverage above $50,000. Life insurance proceeds are exempt from federal income tax. But if the beneficiary receives payment in installments over time instead of in a lump sum, a portion of the installment payments that represents the interest is considered to be taxable income. Life insurance proceeds from an unfunded, self-insured plan are taxable if the lump-sum benefit exceeds $5,000.

The portion of the survivor benefit that is taxable qualifies for taxation at a joint-return rate provided the survivor meets the qualifications for a surviving spouse:

- the survivor's spouse died during one of the two immediately preceding taxable years;

- the survivor did not remarry before the close of the taxable year;

- the survivor was able to file jointly in the year the spouse died; and

- the survivor maintained a home (that is, furnished at least one-half of the cost of maintaining the household) that was the principal place of abode of a dependent of the survivor (as defined by section 152 of the tax code) and for whom the taxpayer is entitled to a deduction in the current taxable year.

Pension Plan Death Benefits

Most pension plans contain provisions for death benefits payable when a participant dies. The Internal Revenue Service requires that these benefits be *incidental* to the plan's main purpose, which is to provide retirement benefits.

Although the Employee Retirement Income Security Act of 1974 (ERISA) and the Retirement Equity Act of 1984 impose certain requirements, there is still a considerable amount of flexibility in designing pension plan death benefits. Plans may provide both preretirement death benefits and postretirement death benefits.

The law requires that once a married participant in a pension plan becomes vested, he or she is covered by preretirement survivor annuity protection unless the participant and spouse elect otherwise. This protection will provide an annuity to a surviving spouse in the event the participant dies before the retirement annuity commences. This is true whether the participant stays with the employer until retirement or terminates employment sooner.

240

The minimum amount of the required preretirement survivor annuity is equal to the survivor portion of a joint and survivor annuity (discussed below). If the participant dies before reaching the earliest age at which annuity payments could begin, the annuity is determined by assuming that the participant terminated employment instead of dying, elected commencement of benefits at the earliest date allowed by the plan (usually age 55), and died immediately thereafter. The plan could provide that no annuity payments be provided to the surviving spouse until the date the participant would have reached the earliest retirement age, had he or she survived. If the participant dies after the earliest retirement age, the survivor annuity is generally determined by assuming that the participant had retired, elected commencement of a joint and survivor annuity at the time of death, and died on the day after retirement.

The law also requires that retirement benefits to married persons be paid as a qualified joint and survivor annuity, unless the participant and spouse elect to receive benefits in some other form or unless the plan meets one of the exceptions granted under the Tax Reform Act of 1986 (TRA '86). Under TRA '86, a plan is exempt from the qualified joint and survivor annuity law if: the plan was established before January 1, 1954, as a result of an agreement between employee representatives and the federal government during a period of government operation, under seizure powers, of a major part of the productive facilities of the industry; and if participation in the plan is substantially limited to participants who ceased employment covered by the plan before January 1, 1976.

Under a joint and survivor annuity, the retired worker receives a benefit during his or her retirement years; after death, benefits continue to be paid to the surviving spouse in the same or a lesser amount. If the spouse dies first, the lesser amount is paid until the retiree's death. The retired worker's benefit is usually reduced to reflect the cost of survivor protection and the ages of the retiree and spouse at the time of retirement. Some plans, however, pay an unreduced amount to the retired worker. If a married participant wants to reject the joint and survivor annuity, his or her spouse must agree to this rejection in writing before a notary public or plan representative.

ERISA also requires that, as a minimum, all *employee* contributions be paid with interest to a beneficiary if a participant dies before receiving benefits.

Other forms of death benefits under pension plans include the lump-sum value of a participant's accrued benefit, a life insurance contract with a face value equal to 100 times the monthly pension benefit the decedent would have received at normal retirement, monthly payments in the amount the decedent would have received as a pension, and lump-sum death benefits designed to meet final illness and funeral expenses (usually such benefits range from $1,000 to $3,000).

Eligibility for survivor benefits may require a couple to have been married for a specified length of time. Or, the beneficiary may be required to be a parent of a dependent child. When there is no surviving spouse, benefits may be paid to dependent children. Some plans pay benefits to other dependent relatives.

Taxation—A death benefit from a qualified pension plan paid as a lump-sum distribution may be eligible for five year forward averaging if it is received after the participant would have attained age 59½. Lump-sum distributions are generally taxed as ordinary income and are eligible for five year forward averaging; they may also be eligible for a $5,000 death benefit exclusion. This provision permits beneficiaries to exclude up to $5,000 in employer-provided death benefits from gross income.

Under certain circumstances, a lump-sum distribution to a surviving spouse may be eligible for rollover to an individual retirement account (IRA) or another qualified plan. Also, if a spouse inherits an IRA, he or she may roll over that account into his or her own IRA without being taxed on the amount.

Bibliography

Mamorsky, Jeffrey D. *Employee Benefits Handbook: 1989 Update.* Boston: Warren, Gorham & Lamont, 1989.

Rosenbloom, Jerry S. *The Handbook of Employee Benefits.* Homewood, IL: Dow Jones-Irwin, 1988.

U.S. Department of Health and Human Services. Social Security Administration. *Your Social Security Rights and Responsibilities, Retirement and Survivors Benefits.* Baltimore, MD: Social Security Administration, 1986.

———. *The Social Security Handbook, 1988.* Washington, DC: U.S. Government Printing Office, 1988.

29. Disability Income Plans

Introduction

Unexpected illness or injury can result in a person's inability to work, creating serious financial problems for the individual and his or her family. The costs of necessary medical treatment can exacerbate these financial problems. Health insurance plans may help to pay for medical care costs, while private and public disability income plans may replace a portion of a disabled worker's lost income.

Disability income plans differ from workers' compensation in that disability plans cover *nonwork*-related injury, while workers' compensation covers only *work*-related injury. Disability plans are public and private programs that cover temporary or permanent illness. Workers' compensation is a public program that pays wage loss benefits and medical benefits.

By the year 2000, disability benefits may cost business and government an estimated $200 billion a year. The average age for the onset of disability was age 44.2 in 1987, compared with 39.6 in 1982. In 1987, the average age for the onset of disability related to back disorders was 40.7 years; for mental illness, 41.3 years; for musculoskeletal disease, 43.4 years; and for heart disease, 50.5 years. The national average cost for rehabilitation was $1,572. Chances are one in three that an employee will have a work-stopping health problem lasting at least one month before he or she reaches age 65.

A 1986 report by the U.S. Bureau of the Census found that 20.6 percent of people aged 15 or over—including 14.1 percent of those aged 16–64 and 58.5 percent of those aged 65 or over—had difficulty performing one or more basic physical activities (U.S. Department of Commerce, 1986). The survey also found that the proportion of women with disabilities was 23.2 percent, compared with 17.7 percent for men. (The difference occurs largely because women outnumber men in the elderly age groups.) Among people aged 16 to 64, the report indicated that about 18.2 million, or 12 percent, had a disability that affected their work, and 8 million had a disability or a temporary disability (lasting less than one year) that prevented them from working.

In the past, many employers offered informal pay-continuation arrangements when disability occurred—especially for salaried employees. Today, *formal* disability income programs have gained wide acceptance. About 63 percent of business and industry employees are covered by some form of private disability income plan. Virtually all workers are covered by mandatory public disability plans (for example, Social Security and workers' compensation).

Disability can be categorized as short-term or long-term and as partial or total. Most plans require disabled employees to be under a physician's care to be eligible for benefits. Benefits must be provided for pregnancy-related disability on the same basis as for any other disability.

Public Programs

Social Security—The Social Security program provides benefits for workers with long-term disabilities (those lasting at least 12 months) who satisfy the following conditions: the worker must have *fully insured* and *disability insured* status;[1] he or she must be under a disability as defined by law; and he or she must have suffered from the disability for at least 12 consecutive months.

The Social Security disability benefit is equal to the primary Old-Age benefit. However, when combined with workers' compensation, it may not exceed 80 percent of *average current earnings* before the disability began.[2] (Employees covered by the Railroad Retirement Act are entitled to disability income benefits under that act rather than under Social Security.) The Social Security program paid $21.4 billion to 2.8 million disabled workers and their 1.2 million dependent children and spouses in 1988.

Workers' Compensation—Workers' compensation provides benefits to workers disabled by occupational injury or illness. These benefits are required by law in every state. In most states, this coverage is provided through private insurance or through employer self-insurance arrangements. However, 20 states offer coverage through state funds and six of these *require* employers to use the state funds. Em-

---

[1]To satisfy the fully insured requirement, a person usually must have earned at least one quarter of Social Security coverage for each year after 1950 (or, if later, the year in which he or she reaches age 21) and before the year of death, disability, or the 62nd birthday, whichever occurs first. To satisfy the disability insured requirement, a person must have earned at least 20 quarters of coverage during the 40 quarter period ending with the quarter in which the disability begins. If a person becomes disabled before reaching age 31, more liberal rules apply.

[2]For purposes of Social Security disability, average current earnings are generally defined as a person's highest-year earnings in the six year period consisting of the calendar year when disability began and the five years preceding that year.

244

ployers pay for workers' compensation through risk-related premiums. The amount and duration of workers' compensation benefits depend on state laws and the extent of the disability.

Nonoccupational Temporary Disability Insurance Plans—Most of these plans are voluntary. However, California, Hawaii, New Jersey, New York, Rhode Island, and Puerto Rico require employers to provide disability income protection for nonoccupational temporary disabilities. Under these compulsory laws, benefits are payable after a short disability period (for example, one week). Depending on the state, temporary disability coverage is provided through state funds, private insurers, or both. Eligibility criteria and benefit formulas vary from state to state. However, a maximum protection period of 26 weeks is generally imposed.

Private Programs

Individual employers, jointly managed (Taft-Hartley) trust funds, and employer associations may offer private disability income plans. Before a private plan is adopted, a number of plan design and administration questions must be answered. For example: What benefit level should be provided? How long should benefits be provided? What portion of the benefits should be paid by employers (that is, indirectly by stockholders and customers), and what portion should be paid by employees?

Employers are legally required to contribute to the public disability plans discussed in the previous section. To avoid costly duplication, private plan sponsors must recognize all sources of disability income when determining benefit levels. This is usually accomplished by a benefit *integration* provision. Integration is intended to limit combined disability benefits to a reasonable *income replacement level* (that is, the portion of a worker's income prior to disability that is replaced after disability).

There are two primary types of private disability income plans: short-term disability plans (in which benefit payments usually are provided for 26 weeks or less) and long-term disability plans (in which benefit payments are usually provided after short-term benefits have ended). Long-term benefits are generally paid until age 65 or the normal retirement age. Under the 1986 amendments to the Age Discrimination in Employment Act, which abolished mandatory retirement, plans that provide disability benefits cannot impose an upper age limit on active employees' eligibility for these benefits. The benefits may be paid to employees aged 65 or over who become disabled, based on age-related cost considerations. Employers must either provide equal benefits to employees regardless of age, or—as is usually the case—provide benefits that are equal in cost to employees of all ages. Since disability costs rise with age, this means that employees who are disabled at older ages may be paid disability benefits for a shorter duration or lower benefits for the same duration, relative to younger employees.

Short-Term Disability Plans—A short-term disability is usually defined as *an employee's inability to perform normal occupational duties*. Under most short-term disability plans, such as sickness and accident insurance plans, the disability must exist for at least one week before a worker becomes eligible for benefits. This waiting period is intended to control plan costs. Often, paid sick leave is available to the employee without any waiting period, and it may be used during the interim before sickness and accident insurance payments begin.

Short-term disability protection may thus include sickness and accident insurance benefit programs as well as paid sick leave. Under these programs, sick leave usually provides 100 percent of a worker's normal earnings; sickness and accident insurance usually replaces 50 percent to 67 pecent of pay during limited disability periods. Sick leave plans frequently specify a number of covered days each year that are permitted for paid sick leave.

Sickness and accident insurance plans may be used instead of, or in conjunction with, sick leave plans. When used in conjunction with sick leave plans, sickness and accident plans provide benefits after sick leave benefits are exhausted. The level of sickness and accident benefits for short-term disability may be expressed as a specified weekly dollar amount or as a percentage of straight-time pay. The level and duration of benefits may increase with service. Generally, benefits replace between one-half and two-thirds of a person's pre-disability gross weekly income. Many believe that a higher replacement rate would create a disincentive for employees to return to work.

Employers usually pay for short-term disability plans. These plans may be financed under a group insurance contract with a private insurance carrier, an employer self-insurance arrangement, an employer-established employee benefit trust fund, a Taft-Hartley multiemployer welfare fund, or general corporate assets (for example, for a sick leave plan). Short-term disability plans may be administered by an employer, an insurance carrier, or the board of trustees of a Taft-Hartley plan.

The duration of short-term disability benefits ranges from 13 weeks to 52 weeks, although most workers are covered for up to 26 weeks.

Short-term disability plans usually specify when successive periods of disability are considered to be separate disabilities and when they are considered to be a continuous disability.

Long-Term Disability Plans—Many employers offer long-term disability benefits. Approximately 40 percent of the U.S. labor force has employer-sponsored insured or self-insured group long-term disability coverage or purchased private coverage. It is estimated that 85,000 group long-term disability policies were in force in the United States in 1987. In 1989, 45 percent of employees in medium-sized and large establishments in the United States had long-term disability coverage (U.S. Department of Labor, 1990). It is estimated that 35 percent of all U.S. businesses currently offer long-term disability insurance to their employees.

In most long-term plans, disability for the first two years is defined in the same way as disability under short-term plans (for example, an employee's inability to perform normal occupational duties). If the disability continues for more than two years, the definition of disability usually changes to *the inability to perform any occupation that the person is reasonably suited to do by training, education, and experience*. Some plans use the payment of Social Security disability benefits as the sole test for ascertaining whether a participant should receive long-term disability benefits under the plan.

Long-term disability plans generally provide benefits after short-term disability benefits expire. Like short-term benefits, long-term disability benefits are integrated with benefits from other sources to produce reasonable replacement rates and to control costs.

Private sources of long-term disability benefits include disability provisions under long-term disability plans, group life insurance, employer-sponsored pension plans, and other insurance arrangements (for example, individual insurance protection). Generally, these plans pay benefits amounting to from one-half to two-thirds of a person's predisability gross weekly income. Some plans, however, provide as much as 70 percent to 80 percent of predisability pay. Additionally, some plans contain a provision stating that private-sector long-term disability benefits, plus Social Security disability benefits, cannot exceed a stated amount (for example, 75 percent of salary). The cost of long-term disability benefits may be financed by employer contributions, employee contributions, or employer/employee cost sharing.

Although long-term disability plans may limit benefits to a specified period (for example, 5 to 10 years), most provide benefits for the length of a disability, up to a specified age (for example, age 65, when

Social Security and employer-provided retirement benefits usually begin). Similar to short-term disability plans, long-term plans usually specify when successive periods of disability are considered to be separate disabilities and when they are considered to be a continuous disability. Also, some long-term plans provide for continued payment of at least some disability benefits to long-term disabled persons who engage in rehabilitative employment.

An increasing number of businesses are establishing programs to rehabilitate disabled workers. According to one estimate, rehabilitation programs may save employers $60 in benefits for every $1 spent on rehabilitation—as well as help the individual to resume a productive life.

Bibliography

Berkowitz, Monroe, and Anne M. Hill. *Disability and the Labor Market.* Ithaca, NY: ILR Press, New York State School of Industrial and Labor Relations, Cornell University, 1986.

U.S. Department of Commerce. Bureau of the Census. *Disability, Functional Limitation, and Health Insurance Coverage: 1984/85.* Washington, DC: U.S. Government Printing Office, 1986.

U.S. Department of Labor. Bureau of Labor Statistics. "Employee Benefits Focus on Family Concerns in 1989." USDL news release 90-160, 30 March 1990.

Additional Information

Workers' Compensation Research Institute
245 First Street, Suite 1402
Cambridge, MA 02141
(617) 494-1240

30. Education Assistance Benefits

Introduction

During the last 40 years, participation in higher education has grown. One reason has been the demand for more skilled workers to meet the challenges of high-technology industries. Another factor has been the passage of the World War II GI bill, which entitled World War II veterans to a higher education—previously virtually an impossibility for low-income veterans. In the late 1950s and the 1960s, higher education also became more accessible to minorities and low-income individuals as a result of government grant, job, and loan programs, most of which were established under the Higher Education Act of 1965.

Higher education is more expensive today than it has been during any previous period in U.S. history. Many individuals who cannot afford to finance their education in full look to federal loan and grant programs for financial assistance. However, some of these programs are only available to students who are enrolled at least half time. Many part-time students, therefore, may not receive government assistance. For these individuals, employer-provided education assistance is an important benefit in furthering their educational pursuits.

Availability

Education assistance benefits can facilitate career advancement for employees at all income levels, but they are particularly important for lower-paid employees, many of whom are women and minorities. These programs are widely used by employers; a recent survey found that 74 percent of private-sector employers provided this benefit in 1988 (U.S. Chamber of Commerce, 1989). Another report indicated that in the same year 70 percent of private full-time workers in medium-sized and large establishments (20 million employees) were eligible for job-related education assistance and 18 percent (6 million employees) were eligible for nonjob-related education assistance (U.S. Department of Labor, 1989).

The cost of employer-provided education assistance accounts for approximately 0.2 percent of total employee wages and salaries, a small proportion of total compensation costs. Surveys have shown that education benefits can contribute to reduced employee turnover, increased productivity, and bolstered morale and motivation. One survey of the restaurant industry—which experiences high turnover and labor shortages—found that the turnover rate of employees participating in education assistance programs dropped from a preprogram high of 180 percent to 58 percent after the program. The industry norm for turnover ranges from 200 percent to 300 percent (Enterprise Communications, 1989).

Program Design and Types of Assistance

Employers can design their education assistance plans in a variety of ways. They may reimburse for job-related courses only, for courses relating to future jobs within the company, for degree-related courses, and/or for nonjob-related courses.

Some employers pay all of the education expense; others pay a percentage of it. Many employers require the employee who receives education assistance to obtain a certain grade on completion of the course he or she is taking before the cost will be reimbursed. Others reimburse a greater proportion of the cost for a higher grade. Some employers require the employee to stay with the firm for a certain number of years after completing the course, or to repay the course costs.

A recent survey found that the mean amount of assistance provided was $621 per year, with the average payments concentrated below $1,000 (Bureau of National Affairs, 1989).

The status of the assistance as "job related" or "nonjob related" is important and determines the tax treatment for the employee and the employer.

Job-Related Education—On-the-job training, coursework, seminars, or other types of education assistance that "maintain or improve skills required by the employee's employment or meet the express requirements imposed as a condition of *retaining* employment" qualify as job-related assistance, according to the U.S. Department of the Treasury. These expenses are not taxable to the employee, and the employer is not required to withhold income or employment taxes on the amounts paid (Internal Revenue Code (IRC) section 162).

An individual may claim an income tax deduction for job-related education expenses not reimbursed by the employer. Deductible expenses include tuition, books, supplies, laboratory fees, correspondence courses, tutorial instruction, and research undertaken as part of the education. The costs of travel, meals, and lodging are deductible expenses as long as they are not personal in nature. Transportation expenses are also deductible if they are directly related to education expenses. These expenses are treated as a miscellaneous business expense, deductible to the extent they (and other expenses in this category) exceed 2 percent of adjusted gross income.

An education expense is not job related, however, if it leads to qualification for a new position, trade, or business. U.S. Department of the Treasury regulations (1.162-5) provide a number of examples of job-related training and include the trade and business test.

Nonjob-Related Education—If an employer pays or reimburses expenses incurred by an employee that are *not* job related, the amount is not taxable to the employee under IRC section 127 if certain conditions are met: the assistance must be provided under a nondiscriminatory plan; the assistance must be limited to $5,250 per person per year; the assistance may not involve sports, games, or hobbies unless related to the business of the employer or required for a degree program, and the assistance is not for graduate-level courses. An exception to the latter is allowed for tuition assistance for graduate teaching and research assistants.

Employers offering section 127 education assistance benefits must file an information return with the U.S. Department of the Treasury that shows: the number of employees in the firm; the number of employees eligible to participate in such a program; the number of employees participating in general; the program's total cost during the year; and the name, address, and taxpayer identification number of the employer and the type of business in which the employer is engaged.

Any amounts provided over $5,250 are taxable to the employee. When an employee has multiple jobs, the annual limit applies to education assistance from all employers.

Originally legislated through the Revenue Act of 1978, section 127 education assistance benefits were made explicitly nontaxable from December 31, 1978, through December 31, 1983. Subsequently, Congress extended the provision for periods of one year, and added dollar limits on excludable amounts.

The Omnibus Budget Reconciliation Act of 1989 extended the tax exclusion for employer-provided education assistance benefits through September 30, 1990. This exclusion is an impermanent provision of the tax code and must be extended by Congress to continue the tax-free status.

Scholarships, Loans, and Leave—These are other ways employers can assist in furthering employees' education. Scholarships are nontaxable, and leave may be paid or unpaid.

Federal Education Assistance Programs

The U.S. Department of Education offers six major student financial aid programs: Pell grants, Supplemental Educational Opportunity Grants (SEOG), College Work-Study (CWS), Perkins loans (formerly known as National Direct Student Loans), Stafford loans, and PLUS Loans/Supplemental Loans for Students (PLUS/SLS).

Pell Grants—Pell grants help undergraduates to finance their college education. This is the largest federal student aid program. If a student is enrolled in two different schools, he or she may not receive Pell grants for duplicative costs. For these grants, each participating school (that is, one that meets requirements) is guaranteed to receive enough money to pay for the Pell grants for each qualifying student. A student must show financial need to qualify.

Supplemental Educational Opportunity Grants—SEOGs are also financial awards for college undergraduates. Unlike Pell grants, however, the SEOG program allocates a set amount of money each year to an institution. Thus, there is no guarantee that each qualified applicant will receive an award. Like Pell grants, these awards are based on financial need.

College Work Study—The CWS program, which is for both undergraduate and graduate college students, pays students to work on- or off-campus. It is a combined contribution program sponsored by the government and an employer, college, institution, or off-campus agency. A CWS job must always be with a public or private nonprofit organization.

Perkins Loans—Perkins loans are low-interest loans available to undergraduate and graduate college students through a school's financial aid office. Repayment begins six months after the student graduates, leaves school, or drops below half-time student status. The definition of half-time status is determined by the college or institution. The amount a student may borrow depends on his or her need, the availability of Perkins loan funds at the school, and the amount of other aid received. A Perkins loan is generally repaid monthly over a total repayment period of 10 years, with some exceptions.

Stafford Loans—Stafford loans (formerly Guaranteed Student Loans) are also low-interest loans—financed through banks, credit unions, savings and loan associations, and other eligible lenders—that are available to undergraduate and graduate students attending school at least half time. The amount a student can borrow depends on his or her financial need and student status, not to exceed certain limits. (Also see following discussions of PLUS/SLS loans.)

PLUS/SLS Loans—PLUS loans are available to parents of dependent students; SLS loans are for student borrowers. PLUS/SLS loans are similar to GSLs, but they are available at higher interest rates. Unlike GSL borrowers, PLUS/SLS borrowers do not have to show need for their loan.

GSL and PLUS/SLS programs are administered by a state or private nonprofit agency referred to as a "guarantee agency." Each state has its own guarantee agency, which usually charges an origination fee and an insurance premium at the time the loan is disbursed. Interest repayments for an SLS begin within 60 days unless the applicant has qualified for a deferment and the lender agrees to allow the interest to accrue until the deferment ends. There are no deferments for a parent borrower. (For more information on grant, job, and loan programs and state guarantee agency information, contact the U.S. Department of Education, Office of Student Financial Assistance, Washington, DC 20202.)

State Student Incentive Grant Program

The State Student Incentive Grant Program is a combination state and federal tuition assistance program. The government allocates funds to each state guarantee agency based on its enrollment of students in postsecondary education. The state agency must contribute at least 50 percent of the total grant awards made available to students.

Other Federal Assistance Programs

The Veterans Administration offers two types of education assistance programs. For veterans of the Korean and Vietnam wars with service between February 1, 1955, and December 31, 1976, assistance is available under the GI bill. Veterans have 10 years from the last day of active duty to use the benefit. Veterans who served after 1976 receive assistance under a contributory plan. For more information on these programs, contact the Veterans Administration, Washington, DC 20420.

Conclusion

Like most other employee benefits, education assistance is often a combined effort of employers, the federal government, and individuals. Employers usually provide education assistance that can enrich their employees' skills and careers. The federal government provides

253

grants, loans, and work-study programs to undergraduate students and loans and work-study programs for graduate students seeking a degree or certificate. Employees, with or without federal or employer assistance, also enrich their job skills and careers by pursuing education on their own. This individual effort, in turn, is subsidized by the tax code if conditions set out in the IRC are met.

Bibliography

Bureau of National Affairs. "Benefit Distribution Parallels Workforce Earnings, Study Finds." *BNA Pension Reporter* (7 August 1989): 1448.

Cranford, Sharon H., and James E. Connor. "Employer-Provided Educational Assistance Plans." *Journal of Compensation and Benefits* (March-April 1989): 304–305.

Enterprise Communications. "Part-Timers Eat Up Education Program." *Employee Benefit News* (February 1989): 14–15.

Norback, Craig T. *The Human Resource Yearbook*. Englewood Cliffs, NJ: Prentice-Hall, 1989.

U.S. Chamber of Commerce. *Employee Benefits: 1989 Edition Survey Data from Benefit Year 1988*. Washington, DC: U.S. Chamber of Commerce, 1989.

U.S. Department of Education. Office of Student Financial Assistance. *Federal Student Aid Fact Sheet, 1990–91*. Washington, DC: U.S. Department of Education, n.d.

U.S. Department of Labor. Bureau of Labor Statistics. *Employee Benefits in Medium and Large Firms, 1988*. Washington, DC: U.S. Government Printing Office, 1989.

Additional Information

American Society for Training and Development
1630 Duke Street
Alexandria, VA 22313
(703) 683-8100

Federal Student Aid Information Center
(800) 333-INFO

National Institute for Work and Learning
1200 18th Street, NW, Suite 316
Washington, DC 20036
(202) 887-6800

31. Legal Services Plans

Introduction

According to an American Bar Association (ABA) survey, 80 percent of the public is uncertain about how to obtain legal advice. Employed persons usually do not qualify for legal aid or the services of public defenders. Most people tend to postpone seeking legal information and assistance until their needs become acute and, typically, more costly. Thus, wills go unwritten and legal documents go unchecked. Legal services plans can provide affordable legal representation and consultation for many who would otherwise not obtain such services.[1]

Legal services plans are arrangements between a group of people and one or more lawyers to obtain legal assistance. Although they have been in existence since the late 1800s, their development was hindered well into the 1900s by the ABA, which opposed the plans out of concern that they constituted a form of client solicitation. Four U.S. Supreme Court decisions between 1963 and 1971 recognized the constitutional right to associate to obtain legal advice, however, and the Court ruled that bar associations could not interfere with the establishment of legal services plans.

The U.S. Department of Labor reports that 4 percent of full-time employees in private-sector medium-sized and large establishments, or 1.2 million workers and their family members, were eligible for employer-sponsored legal services benefits in 1988 (U.S. Department of Labor, 1989).

Legal services plans primarily provide preventive assistance by making legal information and advice readily available. By preventing questions or simple legal matters from becoming complex problems, they offer the potential for reducing legal expenses; in addition, plan members often receive discounted rates.

Plan Design and Cost

Legal services plans encompass a broad spectrum of designs and costs, ranging from plans that offer free consultations and discounts

---

[1]Legal services plans are sometimes known as prepaid legal services plans or group legal services plans.

to those that cover a wide range of legal services. Most plans are group plans.

Access plans provide members access to legal advice and services. They typically include unlimited in-office or telephone consultation with a lawyer; follow-up services, such as correspondence; review of legal documents; and fee discounts for more complex matters. Access plans can cost up to $150 per family per year (Bolger, 1987).

In addition to the services provided in access plans, *comprehensive plans* provide other services—such as legal representation in a divorce, the sale or purchase of real estate, or a civil or criminal trial—in return for a fee or premium. Benefits and fees vary considerably among these plans, but the cost is usually $100–$150 per family per year, and is usually paid by employers or through employees' union dues (Bolger, 1987).

Enrollment—In group plans, enrollment may be *automatic* or *voluntary*. In an automatic enrollment plan (also known as a "free plan"), all members of the group are automatically members of the plan. In a voluntary enrollment plan, only those members who choose to enroll are covered, on a prepaid basis. Household members typically are also covered.

In addition to group plans offered to members of defined groups, *individual* enrollment plans may be offered by businesses to their customers, also on a prepaid basis.

Delivery of Benefits

The structures for delivering benefits vary as much with legal services plans as with health insurance plans, but can be classified under three broad categories: open panel plans, closed panel plans, and modified panel (or combination) plans.

Open Panel Plans—Under an open panel plan (the least common), a member may use any licensed attorney. Payment for services is usually made according to an established fee schedule, with fees varying depending on the type of service provided. The plan participant is responsible for attorney fees in excess of the scheduled amount. Open panel plans may also use legal services trust funds.

Open panel plans offer advantages and disadvantages. While a participant is able to choose his or her own attorney, the attorney selected is not obligated to accept the case, particularly if the attorney's caseload is heavy or the case is outside of his or her area of expertise. Administrative costs are generally higher in open panel plans because the administrator must keep records of all services provided by the

256

various attorneys. Since the sponsoring employer has no control over the attorneys' fees, sponsors often restrict coverage to selected services and/or impose maximum coverage limits.

Closed Panel Plans—There are two types of closed panel plans: staff plans and participating attorney plans. *Staff plans* provide benefits through a full-time, salaried staff of lawyers who are hired specifically to handle the group's needs. In *participating attorney plans*, a plan sponsor contracts with a number of law firms to provide access to legal services to a group of participants who are geographically dispersed. The law firms agree to provide certain types of legal services for a set fee per participant, with little restriction on the amount of time that can be spent.

Administrative costs under closed panel plans are generally lower than under open panel plans. Since a smaller number of attorneys is involved, there are fewer records to manage and payment for services may be easier. The lawyers in a closed panel plan often acquire special expertise in areas associated with the covered group's most common problems. Unions usually favor closed panel plans, under which they are able to control the quality of the legal work by controlling the selection of attorneys. Closed panel plans frequently can offer more efficient legal services at lower rates than open panel plans. Despite the salary arrangement between the attorney and the plan, attorneys may reject cases for sufficient reason (again, if the attorney's caseload is heavy or the case is outside of his or her area of expertise).

Modified Panel or Combination Plans—These plans, the most common, offer combinations of the characteristics of open panel and closed panel plans. Generally, they permit employees to choose from among a small number of lawyers and law firms, which the plan sponsor selects, or from attorneys who practice in a specified geographic area.

Scope of Services

Types of Services Covered—There are four broad service categories under typical comprehensive service plans: consultation, general nonadversarial, domestic relations, and trial and criminal.

- *Consultation*—Legal services plans are used most frequently for legal information and advice (most legal matters require no more). They may deal with virtually any type of legal issue, including consumer matters, landlord-tenant disputes, and domestic disputes (for example, overdue child support payments and visitation rights). Here, the attorney counsels the participant, either by telephone or in the office, on appropriate legal action, or may provide self-help information so the plan participant may resolve the problem on his or her own.

- *General Nonadversarial*—These services are generally performed in an attorney's office. They deal with such matters as reviews of documents, wills, and adoption papers; guardianship; name changes; personal bankruptcy; real estate transfers; estate closings; and Social Security, unemployment, and other benefit claims.

- *Domestic Relations*—Legal separations and divorces are the most expensive—and most common—services covered by legal services plans. Most plans that cover these services also cover the costs of modifying divorce and separation agreements (such as changes in the terms of child custody agreements, visitation agreements, child support, or separate maintenance arrangements). Due to the high cost that is often associated with domestic relations legal problems, many plans limit these types of services.

- *Trial and Criminal*—This type of service includes adversarial legal matters, such as contested adoptions and guardianship, civil suits, and contested domestic relations matters; and minor criminal matters, such as suspension or revocation of driver's licenses, juvenile court proceedings, and misdemeanors. Although infrequently utilized, these services usually incur the highest plan cost per claim; thus, many plans do not cover them.

Exclusions and Limitations—Legal services plans may be subject to abuses, such as excessive attorney fees and unnecessary services. Plan sponsors, therefore, may build in cost controls by excluding coverage for certain types of services, such as: actions against employers and unions; services for legal problems existing before the plan's effective date; lawyers' contingency fees; and court expenses such as fines, court costs, filing fees, subpoenas, assessments, penalties, and expert witness fees.

Plans may also use closed lists of eligible procedures, which automatically exclude some legal services from the schedule of benefits; limit the number of hours or dollar amount of services rendered; limit the frequency of coverage for a particular service over a specified time; or place maximum limits on the hourly fees of attorneys, usually less than the prevailing rate.

Taxation

Initially, legal services plan benefits were counted as gross income to the employee. Employers, however, were allowed to take a tax deduction for their contributions. Subsequent legislative changes removed many of the initial deterrents to establishment of these plans, particularly their explicit exclusion from taxation under the Tax Reform Act of 1976, which added section 120 to the Internal Revenue Code (IRC). The original law expired at the end of 1981, but subsequent tax laws in 1981, 1984, 1986, 1988, and 1989 extended the tax exclusion, sometimes retroactively. The extension included in the 1989 law is set to expire on September 30, 1990. Some observers believe that the impermanence of the tax exclusion for legal services plans may discourage their widespread development and use.

In a qualified plan under IRC section 120, employer contributions for legal services benefits of up to $70 per year are excludable from income tax. To qualify for favorable tax treatment, the plan must meet the following requirements.

- An application for qualification must be filed with the Internal Revenue Service.

- The employer must establish a separate written plan for the exclusive benefit of employees (and their spouses or dependents); the plan must provide *only* legal services.

- The plan must provide *personal* legal services; it cannot provide legal services related to an employee's trade or investment property.

- The plan cannot discriminate in favor of shareholders, officers, or highly paid employees. In determining whether the plan is discriminatory, certain employees may be excluded from consideration—specifically, those covered by an agreement determined by the Secretary of Labor to be a collective bargaining agreement, providing there is evidence that group legal services benefits were the subject of good faith bargaining. Certain limits also apply to contributions made on behalf of shareholders and owners who have more than a 5 percent interest.

- The employer must transmit its plan contributions to designated recipients (for example, insurance companies, tax-exempt trusts, or authorized service providers).

All legal services plans maintained by a private employer or employee association are classified under the Employee Retirement Income Security Act of 1974 (ERISA) as employee welfare plans and are subject to certain requirements (discussed in chapter 3). Legal services plan sponsored by public employers are not subject to ERISA.

Bibliography

Billings, Roger D. *Prepaid Legal Services*. Rochester, NY: Lawyers Cooperative Publishing Co., 1981 (updated supplements issued annually).
Bolger, William A. *How to Start a Free Legal Services Plan for Your Group*. Falls Church, VA: National Resource Center for Consumers of Legal Services, 1987.
U.S. Department of Labor. Bureau of Labor Statistics. *Employee Benefits in Medium and Large Firms, 1988*. Washington, DC: U.S. Government Printing Office, 1989.

Additional Information

American Prepaid Legal Services Institute
1155 E. 60th Street
Chicago, IL 60637
(312) 988-5751

National Resource Center for Consumers of Legal Services
1444 Eye Street, NW, 8th floor
Washington, DC 20005
(202) 842-3503

32. Dependent Care

Introduction

Since World War II, women have assumed an increasingly significant role in the work place, and by the year 2000 they are expected to account for approximately two-thirds of the new entrants into the labor force (Saltford, 1989).

One of the most significant labor force changes in the last 30 years is the increase in the number of working mothers with young children. In 1950, 12 percent of women with children under age 6 were in the labor force; in 1987, 57 percent of these women were employed (Saltford, 1988). The increasing labor force participation among women means that men are no longer the sole wage earners in many families. Differences in employment patterns for women according to marital status and the presence and age of children have almost disappeared.

In 1989, the husband was the sole earner in only 27 percent of married-couple families, down from 33 percent in 1970. At the same time, husband and wife two-earner couples have increased from 34 percent of all married-couple families in 1970 to 52 percent in 1989 (U.S. Department of Labor, 1989b). Many of these families require child care to support their participation in the labor force. High rates of separation and divorce have contributed to single parenthood, resulting in a growing number of single-headed households with young children. In 1988, 5 million children under age 6 lived with one parent (U.S. Department of Labor, 1989a). Some form of child care assistance is critical if these low-income women are to remain in the work force.

In response to changing work force and family patterns, child care is emerging as a valuable employee benefit that is offered by a relatively small but growing number of employers.

Children of Working Parents

In 1988, more than 11.3 million children under age 6 had mothers in the labor force (Wider Opportunities for Women, 1989).

The types of child care arrangements available to parents vary by locality but often include in-home care, in which a person, sometimes a relative, comes to the child's home; family care, in which

TABLE 32.1
Distribution of Principal Child Care Arrangements of Children under Age 5 of Working Mothers, Fall 1986

Arrangement	Percentage
Number of Children	
(in thousands)	9,046
Percentage	100.0%
Care in Child's Home	29.7%
By father	14.2
By grandparent	6.7
By other relative	2.7
By nonrelative	6.1
Care in Another Home	41.3
By grandparent	11.5
By other relative	6.0
By nonrelative	23.8
Organized Child Care Facilities	22.3
Day/group care center	14.7
Nursery school/preschool[a]	7.6
Parent Cares for Child[b]	6.7

Source: U.S. Department of Commerce, Bureau of the Census, news release CB 89-119, 27 July 1989.
[a]Includes a small number of children enrolled in kindergarten.
[b]Includes women working at home or away from home.

a child is taken to another home where the provider often takes care of several children; or child care centers, which are organized facilities that care for many children. Most children are cared for in another home by a nonrelative. The U.S. Bureau of the Census reported that 41 percent of children of working mothers under age 5 were cared for in this way in 1986 (table 32.1) (U.S. Department of Labor, 1989b); 30 percent of the children were cared for in another home; and 22 percent attended a day care center, preschool, or kindergarten. In some cases, mothers cared for children at work (7 percent of children).

Child care arrangements vary over the course of a year, especially for school age children. Parents often use multiple arrangements and providers to try to guarantee supervision through the day. The cost of child care varies widely, averaging $45 per week in 1986, according to the U.S. Bureau of the Census. For toddlers under age 2, the average was higher at $52 per week.

Child Care and the Employer

The nature of employees' responsibilities at home and at work varies with the number, age, and health of their dependents and the employees' particular work loads at any given time. Yet, when child care arrangements are inadequate, inappropriate, or unavailable, parents can experience increased stress and decreased morale, lose time from work, and be less productive.[1] A recent study based on a poll of men and women with children under age 12 found child care problems to be the strongest predictors of absenteeism and unproductive time at work (Chapman, 1987). More than two-fifths of parents surveyed had lost one day's work because of family matters in the three months prior to the poll, and nearly 10 percent had been absent from three to five days.

Many employers have become involved in child care, especially those with a high proportion of younger employees and women and those with high turnover rates and problems with absenteeism.

Employer-sponsored child care programs may take a variety of forms. Programs range from company owned and operated day care centers to resource and referral services to direct financial assistance through vouchers or discounts at local child care facilities or through cash subsidies.

Employer-sponsored child care benefits are not common but are growing. They are most often provided in the service industries (for example, hospitals, banks, and insurance companies). About 4,177 of 6 million private employers provided some form of child care assistance in 1989 (The Conference Board, 1989). A survey that included public as well as private employees found that 11 percent of 1.2 million firms with 10 or more employees had established child care programs in 1988 (U.S. Department of Labor, 1988).

Types of Assistance

Child care centers at or near the work place are the most visible form of assistance. They can be company operated, contracted out, or operated by parents. Sometimes employers contract with other employers or municipal governments to establish facilities. However, start-up costs for centers are high, and continuing labor costs can be higher.

---

[1] For a review of studies examining these relationships, see Berkeley Planning Associates, 1989.

Some firms support community child care programs. When an employer chooses to finance a community day care center rather than to create an on- or near-site service, the employees of the participating company may receive preferential admission, reduced rates, or a reserved space in the day care center in exchange for the employer's financial support to the center. In this way, the employer avoids the administrative and legal responsibilities but still offers support services. However, support or maintenance of child care centers is not as common as other forms of employer-provided assistance.

Resource and referral services are more common. These services can help parents obtain information on child care and, in many cases, refer them to the most appropriate form in their community. Most companies contract with an existing referral agency in the community; others have an in-house hotline capacity. A growing number of employers sponsor educational seminars on parenting issues. Although this form of assistance may not include access to a child care center, it can help the employer estimate the potential demand for child care services before investing in other forms of child care support.

Direct financial assistance with child care expenses is typically provided through employers' flexible benefit plans. Sometimes called "cafeteria plans," those arrangements allow employees to choose among a variety of benefit options paid for by employer contributions, employee contributions, or both. There are various approaches to design, but often flexible benefit plans provide credits that employees can use to purchase benefits of their own choice. When child care benefits are offered in this type of arrangement, those employees who need and want them can purchase them. Those who do not may choose other benefits. Flexible benefit plans allow flexibility to meet the needs of different lifestyles and at the same time satisfy equity considerations among a diverse work force.

Flexible spending accounts—also known as reimbursement accounts—provide a way to finance child care and other benefits, either within flexible benefit plans or separately as stand-alone plans. These accounts are funded by employee salary reduction arrangements, employer contributions, or both. Under a salary reduction arrangement, the employee makes a pretax contribution to a spending account, which reduces the amount of salary subject to federal income and Social Security taxes. Employees must determine how much they wish to contribute in advance and forfeit any unused dollars at the end of the year. (For more information on flexible benefit plans and flexible spending accounts, see chapter 33.)

TABLE 32.2

Type of Child Care Benefits and Work-Schedule Policies Aiding Child Care among Establishments with 10 or More Employees, by Number of Employees, Summer 1987

Child Care Benefits and Work-Schedule Policies	Total	Size of Establishment		
		10–49 employees	50–249 employees	250 + employees
Total Establishments (thousands)	1,202	919	236	47
Percentage Providing Child Care				
Benefits or Services	11.1%	9.0%	15.3%	31.8%
Day care centers	2.1	1.9	2.2	5.2
Assistance with child care expenses	3.1	2.4	4.7	8.9
Child care information and referral services	5.1	4.3	6.3	14.0
Counseling services	5.1	3.8	7.6	17.1
Other child care benefits	1.0	0.7	1.6	2.9
Percentage with Work-Schedule				
Policies Aiding Child Care	61.2	62.0	58.1	59.4
Flextime	43.2	45.1	37.7	34.9
Voluntary part time	34.8	36.0	32.0	25.1
Job sharing	15.5	16.0	13.7	15.7
Work at home	8.3	9.2	5.6	3.8
Flexible leave	42.9	43.8	39.9	40.2
Other leave or work-schedule policies	2.1	1.9	2.9	3.1
Percent with No Child Care Benefits or Policies Aiding Child Care	36.8	36.7	38.1	32.5

Source: U.S. Department of Labor, Bureau of Labor Statistics, news release USDL 88-7, 15 January 1988.

Note: The individual categories will sum to more than 100 percent because many employers provided more than one benefit or policy.

Certain *work schedule policies* such as flextime, job sharing, and part-time work (table 32.2) can also be valuable to working parents and are implicitly a form of child care support. These policies were offered at 43 percent of work places in 1989, up from 11 percent in 1987. Many more employers provide this form of child support than offer traditional child care assistance programs.

Taxation

The Economic Recovery Tax Act of 1981 (ERTA) provided tax incentives for employer-sponsored child and dependent care benefits. Dependent care assistance programs (DCAPs), qualified by the Internal Revenue Service under section 129, provide tax incentives to both employers and employees.

Employers may deduct from income tax the cost of providing child care benefits. Employees may exclude the value of child care benefits from taxable income. The cost of service is not treated as part of employee wages, so neither the employee nor the employer pays FICA or other payroll taxes on this amount. An employee (single or married) may exclude from income up to $5,000 annually or $2,500 for a married individual filing separately, but the amount of dependent care assistance cannot exceed the income of the employee or spouse, whichever is lower. The limits are applicable to the taxable year in which the services are incurred, not the year in which the employee is billed or reimbursed. Eligible expenses are limited to dependents under age 13, disabled spouses, and disabled dependents.

To qualify for tax-free status under section 129, the program, regardless of the type—child care center, direct payment to a child care provider, or resource and referral service—must be available to all employees and cannot discriminate in favor of employees who are officers, owners, or highly compensated.

An employer must also prepare a written plan setting forth eligibility requirements and the method of payment. Eligible employees must be notified of the plan's availability and terms. Each year, on or before January 31, the employer must give each employee a written statement showing the amounts paid or expenses incurred by the employer in providing dependent care assistance to the employee during the previous calendar year.

Section 21 of the Internal Revenue Code permits a federal income tax credit for qualified child care expenses not covered or paid for by an employer-sponsored DCAP. A credit is allowed for eligible children when both spouses work full time or when one spouse is a student and the other is employed. A single parent must be employed or be a student. Qualified expenses are limited to $2,400 for one child and $4,800 for two or more children and cannot exceed the earned income of the individual, if single, or the income of the lesser-earning spouse of a married couple.

A credit equal to 30 percent of eligible expenses is available to individuals with adjusted gross incomes of $10,000 or less, with the credit reduced by one percentage point for each $2,000 of income between $10,000 and $28,000. For individuals with adjusted gross incomes above $28,000, the credit is limited to 20 percent of qualified expenses.

Employees claiming a tax credit or excluding employer DCAP expenses must provide the name, address, and Social Security number or other taxpayer identification number of the care provider on their tax forms. Nonprofit 501(c)(3) organizations, such as day care centers operated by nonprofit religious or educational organizations, are not required to provide a taxpayer identification number.

The use of both the federal tax credit and employer-sponsored DCAP for child care expenses is restricted. Expenses claimed for the tax credit are reduced dollar for dollar by the amounts excluded under an employer's DCAP. Prior to 1989, an individual could use one form of tax relief (either the tax credit or income exclusion) up to its maximum, then use the other for expenses exceeding that amount. The ability to use either provision independently has not been changed.

Parental Leave

The United States does not require employers to follow a standard parental leave policy. Rather, the focus of federal policy with regard to employer-provided parental leave is on the prohibition of discrimination among employees in the provision of this benefit. Parental leave benefits (maternity and/or paternity) that do exist are either voluntarily provided by employers or are related to state-mandated disability insurance or collective bargaining agreements. The only relevant federal legislation is the Pregnancy Discrimination Act (PDA) of 1978.

Although federal law does not mandate employer provision of disability plans, PDA requires that employers who choose to offer such plans treat pregnancy and childbirth as any other disability, with the same employee benefit provisions. PDA covers businesses with 15 or more employees.

As of this writing, five states—California, Hawaii, New Jersey, New York, and Rhode Island—and Puerto Rico have adopted mandatory short-term disability insurance for employers in those states. Seven states—California, Connecticut, Iowa, Louisiana, Massachusetts, Montana, and Tennessee—have mandated maternity disability leave. Five states—Oregon, Hawaii, Kansas, New Hampshire, and Washington—provide maternity leave through state antidiscrimination laws. States that have enacted broader policies mandating employers to provide unpaid leaves of absence, with continuation of benefits and a guarantee of a comparable job, include California, Iowa, Maine, Minnesota, Oregon, Rhode Island, Wisconsin, and Tennessee; a Connecticut law that applies only to state employees became effective in July 1988.

Most parental leave benefits provided by employers are unpaid. The leave typically can be used for a certain period after regular paid leave (short-term disability, personal days, and vacation) has been exhausted. In 1988, 33 percent of full-time employees in medium-sized and large establishments were eligible for unpaid maternity leave, 16 percent were eligible for unpaid paternity leave, and a small percentage were eligible for paid leave (U.S. Department of Labor, 1989a). The length of leave (maternity or paternity) allowed under an employer's plan ranged from under 1 month to slightly more than 12 months, with an average of 4.4 months.

Adoption Benefits

Adoption benefits include direct financial assistance or reimbursement for expenses related to the adoption of a child and/or the provision for paid or unpaid leave for the adoptive parent employee. Such benefits are increasing in popularity but are only available in a limited number of companies. Financial assistance varies widely, with cash amounts up to approximately $2,000 per adoption (*Working Mother*, 1989). ERTA allowed for the first time a deduction of up to $1,500 for the adoption of a "special needs" child (that is, one who is aged 5 or older or handicapped) or children belonging to a sibling set. Since this tax revision, a number of legislative proposals have been considered to broaden tax deductibility for cash assistance and/or expenses related to adoption. Currently, the taxability of such cash awards made by employers remains an issue.

Conclusion

The demand for child care services is growing in the United States as a result of a combination of factors, including increases in the child population, in two-wage-earner families, and in single-headed households. Although some employers are providing child care benefits, individuals still pay most day care expenses. The federal government is currently exploring new roles in child care. As the needs of employees change and as employers try to satisfy these needs, both the private sector and the federal government may choose to take an expanded role in the provision of child care benefits.

Bibliography

Employee Benefit Research Institute. *Business, Work and Benefits: Adjusting to Change.* Washington, DC: Employee Benefit Research Institute, 1989.

Berkeley Planning Associates. *Employer-Supported Child Care: Measuring and Understanding Its Impacts on the Workplace.* Report prepared for the U.S. Department of Labor, Employment and Training Administration. Oakland, CA: Berkeley Associates, 1989.

Chapman, Fern Schumer. "Executive Guilt: Who's Taking Care of the Children?" *Fortune* (16 February 1987): 30–37.

The Conference Board. *Employers and Child Care: Benefiting Work and Family.* New York: The Conference Board, 1989.

Lakeshore Curriculum Materials. "Kids & Companies: The Employer's Guide to Child Care Solutions." Unpublished. Carson, CA: 1989.

9 to 5 (National Association of Working Women). Fact sheet. Cleveland, OH: 9 to 5, 1989.

Saltford, Nancy C. Employee Benefit Research Institute. "Dependent Care: Meeting the Needs of a Dynamic Work Force." *EBRI Issue Brief* no. 85 (December 1988).

Saltford, Nancy C., and Ramona K.Z. Heck. *An Overview of Employee Benefits Supportive of Families.* EBRI Special Report. Washington, DC: Employee Benefit Research Institute, 1990.

U.S. Congress. House. *Act for Better Child Care Services of 1988.* Report 100-985. 100th Cong., 2nd sess., 27 September 1988.

U.S. Department of Commerce. Bureau of the Census. *Marital Status and Living Arrangements: March 1988.* Current Population Reports. Series P-20, no. 433. Washington, DC: U.S. Government Printing Office, 1989a.

_____. News release CB89-119, 27 July 1989b.

U.S. Department of Labor. *Child Care: A Workforce Issue. Report of the Secretary's Task Force.* Washington, DC: U.S. Government Printing Office, 1988a.

U.S. Department of Labor. Bureau of Labor Statistics. *Employee Benefits in Medium and Large Firms, 1988.* Washington, DC: U.S. Government Printing Office, 1989a.

_____. *Employment and Earnings.* Washington, DC: U.S. Government Printing Office, 1989b.

_____. News release USDL 88-7, 15 January 1988b.

Wider Opportunities for Women. National Commission on Working Women. Fact sheet. Washington, DC: Wider Opportunities for Women, 1989.

Working Mother. "The 60 Best Companies for Working Mothers" (October 1989).

Additional Information

Catalyst
250 Park Ave. South
New York, NY 10003
(212) 777-8900

269

The Conference Board
845 Third Ave.
New York, NY 10022
(212) 759-0900

Family Resource Coalition
230 Michigan Ave., Suite 1625
Chicago, IL 60601
(312) 726-4750

33. Flexible Benefit Plans

Introduction

In recent years, family relationships, lifestyles, a trend toward early retirement, and increased longevity have raised questions about the efficacy of conventional benefit plans. The work force has experienced an influx of young workers and female workers whose lifestyles and values are different from those of the male breadwinners of 20 years ago. Changes in social and economic circumstances have affected workers' needs and preferences.

Most employee benefit programs are designed to satisfy the traditional family's needs. Workers' benefit needs are largely determined by their age, marital and family status, and compensation levels. Traditional programs may not reflect the circumstances of single workers with no dependents, two-earner couples, and single-parent workers; additionally, they may not anticipate changes in workers' needs over time.

Some employers have implemented flexible benefit plans to respond to their workers' differing needs. The central idea in flexible plans is that they allow employees to make choices about their benefits that previously were made by their employers. Within the plan's rules, some flexible plans allow an employee to determine how the employer's contributions will be allocated among the benefits offered. Depending on plan specifications, employees may also elect to reduce their salaries to purchase additional benefits. Because of the choice accorded employees, flexible benefit arrangements are often called "cafeteria" plans.

Tax Status

Flexible benefit or cafeteria plans are governed by section 125 of the Internal Revenue Code (IRC). Prior to the enactment of this section in 1978, employees could not choose between taxable forms of compensation (including cash) and nontaxable benefits without rendering the latter taxable. Section 125 provided that the opportunity to choose would not alter the tax status of the benefit chosen. Thus, its enactment made a choice between cash and nontaxable benefits and between taxable and nontaxable benefits feasible. Employee choice in

271

benefit programs had previously been limited to a choice among options within a benefit category, such as health insurance.

Benefits That May Be Included in a Flexible Benefit Plan

In March 1989, the Internal Revenue Service (IRS) released proposed regulations on cafeteria plans that update and supplement the regulations issued in 1984. Under the 1989 proposed regulations, the following nontaxable and taxable benefits (including cash) may be offered under a cafeteria plan:

- accident and health plans, including health care spending accounts;
- group term life insurance (including taxable coverage over $50,000) and dependent coverage;
- disability benefits and accidental death and dismemberment plans;
- employee contributions to section 401(k) plans or other thrift or savings plans, either pretax or after tax;
- dependent care assistance plans, including dependent care spending accounts;
- otherwise qualified benefits that are taxable because they fail to satisfy nondiscrimination requirements;
- vacation days;
- group legal services (although these plans are usually offered separately); and
- any taxable benefit that is purchased by the employee with after-tax dollars, such as group automobile insurance.

Flexible plans may not be used to defer compensation or to defer benefits from one year to another, except for 401(k) deferrals. Benefits that may not be included under a cafeteria plan include scholarships, education assistance benefits, employee discounts, and other fringe benefits, whether or not taxable.

Funding

Flexible benefit plans may be funded by employer contributions, employee contributions, or both. Some plans utilize salary reduction, which enables employees to use pretax dollars to fund certain benefits. (When an employee agrees to a salary reduction, the reduction amount is not part of his or her taxable income and is treated, for most purposes, as an employer contribution.)

Salary reduction is frequently used to fund health care and dependent care spending (reimbursement) accounts and to convert the contributions employees make to health insurance premiums to employer contributions, thus rendering them nontaxable. Salary reduction amounts under flexible plans are excluded from Social Security (FICA) and unemployment (FUTA) taxes unless the amounts are contributed to 401(k) plans. Flexible benefit plans may also permit employees to purchase benefits with after-tax dollars.

Types of Plans

As the term implies, flexible plans present a variety of design alternatives. Some plans consist entirely of "stand alone" spending accounts. Others offer a choice among a broad range of permissible benefits. In some plans all or part of the employer contribution is translated into flexible credits to be allocated as employees choose. In others, a mandatory core of benefits (usually consisting of minimum levels of health, life, and disability insurance and vacation leave) is prescribed, and employees are given additional credits to spend as they choose. They may use the additional credits to buy greater coverage in the core benefit areas or to buy benefits in other areas, such as dental care or spending accounts. While there appears to be a trend toward "unbundling" benefits, another approach involves allowing employees to choose among several benefit packages, with all packages representing equal value but designed to meet the needs of different lifestyles. Spending accounts, funded partially or wholly by salary reduction, may be combined with any of these design alternatives.

Impact on Cost

Some employers have used flexible benefit plans to reduce their benefit costs or the rate of increase in these costs. When flexible credits are used, the amount of credits accorded each employee does not necessarily increase each year or move in tandem with the most inflation prone benefit (health care). Thus, the full impact of inflation may not be reflected in the employer's costs. Flexible plans may also encourage cost conscious behavior on the part of employees. Employees have more control over employer contributions under flexible plans than they have when benefits are offered on a "take it or leave it" basis, and they may opt for less expensive coverage in one area (health) in order to release funds for another desired benefit or cash. Salary reduction agreements can produce savings for both employees and employers. Employees "save" the amount of the tax they would have paid on the salary reduction amount, while both employees and employers save on FICA taxes associated with the amount. The employee's savings are counterbalanced by the fact that benefits based on pay (for example, Social Security) may also be reduced.

IRS Requirements

The design of flexible plans is constrained by a number of requirements in the IRC and its supplementing regulations. A few of the more important requirements are listed below.

- In order to obtain favorable tax status, flexible benefit plans must not discriminate in favor of highly compensated or key employees (as defined in law and regulation). Three tests are applied. The first requires that no more than 25 percent of the tax-favored benefits provided under the plan be provided to key employees. The second requires that the flexible plan be available to a classification of employees that does not discriminate in favor of the highly compensated. Third, the flexible program must not discriminate in favor of highly compensated employees with regard to contributions and benefits. In addition, specific benefits offered under a flexible plan may be subject to special nondiscrimination rules applicable to that benefit.

- Employees must make their elections under flexible benefit plans before the coverage period begins. Generally, these choices cannot be revoked after the start of the plan year. The 1989 proposed regulations clarify and expand the circumstances under which an employee may make election changes. However, a plan is not required to allow these election changes. In general, election changes may be made when a change in family status occurs (provided the change is consistent with the altered family status) and when a health plan provided by an independent third party undergoes a significant change in cost or coverage. Also, to the extent that an employee is allowed to make changes in contributions to a 401(k) plan, these changes are permissible under a cafeteria plan. Elections may be revoked when an employee separates from service or stops making premium payments.

- To assure that the regulations are satisfied, the coverage period for each benefit should be a full year, and all coverage periods should coincide with the cafeteria plan year.

- Flexible plans must not be used to defer compensation (except in the case of section 401(k) arrangements). Unused credits or benefits, including unused vacation days, may not be carried over to a subsequent plan year. Unused funds in flexible spending accounts must be forfeited.

- Funds allocated to one flexible spending account, such as a health care reimbursement account, cannot be used to reimburse other types of claims, such as dependent care expenses.

- In the case of health care reimbursement accounts, the coverage must be uniform throughout the year (that is, the full amount for the benefit year must be available regardless of how much has actually been contributed at a particular point during the year).

- Claims for reimbursement from flexible spending accounts must be documented with a written statement from an independent third party (i.e., physician or day care center) specifying that the expense has been incurred and the amount. The employee must certify that the claim has not been reimbursed through any other coverage (or, in the case of dependent care, that the charge is an eligible expense under the plan).

Advantages and Disadvantages of Flexible Benefit Plans

Flexible benefit plans offer employees and employers a number of advantages.

- Employees may receive more benefit value because they can tailor their benefits to their needs. Employees can change benefits as their lives change (for example, when they marry or divorce, as their salaries increase, or as their children mature and leave home).

- Employees become more aware and appreciative of their benefits. This may improve employee morale and productivity.

- Employees may become more involved in controlling benefit costs. Moreover, when employees want a new benefit, they are asked to trade another benefit for it rather than to expect their employer to provide an additional benefit.

- Flexible compensation plans can be used to convert workers' earnings into tax-free employee benefits, thereby producing a more valuable compensation dollar.

Flexible compensation plans also present potential disadvantages to employees and employers (although most of these can be minimized by careful planning).

- Some employees may not understand their choices well enough to choose the most needed benefits; thus, families could suffer from losses in areas where they did not select adequate coverage. This problem can be addressed, in part, by a mandatory core program that assures basic protection and also by an effective communications program.

- Effective employee benefit communication—which is always important—is critical in a flexible benefit plan. Therefore, the introduction of these plans must be accompanied by a more thorough communications effort than is required for traditional plans.

- Flexible plans may result in increased utilization and adverse selection, both of which may cause problems with group insurance underwriting requirements and result in higher benefit costs. Plan features can be added to minimize adverse selection (for example, limits can be placed on coverage levels and the frequency of election periods). The pricing of the options can prevent the higher costs that can be caused by adverse selection.

- The requirement for health care spending accounts to provide uniform coverage throughout the plan year could expose an employer to additional liability if employees incur large claims early in the year and terminate employment before fully funding their accounts. This danger can be minimized by plan design features, defining lower annual maximums, or limiting midyear changes.

- Greater benefit flexibility is likely to result in greater administrative complexity and costs. To some extent, administrative costs can be controlled by restricting employee options and the frequency of benefit election periods. These restrictions limit the amount of flexibility under the plan, however. A number of available packaged computer systems for handling enrollment, benefit payment, and recordkeeping can reduce the time and costs of implementing flexible benefit plans.

Deciding on a Flexible Plan

Before deciding to offer a flexible benefits plan, an employer should determine whether this type of plan is consistent with the organization's overall philosophy and is likely to advance its management goals and objectives. The design of a specific plan is often preceded by a survey to determine whether employees are receptive to the concept of flexible benefits and to identify the benefit choices employees most need and want. Once a decision is made to proceed, the employer must confront a number of basic issues. The most basic issue is probably, "How much do I want to spend and how can I maximize employee satisfaction or minimize employee dissatisfaction while limiting costs to that figure?" Some questions plan designers should decide are whether, and how, to include currently offered benefits in the plan; whether to provide a core of benefits; what benefits to make optional; what value to place on each option; how to distribute flexible credits; how to prevent adverse selection; and under what circumstances to permit employees to change elections.

Conclusion

Flexible benefit plans are attracting great interest among employees and employers. According to a recent survey of full-time employees in private medium-sized and large establishments, 9 percent of all workers were eligible for flexible benefit plans and 23 percent were eligible for reimbursement accounts in 1989 (U.S. Department of Labor, 1990). Furthermore, the number of employers offering flexible benefit plans is growing. A 1989 survey of flexible compensation found that a total of 1,001 flexible benefit programs were expected to be in effect as of January 1, 1990, compared with 19 in 1981 (Hewitt Associates, 1989). The growth of flexible programs has been particularly strong in recent years. According to the foregoing survey, 55 percent of the top 100 industrial companies, 57 percent of the top 100 commercial banks, and 40 percent of the top 50 life insurers planned to have flexible programs in place in 1990.

Bibliography

A. Foster Higgins & Co., Inc. *A Survey of Flexible Benefit Programs, 1988.* Princeton, NJ: A. Foster Higgins & Co., Inc., 1988.

Hewitt Associates. *Survey on Flexible Compensation Programs and Practices.* Lincolnshire, IL: Hewitt Associates, 1989.

_____. *Fundamentals of Flexible Compensation.* Lincolnshire, IL: Hewitt Associates, 1988.

U.S. Department of Labor. Bureau of Labor Statistics. "Employee Benefits Focus on Family Concerns in 1989." USDL news release 90-160, 30 March 1990. Washington, DC: U.S. Government Printing Office, 1989.

Additional Information

Charles D. Spencer & Associates, Inc.
250 S. Wacker Drive, Suite 600
Chicago, IL 60606-5834
(312) 993-7900

Employers Council on Flexible Compensation
927 15th Street, NW, Suite 1000
Washington, DC 20005
(202) 659-4300

34. Guidance on Evaluating an Employee Benefit Package

Introduction

Employee benefits make up a sizable portion of total compensation, and it is important not to overlook their worth. If an employee accepts a higher-paying job and as a result pays more expenses out-of-pocket to duplicate benefits received at the prior job, he or she may not have realized financial gain after all. To utilize the full value of a benefit package, one must understand the benefits provided and the role they play in total compensation.

Even though a particular benefit may not match an employee's needs, the package as a whole may be quite valuable. Moreover, benefits an employee may not be interested in today may become important to him or her in the future. It is important, therefore, to focus on the entire benefit package and not only on its individual parts.

What to Expect

Employers offer a wide variety of benefits. Some are legally required and others are offered voluntarily. Legally required benefits include Social Security, Medicare, unemployment insurance, and workers' compensation. Additional benefits offered voluntarily by employers vary. U.S. Department of Labor statistics show that, among full-time workers in medium-sized and large establishments in 1989, 92 percent participated in employer-sponsored medical plans, and 94 percent had employer-sponsored life insurance. Sixty-six percent participated in dental plans, 45 percent had long-term disability benefits, and 41 percent participated in 401(k) plans. Nine percent were eligible to participate in flexible benefit programs. Unpaid maternity leave was available to 37 percent of employees and unpaid paternity leave to 18 percent. Five percent were eligible for employer-subsidized child care benefits (U.S. Department of Labor, 1990).

Levels of benefits vary by industry and employer size. The value of the benefits package can range from less than 15 percent of pay to more than 45 percent, according to a 1989 survey of 1,943 private employers (A. Foster Higgins & Co., Inc., 1989). The average value of benefits included in the survey was 26.5 percent of pay. The U.S.

Department of Commerce's Survey of Current Business, which includes both public and private employers, found the proportion of total compensation spent on benefits to be 16.3 percent in 1988 (Betley, 1989).

Part-time employees and those working for small employers often receive fewer benefits. Generally, benefits legally required for full-time workers are also required for part-time workers. But there is considerably more variation among benefits offered voluntarily by employers. In general, the more hours an employee works during the year and the more years of service he or she has with an employer, the greater the likelihood of earning voluntarily provided benefits. Those who work 30 hours a week or more are more likely to receive major voluntary benefits such as medical insurance, life insurance, and paid leave. Those working less than half time (fewer than 17½ hours per week) do not generally receive these voluntary benefits because they can be expensive to provide.

How to Get Started

Evaluating an employee benefit package requires detailed knowledge of the benefits offered and a clear understanding of one's own personal and family situations. A good way to start is by reading the preceding chapters for basic explanations of various benefits. Also, private-sector employers must provide employees with a summary plan description (SPD) of most types of benefit plans they provide. More detail is usually available from the plan administrator on request.

When evaluating a benefit package, employees should consider family composition, career plans, age, and the tax status of the benefits. An employee with a family should find out which benefits cover dependents, since employers are not required to offer dependent coverage. It is also important to look for benefits specifically for dependents when considering the value of a benefit package. Other coverage may be available to the employee through a spouse or through individual insurance.

Benefit coverage sometimes overlaps in families where more than one person is in the work force. To make the most efficient use of benefits, employees should be aware of when and how they are covered under another family member's benefit plan. Knowing how a plan's coverage works is especially relevant when an employee participates in a flexible benefit plan and can choose from among a variety of benefits. (For more information on flexible benefits, see chapter 33.) For example, if covered under a spouse's medical plan, an employee may want to choose a less generous medical benefit under his or her own plan and take cash or another benefit instead. Balancing employee benefits in this way maximizes the value of a benefit package.

The value of a benefit package varies with career plans and age. For employees who plan to change jobs frequently—as younger employees tend to do—shorter pension vesting requirements and waiting periods for other benefits are important. Currently, most plans vest 100 percent after five years of service or vest gradually between three and seven years. Older workers may prefer defined benefit retirement plans, which allow a more rapid accrual of benefits, and health plans that will continue coverage during retirement. In addition, older workers are more likely than younger workers to make large contributions to a pension or savings plan to finance their approaching retirement.

The value of a benefit can be enhanced by its tax treatment. Some benefits are taxed as ordinary income, whereas others are tax deferred or tax exempt. (See specific chapters for tax treatment of various benefits.)

An employee benefit package should be evaluated periodically to keep up with changes in individual circumstances. Most employers allow certain changes in plan choice at specified intervals or events. More frequent evaluations of a benefit package are necessary if an employee has a change in position, employer, family status, or retirement plans.

Pension Plans

An employer-sponsored pension is probably the largest single benefit an employee may receive in terms of the percentage of his or her total compensation that goes into the plan. Almost all workers qualify for Social Security benefits, but Social Security only provides a minimum floor of protection—a foundation on which to build. Most people want more than a minimum income when they retire. They want to continue in the lifestyle they were accustomed to during their working years. An employer-sponsored pension plan can make the difference between a "bare bones" retirement lifestyle and a comfortable one.

The first step in evaluating a pension plan is to understand how it works. Employees should obtain a copy of the summary plan description from the employer or plan administrator. It will explain eligibility requirements for participation in the plan, vesting (the years of service required before a benefit becomes irrevocable), what the benefit at retirement will be, and at what ages employees may claim benefits. Employees also need to know whether there are any adjustments in their pension benefits or contributions because of their Social Security coverage. (For more information on integrating pension plans with Social Security, see chapter 16.)

Most pension plans also offer other benefits in the event the worker dies or becomes disabled. Employees should inquire whether these are available through their plan.

There are two general types of pension plans: defined contribution and defined benefit. (The differences between defined benefit and defined contribution plans are discussed in chapter 5.) It is important to understand the differences. In a defined benefit plan, a formula—typically based on years of service and salary—indicates how much an employee will receive at retirement. The employer must fund the plan following detailed federal regulations and using complex calculations. The employer invests the amount with which it funds the plan, and the earnings on the investment may reduce the amount the employer needs to put in the plan to keep it adequately funded. On the other hand, if the investments do not perform well, the employer may have to increase the funding to provide the promised retirement benefit.

A defined contribution plan is fundamentally different. The employer is committed to contributing a specific amount to this type of plan regularly. The allocation is usually equal to a percentage of each employee's earnings. The benefit payable at retirement is based on the money that has accumulated in each employee's account. This accumulated money reflects employer contributions, employee contributions (if any), and investment gains or losses. Usually, the employee has the opportunity to select among several investment options. If the investment performance is better than expected, the employee's retirement income will be higher. If the investments do not do as well as expected, the retirement benefit will be lower. Thus the employee accepts the potential risk—and reward—of the investment performance.

Defined contribution plans include savings and investment plans—known as 401(a) plans and pretax savings plans (401(k) plans). (For more information on 401(k) plans, see chapter 9.) Employee stock ownership plans (ESOPs) are also a form of defined contribution plan. (For more information on ESOPs, see chapter 10.)

Defined contribution plans are often more popular with employees because these plans set up an individual account for each worker that allows him or her to monitor the assets. Another appeal of a defined contribution plan is its "portability"—the employee can take the vested account balance if he or she changes jobs.

Both defined benefit and defined contribution plans are valuable, each having certain advantages depending on an employee's age, previous work history, anticipated longevity with the employer, and future years of service before retirement. Many employers offer both types of plans.

The tax status of the pension plan is also important. Qualified plans—those complying with Internal Revenue Service regulations—allow employer contributions and some types of employee contributions to accumulate tax free until the benefit is paid to the worker. The Tax Reform Act of 1986 imposed a penalty for lump-sum withdrawals made before age 59½, with some exceptions (such as early retirement), to encourage workers to save adequate benefits for retirement rather than spend them beforehand. Favorable tax treatment of a pension benefit can have a major effect on the final benefit received in retirement, so employees should keep abreast of any tax law changes and make appropriate adjustments in financing their retirement.

Health Plans

An employer-sponsored health plan is probably the benefit most used and most valued by workers and their families. Without some form of health care coverage, a hospital stay or prolonged illness could financially devastate a family.

When employers began offering health coverage, it was intended to protect the employee from the catastrophic financial loss that can accompany serious illness or injury. Over time, coverage was extended to family members and additional features were added to many plans. Some plans have paid for nearly every routine medical expense for employees.

In recent years, the cost of providing health care has been skyrocketing, rising much faster than the general rate of inflation. In 1984, employer health care costs (including medical, dental, prescription drug, vision, and hearing benefits) averaged $1,654 per employee, according to one survey. Five years later, the cost had jumped to $2,748—an increase of 66 percent (A. Foster Higgins & Co., Inc., 1989).

It is not uncommon for the cost of health plans to jump 30 percent or more in a single year.

In response, many employers have taken steps to help control overall costs and to share more of the cost with employees. For some employers, the alternative may be to eliminate coverage altogether.

To evaluate a health plan, it is important to understand how it works. (The various health care plans are explained in detail in chapters 19, 20, 21, 22, 24, 25, and 26.) A description of the employer's health plan usually provides information on eligibility requirements, expenses that are covered, plan financing, and the effect of eligibility for other health plans on an employee's participation. Some plans now coordinate with any plans that an employee or dependent *could* be covered under, whether or not he or she actually selected it. And while other coverage may "limit" benefits, it may also free an employee to elect a lower level of coverage—or to opt out completely—under a flexible benefit plan.

Employers generally offer two types of health plans: prepaid plans, such as health maintenance organizations, and fee-for-service plans. Increasingly, employer plans are adopting "managed care" approaches for their fee-for-service plans in an effort to contain health care costs and provide high-quality care. These approaches allow employers to monitor providers to ensure that their patterns of medical practice are appropriate and cost effective. Preferred provider organizations, for example, are contractual arrangements between health care providers and an employer or insurance company to provide fee-for-service health care at a prenegotiated rate. In addition, many employers now require a second opinion before their health plan will cover certain types of elective procedures, while others use precertification—an independent evaluation of whether hospitalization is necessary or an alternative might be preferable and more cost effective.

Increasingly, employees are given a choice among types of health plans or levels of coverage, particularly when a flexible benefit plan is offered. There are a number of factors to consider when selecting a health plan, including the number and age of dependents, medical history, coverage that might be available elsewhere (through a spouse's employer, for example), ability to take some financial risk, and personal preference. Those with families who make frequent medical and dental visits may prefer a prepaid plan in which costs are limited regardless of the number of visits or services needed. Other employees and their dependents may have or may develop a medical condition requiring specialized services and may want to keep or choose their own doctors. Employees have always been able to choose their own physicians under fee-for-service plans, and this is sometimes now an option under prepaid plans as well.

While cost is an important consideration in selecting a health plan, it is important that employees look at the whole picture rather than just at their monthly contribution. Each person's situation is different, as are his or her willingness and ability to accept some financial risk. In addition to the employee's monthly plan cost (or premium, if the plan is insured), the employee typically incurs a cost for using medical services.

The *deductible* is the amount an individual pays before the plan begins to pay. The deductible may apply to all covered charges or to specific types of services. Some plans have a deductible per covered person, with a maximum deductible for a family. Deductibles are most often applied on a yearly basis.

Coinsurance refers to the portion of covered medical costs the employee pays after he or she meets the deductible. For example, a plan may pay 80 percent of expenses and the employee 20 percent after the deductible is met.

The *maximum out-of-pocket expense* is the cap on the employee's share of expenses in a year. This may be an amount per covered person or an amount per family. The intent is to protect the employee from catastrophic medical expenses.

Covered expenses are defined by each plan. Some health care plans cover a broader range of services than others.

Most plans will pay *reasonable and customary* charges for medical services or will pay according to a predetermined fee schedule. The fee schedule sets the maximum amount the plan will pay for a given type of service. The schedule may vary by geographic location to take into account differences in costs.

The *lifetime maximum* is the most the plan will pay for all covered expenses during the employee's lifetime.

These potential costs, taken together, define the true cost of a medical plan. Employees should carefully consider all of these elements before deciding which plan or level of coverage to select.

Employers with health plans are required by law to offer continued access to group health coverage to former workers and their dependents. The recipient pays for the coverage if he or she wants it, and the employer's obligation is limited to a specific period of time. Companies with fewer than 20 employees are exempt from this requirement.

Understanding a health plan could mean the difference between adequate and inadequate medical care. Employees should know their options and regularly evaluate how well their plan is meeting their individual and family needs.

Disability Plans

Sudden injury or illness can leave an employee unable to work and lead to serious financial difficulties. Disability income plans are intended to prevent this. Some aspects to consider are the types of disabilities covered, the extent and length of coverage, and the cost of various levels of benefits.

Disability plans are categorized as short-term disability and long-term disability. In short-term disability plans, benefit payments are usually provided for 26 weeks or less. Workers may receive paid sick leave, which typically provides 100 percent of a worker's normal earnings, or sickness and accident insurance, which usually provides 50 percent to 70 percent of normal earnings. In long-term disability plans, benefit payments are usually provided after short-term benefits have ended. They typically provide one-half to two-thirds of an employee's predisability gross earnings, although some plans may replace as much as 70 percent to 80 percent of predisability pay.

Employees should learn their plan's specific definition of disability and be aware of the conditions under which the definition may change. One question to ask is whether the insurance will pay benefits if the employee is unable to work in his or her own occupation regardless of whether he or she can get paid work in another occupation. To qualify for disability under Social Security, which provides only long-term disability benefits, an employee must be unable to do virtually *any* paid work. Employees should also be aware of when successive periods of disability are considered separate disabilities or one disability, since this could substantially affect the duration of benefit payments.

Employers recognize all sources of disability income when calculating a benefit, and there are usually provisions for integrating an employer's voluntary disability benefits with those required by law. Employers are legally required to contribute to workers' compensation and to Social Security. Some states also require employer payments to nonoccupational temporary disability insurance.

The level of benefits an employer pays is often related to each employee's salary, so a disability benefit may increase in value as an employee gains experience or improves his or her position. Some plans also make cost-of-living adjustments.

The duration of benefits also varies and may increase with service. There is no upper age limit on eligibility for disability benefits for

286

active employees. The level and/or duration of benefits may be reduced for older employees, based on age-related cost considerations, provided that older workers do not receive less in benefits than is provided to younger employees.

Another important consideration is whether payments for partial disability are available. This covers employees who continue to work at their own occupation but at a reduced capacity. Some plans require that the employee be totally disabled for a certain period of time to become eligible for partial disability benefits. Other plans require a certain percentage of income loss to have occurred before a worker can qualify. Employees generally experience about a 25 percent decline in income before qualifying for partial disability.

Employees should also understand what portion of the disability premium is paid by the employer and what portion by the employee. One way to reduce costs is to choose a longer waiting period before disability payments begin. Social Security has a waiting period of five full months from the date of onset of the disability before the individual can begin to receive benefits. Plans generally require a waiting period before long-term benefits are paid.

Disability benefits can be one of the most important benefits to consider when evaluating a benefit package. (For more information on disability income plans, see chapter 29.)

Life Insurance

Employers often provide group term life insurance benefits for their employees. Life insurance benefits can make a big difference in the financial stability of an employee's survivors.

When evaluating a group life insurance plan, employees should consider the eligibility requirements, levels and extent of coverage, cost of premiums, and what portion of the cost, if any, employees must pay.

Group term life insurance is generally intended to replace a portion of the deceased employee's earnings for a period of time. It is pure insurance protection, paying a benefit to the beneficiaries only at the employee's death.

Eligibility to participate in a life insurance plan is generally granted after an employee has worked a designated length of time—usually no more than a few months. Coverage may also be available for dependents. They are often entitled to a lower level of coverage, usually at an additional cost, and their coverage may last only for a specified period of time, usually determined by their age.

When employees participate in their employer's life insurance plan, they must designate primary beneficiaries. Contingent beneficiaries are often overlooked but should also be designated. Employees should find out how often beneficiary designations can be changed and keep them up to date.

The amount of coverage received may be a specific dollar amount but is often a multiple of an employee's annual earnings and thus varies for each employee. Additional benefits for accidental death and dismemberment insurance may also be included in a life insurance plan. Also, some plans continue life insurance protection in the event an employee becomes totally and permanently disabled and in the event of retirement (usually at a substantially reduced level). Employees need to know under what circumstances such coverage continues—and at what cost to them.

Employees should also determine how much life insurance they need. The cost of monthly premiums varies, and the cost may be split between the employer and employee. In plans where employees pay all or part of the cost, the premium is often a flat amount for each covered employee, regardless of age. Also, supplemental insurance plans are sometimes available. Employees usually pay for this additional coverage. Workers should be aware of how often and under what conditions supplemental insurance can be purchased.

It is also important to know whether the group insurance can be converted to an individual insurance policy if an employee leaves the company or retires. Workers should also be aware of the conditions under which their employer can cancel the group policy and what their options are if the insurance carrier cancels their employer's policy.

In addition to group term insurance, employers may offer dependent life insurance, the cost of which is usually paid by the employee, and group universal life insurance, which is employee paid but offers advantages not found in group term insurance. (For more information on group life insurance, see chapter 27.)

Dental and Vision Care Plans

Proper dental care and vision care are important for the prevention and treatment of potentially serious health problems, and growing numbers of employers are providing benefits for this care.

When evaluating dental and vision care plans, employees should consider eligibility requirements, services covered, the availability of dependent coverage, and the existence of copayments and deductibles.

A 1989 survey of 1,943 employers showed that 83 percent offered dental coverage to employees (A. Foster Higgins & Co., Inc., 1989). Employee sharing of dental costs has also increased, with 63 percent of plans requiring employee contributions in 1988, compared with 54 percent in 1984, according to other recent surveys (Hewitt Associates, 1989).

The availability of vision care benefits also continues to grow. In 1984, only 26 percent of employers provided vision care benefits through a vision plan or spending account. In 1988, this percentage grew to 54 percent. Similarly, there has been an increase in the provision of hearing care benefits. In 1984, only 16 percent of employers provided hearing benefits through a plan or spending account, while in 1988, 43 percent did so. (For more information on dental and vision care plans, see chapters 20 and 22, respectively.) Eligibility to participate in these plans is usually granted immediately or after a short waiting period.

Employees should consider whether specific procedures they anticipate needing will be covered by their dental and vision care plans. Coverage for certain services may be limited to the employee or provided at a reduced level for dependents. Coverage may also be limited to a certain number of services. For example, in a vision care plan, a participant may only be covered for the cost of a designated number of eyeglasses or contact lenses. In a dental care plan, the amount of coverage may vary by the type of treatment. Treatment and preventive services may also carry differing amounts of coverage. Employees should be aware of the amounts of deductibles and copayments and of how often deductibles must be satisfied (for example, once annually).

Other Benefits

Many employers offer benefits in addition to those discussed above, including parental leave, dependent care plans, financial or retirement counseling, education assistance, and legal services. Another benefit designed to serve a particular need is the reimbursement account, or cash account, from which employees may reimburse themselves on a pretax basis for out-of-pocket health care or dependent care expenditures. Long-term care insurance policies are beginning to be offered by a few companies and will probably increase as the population ages. Although not commonly offered, these benefits can be particularly valuable to some employees.

Conclusion

Today's workers often do not fully understand their benefit packages, but unmet needs and rising costs have forced them to take a closer look at what they have and to take more responsibility for obtaining the benefits they need. The importance of various benefits depends on individual needs and preferences. When evaluating benefits, however, employees should look at their total benefit package, not merely the separate parts. To get the most from their employer-provided benefits, workers must take the time to understand their options.

Bibliography

A. Foster Higgins & Co., Inc. *Foster Higgins Health Care Benefits Survey 1989.* New York: A. Foster Higgins & Co., Inc., 1989.

Betley, Charles. "Employer Spending for Benefits Rises 8.6 Percent in 1988." *Employee Benefit Notes* (October 1989): 5–7.

Hewitt Associates. *Salaried Employee Benefits Provided by Major U.S. Employers: A Comparison Study 1984–1988.* Lincolnshire, IL: Hewitt Associates, 1989.

McArdle, Frank. Employee Benefit Research Institute. "The Tax Treatment of Pension and Capital Accumulation Plans." *EBRI Issue Brief* no. 82 (September 1988).

Project Hope. "Selecting Quality Health Care: Questions to Ask." Brochure. Chevy Chase, MD: Project Hope, 1989.

U.S. Department of Labor. Bureau of Labor Statistics. "Employee Benefits Focus on Family Concerns in 1989." USDL news release 90-160, 30 March 1990.

PART TWO
PUBLIC-SECTOR BENEFIT PROGRAMS

35. The Public-Sector Environment

Introduction

More than 17 million individuals are employed by public jurisdictions in the United States. These public entities include the federal government; state, county, and municipal governments; school districts; and a host of other special-purpose districts and authorities. Approximately 15 percent of the employed labor force, or more than one in seven working Americans, works for a public entity.[1]

Nearly all of these public employees are covered by employee benefit programs. While there is enormous diversity among the programs, taken together, they exhibit a certain family resemblance and differ in important respects from private-sector programs. This chapter highlights these differences and provides an overview of the current status of employee benefits in the public sector.

Many of the differences between public-sector and private-sector benefit plans stem from the different environments in which they operate. Indeed, the environmental differences are so important that some discussion of them is necessary to provide a context for the differences in individual benefits.

Centrality of Politics

The most significant difference between public- and private-sector benefit programs lies in their relationship to the legislative process. Private-sector plans are strongly affected by laws passed by national and state legislatures, but within these constraints private plan sponsors are relatively free to establish, maintain, and modify their plans. Public employee plans, on the other hand, are not so much affected by the legislative process as they are products of that process. These plans' basic features—eligibility, contributions, types of benefits, etc.—are often described in statutes or in local ordinances. (This is especially true in the pension area.) Moreover, even where collective bargaining over benefit issues is allowed, the legislatures generally retain some measure of control. Furthermore, public employee programs usually exist within a highly structured personnel system that is itself prescribed, often in great detail, in public law.

---

[1] EBRI tabulations of the May 1988 Current Population Survey.

Because they are legislative products, public employee benefit plans necessarily reflect the interplay of political forces.[2] Since large sums of public money are involved as well as the welfare of those who implement public policy, it is regarded as entirely appropriate that major benefit issues should be decided through the political process. This process is not the most efficient means of decision making, however, nor is it the best adapted to consideration of complex, technical issues. It inevitably involves the clash of multiple interest groups. Moreover, where public employee benefit plans are concerned, the "interested" groups usually extend far beyond the public administrators and employees (and their unions and associations) that are directly affected to include provider groups, insurers, the business and financial community, and taxpayer organizations.

The influence of organized labor on public employee benefits is particularly strong. Forty-four percent of public employees are represented by labor unions, compared with 14 percent of private employees (U.S. Department of Commerce, 1989). This influence is exercised directly where bargaining over benefit issues is allowed, but it is also exercised indirectly through the legislative process. In fact, where public employee benefits are concerned, labor-management negotiations and legislative politics are often inextricably intertwined.

Relationship to Federal Law

A second fundamental difference in the environment of public employee plans as opposed to those sponsored by private companies is the role played by federal tax and benefits law and regulation. The taxing power of the federal government has been used to encourage the provision of employee benefits by private business since 1916, when corporations were first allowed to deduct payments to retired employees, their families, and dependents as ordinary and necessary expenses (Graebner, 1980). The federal government's taxing power has also been used to compel certain behavior (for example, participation in Social Security) by the levying of payroll taxes. Public jurisdictions are not taxpaying entities, however, and their behavior cannot be influenced by opportunities to reduce federal tax on their revenues.

State and local jurisdictions also coexist with the federal government in a system of federalism, and while the powers and prerogatives

---

[2]For a description of the legislative environment as it affects pension plans, see Bleakney, 1972.

294

of the various levels of government have changed over time, the balance among them is always a politically delicate issue. Even when the federal government has formally asserted that its laws apply to benefit plans for state and local employees, it has for the most part shown little interest in enforcing them. (Attention to public plans has increased in the last several years, however; see chapter 37 for more detail.) For reasons unrelated to federalism, the federal government has also chosen to exclude its own employees' benefit programs from major parts of the law applicable to private plans. The special status of governmental plans can be seen most readily in their relationship to two landmark pieces of federal legislation, the Social Security Act of 1935 and the Employee Retirement Income Security Act of 1974 (ERISA).

Benefit Systems

For many public employees, the immediate employing entity is not the sponsor or the administrator of the benefit plans under which they are covered. Particularly in the pension area, the public sector is characterized by a relatively small number of large systems and a large number of small systems. According to the Bureau of the Census, there are 2,414 state and local retirement systems, with the 201 systems administered by the states accounting for 86.3 percent of the total covered population (U.S. Department of Commerce, 1990). At the federal level, most civilian employees are covered by the Civil Service Retirement System or the Federal Employees Retirement System. Certain relatively small groups—for example, Foreign Service and military personnel—have their own, entirely separate arrangements.

All states operate one or more pension systems for their employees; some require their political subdivisions to participate in state-run systems, while others allow them to participate at their election. These state systems may be primarily administrative arrangements, with costs remaining distinct for each member "plan," or they may be operated as a unified "plan," with a single set of costs distributed among all the member entities. Even where the state does not operate a pension plan to which local jurisdictions belong, the types of plans local entities can develop may be constrained by state law.

Health and life insurance plans are more likely to be operated by each jurisdiction for its own employees and, unlike pension plans, they are often collectively bargained. However, New York and California operate statewide health benefit programs in which local government employees can elect to participate. Where they exist, state-run long-term disability and sickness and accident insurance plans may also be open to local government entities.

Occupational Divisions

Another salient feature of public employment for benefit purposes is that the work force is subdivided along certain occupational lines. In most jurisdictions law enforcement and firefighting employees have their own programs apart from those for other public employees. Alternatively, they may participate in a general system but enjoy special benefit provisions. (These occupations are, of course, unique to the public sector.) Public school teachers also sometimes have separate plans or separate arrangements, whether they participate in a state-run or a local plan. The special status of these occupational groups is partly historical (they were among the first to obtain pension coverage), partly a consequence of the occupations' characteristics and requirements, and partly a reflection of their ability to protect their interests in the political arena.

One characteristic of private-sector plans that is extremely rare in the public sector is the provision of separate benefits for executives. In the public sector, benefit provisions tend to apply equally to all levels of the work force. Even where separate "executive services" have been recognized, separate benefit provisions are rare. This egalitarian tradition does not extend to members of the judiciary or the legislature, however. Judges almost always have their own separate, usually very generous, pension plans, and legislators usually enjoy special pension vesting, eligibility, and computation provisions. The judges' plans are justified on the grounds that the judiciary must be provided a sufficient measure of security to allow them to carry out their responsibilities in an impartial, disinterested way. The special provisions for legislators are justified by the uncertain nature of their tenure.[3]

Commonalities

Finally, in highlighting the differences between public- and private-sector employee benefit plans, the numerous commonalities should not be overlooked. In a competitive marketplace, all employers need to attract and retain workers and to maintain a healthy and vigorous

---

[3]For a discussion of the legal forms and occupational divisions in public-sector pension plans, see McGill, 1984.

work force. To the extent that benefit programs serve these needs, they are based on common motives and directed at common goals. Furthermore, while public pension systems developed early and more or less independently of private business practice, the later addition of health and welfare plans was often a response to the availability of such benefits in private employment. Indeed, in determining many aspects of compensation for public employees, legislators look first to the practices prevailing in the business community. Thus, many developments in private-sector employee benefit plans eventually surface in public employee programs, albeit in a form tailored to the public entity's traditions and circumstances.

Bibliography

Bleakney, Thomas. *Retirement Systems for Public Employees*. Philadelphia, PA: Wharton School, University of Pennsylvania, 1972.

Graebner, William. *A History of Retirement*. New Haven, CT: Yale University Press, 1980.

McGill, Dan. "Public Pension Plans." In Jerry S. Rosenbloom, ed. *Handbook of Employee Benefits*. Homewood, IL: Dow Jones-Irwin, 1984.

_____. *1987 Census of Governments*. Washington, DC: U.S. Government Printing Office, 1990.

U.S. Department of Commerce. Bureau of the Census. *Statistical Abstract of the United States: 1989*. Washington, DC: U.S. Government Printing Office, 1989.

36. Social Security

Introduction

When Congress began to develop a social insurance system in the early 1930s, retirement arrangements for some public-sector workers were already in place. Police officers, firefighters, teachers, federal civilian workers, and some state employees were among the earliest groups to acquire coverage. Thus, while Social Security was envisioned from the outset as a universal system, there was less urgency about extending its benefits to public-sector workers than to private-sector employees, for whom existing coverage was very rare. Furthermore, the new social insurance scheme was to be financed by a payroll tax, and the federal government's constitutional authority to impose a tax on other public jurisdictions was questionable. Thus, the initial Social Security legislation excluded all public-sector workers from coverage.

In 1950, the law was amended to allow state and local employees not already covered under a retirement system to acquire Social Security coverage in a manner consistent with their employers' sovereignty—through voluntary agreements between the state and federal governments. In keeping with the voluntary nature of the coverage agreements, public jurisdictions were allowed to opt out of Social Security after a five year period of participation, if they gave two years' notice. In 1954, groups of employees who were already covered by retirement systems became eligible for Social Security, provided a majority of the members of the group voted for coverage in a referendum. (Police officers and firefighters, at the request of their representatives, were excluded.) Two years later, specified states and interstate authorities were allowed to cover parts of groups (including police officers and firefighters) on the condition that all newly hired members of the group in question would be covered. In 1967, the law was further amended to allow all states to provide Social Security coverage for firefighters (but not police officers) who were already covered under a state or local retirement system (U.S. Congress, 1982).

Participation

Participation in Social Security by state and local government employees reached 72 percent in the early 1970s, dropped off slightly

299

due to withdrawals from the system in the late 1970s, and now appears to have stabilized at approximately 73 percent of the employee population. Entities that are still outside the system seem to show little interest in joining it. Moreover, most federal civilian employment remained outside Social Security until 1984, when (after a losing battle on the part of federal unions) workers newly hired after December 31, 1983, and Congress itself became mandatorily covered.

Social Security versus Public-Sector Pension Plans

Although the benefit per dollar of contribution to Social Security is generally attractive, many public employees (including a majority of federal employees hired before 1984 and most police officers) apparently perceive their existing retirement plans to be superior to any combined Social Security/employer-sponsored plan they are likely to obtain from Social Security coverage. They hold this view despite the fact that a majority of state and local plans are not integrated with Social Security, and the combined benefits yield extraordinarially high replacement rates. Some public employees see the desire to include them under Social Security as motivated not by a concern for their welfare but rather by a need to improve Social Security's revenue base and/or a desire on the part of the employing jurisdiction to save money. It is also true, however, that a majority of public workers were able to enjoy until 1984 some of the more generous features of Social Security whether or not their public employment was covered by the federal program.

At least 70 percent of federal workers and a similar portion of state and local employees whose public employment was not covered by Social Security have obtained Social Security pension benefits and Medicare coverage.[1] Some of these workers acquired benefit entitlement by working a minimum period (40 quarters) in covered employment after or concurrent with their public service careers. Since the formula for computing Social Security retirement benefits did not until recently distinguish between long careers at low salaries and short careers (40 quarters) at higher ones, these workers often received the full value of the Social Security "tilt" toward the lower

---

[1]The estimate for federal workers is based on a computer match of federal retirement system files with Social Security files. See also A. Foster Higgins & Co., Inc., 1988, which cites a survey by the U.S. Department of Health and Human Services indicating that 85 percent of exempt state and local employees aged 65 or over were enrolled in Medicare Part A, based on other employment or through the entitlement of a spouse.

paid. Alternatively, retired public-sector workers were eligible to receive spousal benefits when a husband or wife with a career in covered employment qualified as a Social Security beneficiary.

1983 Amendments to Social Security Act

From the point of view of the Social Security system, public-sector employees who acquired Social Security and Medicare coverage in addition to coverage under public-sector programs were thwarting the law's intent. The Social Security law was designed to provide a floor of benefits to protect workers against poverty in old age and not as an add-on to already rather generous public pensions. In 1983, an amendment to the Social Security law introduced a modified, less generous formula to compute the benefits of workers with less than 25 years (initially 30, but changed by further amendment) of substantial coverage under Social Security *and* who receive a pension from non-Social Security covered employment. (This change is commonly referred to as the elimination of the "windfall" benefit.) The law also reduced the benefit of a person receiving Social Security as a spouse of a covered worker if that person also receives a pension based on his or her own employment with a federal, state, or local government (U.S. Department of Health and Human Services, 1988). The 1983 amendments also required all federal employees to pay the Hospital Insurance tax for Medicare, regardless of whether or not they were covered under Social Security's retirement provisions. In addition, the federal legislation mandated payment of the Hospital Insurance tax for all state and local employees hired after March 31, 1986, but those already employed and not covered by Social Security are exempt.

It remains to be seen whether the recent changes in the Social Security law affecting public employees will lead more state and local jurisdictions to seek coverage. It appears certain that coverage will not be reduced. The 1983 Social Security Amendments rescinded the states' right to withdraw from voluntary coverage agreements but provided that groups previously covered could reenter the agreements.

Bibliography

A. Foster Higgins & Co., Inc. *Pension Commission Clearinghouse, Report on State Pension Commissions*. New York: A. Foster Higgins & Co., Inc., 1988.

U.S. Congress. House. Committee on Ways and Means. Subcommittee on Social Security. *Termination of Social Security Coverage for Employees of*

State and Local Governments and Nonprofit Groups, Appendix A. Committee Print. Washington, DC: U.S. Government Printing Office, 1982.

U.S. Department of Health and Human Services. Social Security Administration. *Social Security Handbook, 1988*. Washington, DC: U.S. Government Printing Office, 1988.

37. Employee Retirement Income Security Act

Introduction

Prior to enactment of the Employee Retirement Income Security Act of 1974 (ERISA), the Internal Revenue Code (IRC) contained eligibility, nondiscrimination, vesting, funding, and fiduciary requirements that pension plans needed to meet to be considered "qualified" for tax purposes. These requirements were generally less rigorous than those later imposed by ERISA but were considered applicable by the Internal Revenue Service (IRS) to public as well as to private plans. In fact, the IRC requirements had very little impact on public plans. While, theoretically, if a public plan failed to "qualify," its employees' vested interest in the plan would become taxable on a current basis, public employers worried very little about qualification, and taxes were not levied on pension plan participants. IRS even wavered in its certainty that some of the provisions applied. In 1977, IRS imposed a moratorium on adverse qualification decisions based on nondiscrimination requirements while it reconsidered whether the requirements applied to state and local plans.[1] In 1989, the moratorium was lifted (see discussion below).

Federal Regulation

ERISA established new vesting, funding, and participation requirements for pension plans, to be administered by IRS, and reporting, disclosure, and fiduciary standards and termination insurance, to be administered by the U.S. Department of Labor (DOL). Except for the IRC provision (section 415) that established limits on benefits and contributions, public employee plans were virtually exempt from this law's provisions. Congress was concerned about public-sector plans, however, and in the ERISA legislation authorized a major study of public employee retirement systems, which was completed four years later.

---

[1] Letter from Internal Revenue Service responding to questions concerning the tax qualification of public employee retirement systems (15 August 1977). See also U.S. Congress, 1978.

This study, *The Pension Task Force Report on Public Employee Retirement Systems*, reported serious deficiencies in public plans—including plans covering federal employees—in the areas of funding, reporting and disclosure, and fiduciary practices. (Later the same year, the federal government imposed reporting and disclosure requirements on pension systems for its own employees.) Based on the study, proposals partly or wholly paralleling ERISA were advanced for federal regulation of other public plans.

State and local governments argued vigorously against federal action to regulate their plans. They felt the task force report greatly exaggerated the deficiencies of state and local plans, and that they were as capable as the federal government of dealing with any existing problems. Federal interest in imposing ERISA-like vesting and funding standards on public plans quickly waned as it became obvious that such action was fraught with implications for the revenue requirements of the various jurisdictions. Even the imposition of reporting, disclosure, and fiduciary standards, as set forth in the Public Employees Retirement Income Security Act of 1980 (PERISA) and the Public Employee Pension Plan Reporting and Accountability Act of 1982 (PEPPRA), was opposed by state and local jurisdictions, which viewed it as an unwarranted and unjustified intrusion on their sovereignty.[2]

The federal government's interest in state and local plans, together with emerging fiscal problems in some jurisdictions (of which New York City's insolvency crisis was the most dramatic example), added impetus to a movement already under way in some states to put their own houses in order. Of particular concern were nonactuarial funding practices (pay-as-you-go plans), the lack of public disclosure of pension system costs, the diffusion of responsibility for pension matters, and ad hoc decisionmaking. To address these problems, the National Council of State Legislatures encouraged the establishment of pension commissions. By 1988 permanent pension commissions and legislative retirement committees had been formed in 21 states for the purpose of providing "guidance to public executives, administrators, and legislators in developing public retirement objectives and principles, identifying problems and areas of abuse, projecting costs of existing systems and modifications to those systems and designing and implementing pension reform programs" (A. Foster Higgins & Co., Inc., 1988). In some cases the pension commissions also oversee

---

[2]See Advisory Commission on Intergovernmental Relations, 1980; U.S. Congress, 1983; and National Council on Teacher Retirement, 1984.

nonpension benefit programs for public employees and serve as a buffer between the legislature and special interest groups.

While some observers continue to believe that state and local plans would benefit from the federal imposition of ERISA-like standards, considerable improvements have been made in state and local plans in the last decade. Several states that had historically taken a laissez-faire attitude toward local government plans have passed laws establishing minimum standards. (Pennsylvania, for example, mandated actuarial funding requirements for many local plans within its jurisdiction.) While seriously underfunded plans can still be found (primarily at the local level), the larger systems tend to be reasonably well financed. A recent study concluded that "although it would be difficult to deny that PERS [public employee retirement systems] have substantial unfunded liabilities, the data also suggest that amounts are being accumulated to cover these liabilities" (Public Pension and Benefits Consortium, 1987). Furthermore, 81 percent of large systems (and 78 percent of all systems) currently set employer contributions on an actuarial basis, with contributions most often established as a level percentage of payroll. Seventy-six percent of all systems conduct actuarial valuations on an annual basis and 97 percent conduct them at least every three years (Public Pension and Benefits Consortium, 1987).

The existence of large public pension funds presents a continuing temptation to financially pressed public executives. Raids on such funds or temporary cessation of contributions are proposed from time to time to alleviate budgetary crises. The difference between today's environment and that of the past is that these proposals are widely reported and publicly debated. ERISA's influence in the private sector and the discussion of ERISA-like requirements for the public sector have raised the level of awareness of pension plan issues generally and of the necessity for sound funding practices in particular.

Investment Practices

Recently, public employee pension systems have gained national attention not for their funding or reporting deficiencies but for their economic power in the marketplace and their investment practices. During the last decade, many jurisdictions have loosened investment restrictions on their pension plans, allowing them to pursue more aggressive investment strategies in order to maximize yield. While the pension plans have been largely successful in that goal, their emergence from the backwaters of public finance into the limelight of the nation's economy has introduced many new issues, including the propriety of using public pension fund investments to further social goals (for example, bringing pressure on the South African government to end apartheid); to shore up the local, state, or regional economy (targeted investing); or to finance such controversial measures as hostile takeovers and leveraged buyouts. Public nonfederal pension funds have combined assets of more than $700 billion, and, although these assets are less than those of private pension plans, they are concentrated in fewer hands and thus can have a more focused impact (Federal Reserve Board, 1989). Recently, some public plans have begun to press for an active role in the corporate governance of the firms in which they invest and to initiate concerted action in support of social goals.

Ironically, public pension plans' great financial success has caused some plan administrators to rethink their opposition to federal regulation, as least in the area of fiduciary standards. Resisting pressure to use pension funds for worthy purposes unrelated to their primary purpose of paying benefits to plan participants can be very difficult at the jurisdiction level. Thus, some plan fiduciaries have begun to see federal regulation establishing fiduciary standards as potentially more protective than intrusive.

Tax Laws and Public-Sector Plans

While enactment of specific federal legislation governing public-sector benefit plans does not appear imminent, the federal government is showing renewed interest in such plans. In May 1989, the IRS addressed public-sector plans by lifting its 12 year moratorium on adverse qualification decisions based on discrimination requirements. The IRS determined that governmental and church plans must satisfy certain nondiscrimination requirements (*Federal Register*, 1989). Furthermore, in May 1990, rules issued by IRS on coverage, participation, and general nondiscrimination explicitly provide transition rules for governmental plans to give these units sufficient time to come into compliance (*Federal Register*, 1990). On the legislative level, a series of tax laws enacted in the mid and late 1980s modified the legal framework for benefit plans, and many of their provisions—unlike those of ERISA—were made applicable to governmental plans. The Tax Reform Act of 1986 (TRA '86) was particularly significant for the public sector.

Most public employee retirement plans are contributory, and TRA '86 repealed a special "three year recovery" of contributions rule that had applied primarily to public employees. Where public employees had earlier been granted up to three years of tax-free benefit payments to recover their own post-tax investment in pension plans, TRA '86 stipulated that their benefits were to be treated as partly taxable and partly tax free, based on an "exclusion ratio." Furthermore, if those employees received a preretirement starting date distribution, even if the distribution equaled their accumulated contributions, it would be treated as partly a tax-free return of contributions and partly a taxable distribution.[3] The ratio of the tax-free to the taxable part of the distribution would reflect the ratio of the total employee contributions to the total value of the plan's expected benefits. In effect, the favorable tax situation that many public employees in contributory retirement systems had enjoyed at the time of retirement was virtually eliminated.

While TRA '86 imposed strict new requirements on public plans in some areas, it continued to recognize the special status of governmental plans in others. Specifically, governmental plans were allowed to remain under pre-TRA '86 section 415 limits regarding maximum benefits and actuarial reductions for retirement before a specified age. Because retirement at younger ages (for example, age 55) is common in the public sector, compliance with the new, more severe section 415 rules would have forced some public jurisdictions to reduce benefits to current employees below promised amounts, violating pension plan law and in some cases constitutional law that prohibits cutbacks in public employees' benefits. Special section 415 rules were also enacted for police and firefighters, who typically retire at even younger ages than other public workers.

Because some state and local plans had promised benefits even beyond those allowed under pre-TRA '86 limits, an additional option was provided under the Technical and Miscellaneous Revenue Act of 1988 (TAMRA). This law allowed jurisdictions to "grandfather" and excuse any section 415 violations resulting from benefit payments made to employees who became plan members before January 1, 1990, *provided* the jurisdiction elected to apply the new section 415 limits applicable to private plans to all future plan members. Understandably, many state and local plans viewed the TAMRA election opportunity as a mixed blessing.

---

[3]A group of federal retirees is challenging the taxation of the lump-sum payment of their post-tax contributions to the Civil Service Retirement System in the U.S. courts.

Conclusion

How vigorously IRS will enforce its new requirements on public pension plans and how much further Congress may be willing to go in regulating the compensation practices of other public entities is unclear. It does appear, however, that the days of "benign neglect" are over. While public employee pension plans continue to be governed primarily by the specific laws of the jurisdiction authorizing them, plan administrators are beginning to feel the constraint of federal tax law in ways that their private-sector counterparts have experienced for many years.

Bibliography

A. Foster Higgins & Co., Inc. *Pension Commission Clearinghouse, Report on the State Pension Commissions*. New York: A Foster Higgins & Co., Inc., 1988.

Advisory Commission on Intergovernmental Relations. *State and Local Pension Systems*. Washington, DC: Advisory Commission on Intergovernmental Relations, 1980.

Federal Register (18 May 1989): 21437.

Federal Register (14 May 1990): 19897, 19935, and 19947.

Federal Reserve Board. *Flow of Funds, Quarterly Levels, December 1989*. Washington, DC: Federal Reserve Board, 1989.

National Council on Teacher Retirement. *Report of the National Council on Teacher Retirement on State Law Conformance with PEPPRA*. Austin, TX: National Council on Teacher Retirement, 1984.

Public Pension and Benefits Consortium. Government Finance Research Center of the Government Finance Officers Association. *Public Pension Accounting and Reporting: A Survey of Current Practices*. Chicago: Government Finance Officers Association, 1987.

U.S. Congress. House. Committee on Education and Labor. *Pension Task Force Report on Public Employee Retirement Systems*, Appendix A. Washington, DC: U.S. Government Printing Office, 1978.

U.S. Congress. House. Committee on Education and Labor. Subcommittee on Labor-Management Relations. *Hearings on the Public Employee Retirement Income Security Act of 1982*. Washington, DC: U.S. Government Printing Office, 1983.

38. Defined Benefit Pension Plans

Introduction

According to a 1987 survey of state and local governments, 93 percent of all state and local employees are covered by defined benefit pension plans (U.S. Department of Labor, 1988). Approximately 100 percent of federal workers serving under nontemporary appointments are also covered by these plans.

Public employee defined benefit plans as a group are readily distinguishable from private pension plans as a group by six salient characteristics.

Contributions

The majority of public employees are required to contribute to their defined benefit plans (78 percent of state and local plan participants and participants in both major federal plans for civilian employees). Virtually all participants pay a specified percentage of earnings. Teachers frequently contribute from 6 percent to 8 percent of pay, and police and firefighters contribute at even higher rates (U.S. Department of Labor, 1988). Contributions for other state and local employees tend to fall in the 3 percent to 6 percent range. Federal workers in the major stand-alone retirement system contribute 7 percent of pay, while those in the newer plan for employees subject to Social Security pay 0.8 percent of pay, up to the maximum Social Security wage base ($51,300 in 1990).

Most public employees contribute on an after-tax basis. In 1987, contributions to defined benefit plans reduced taxable income for only 13 percent of participants in state and local plans (U.S. Department of Labor, 1988). Contributions to federal defined benefit plans are also made on an after-tax basis.

There is some indication that the number of state and local employees making pretax contributions may be increasing significantly. Prior to 1981, the Internal Revenue Code (IRC) did not allow pretax contributions to defined benefit plans to which the employers also made contributions. Such contributions are now possible under section 414(h). Under this provision, the employee's salary is reduced by the contributed amount, which the employer "picks up" and transforms into an employer contribution. (These plans are referred to as employer "pick up" plans.) The number of state systems that allow employers to pick up employee contributions has grown from 8 out of 85 surveyed in 1984 to 59 out of 85 in 1989, according to a recent study (Testin and Snell, 1989). It is possible that employer "pick up" plans may become even more popular now that the tax-free recovery of contributions at the time of retirement (the three year rule) is no longer allowed.

Retirement Age

Public employee retirement plans are characterized by the availability of unreduced benefits to workers at relatively early ages. Thirty-eight percent of all state and local employees can retire without regard to age after satisfying a service requirement, which is usually 30 years. Twenty-two percent can retire on attaining age 55, usually with a 30 year service requirement (U.S. Department of Labor, 1988). The vast majority of all federal civilian employees can also retire at age 55 with 30 years of service, although for post-1983 hires covered under the Federal Employees Retirement System the minimum age will eventually increase to 57. Even earlier retirement eligibility (sometimes with no minimum age) is common for law enforcement and firefighting personnel at all levels of government, usually on completion of a service requirement of 20 to 25 years. Not all public employees are eligible for retirement at younger ages, however. Nearly one-third of state and local employees are in plans with minimum age requirements of 60 to 65 (U.S. Department of Labor, 1988).

Benefit Formula

There is near unanimity in the public sector in the use of terminal earnings based formulas for benefit computations. Terminal earnings are usually defined as the average of three years, with the three consecutive highest-earning years of a career the most often designated. (For law enforcement and firefighting personnel, the final year's earnings are sometimes used, with earnings including basic salary plus other items such as overtime pay.) Terminal earnings formulas pay a flat percentage of earnings per year of service. The percentage may vary by service or by earnings but usually falls between 1.5 percent and 2.25 percent (for police and firefighters between 1.5 percent and 2.75 percent) (U.S. Department of Labor, 1988). Since terminal earnings formulas base the employee's retirement benefit on his or her most recent (or highest) salary, they implicitly compensate for all of the wage inflation that has occurred during the employee's career and operate to replace a portion of his or her income at the time of retirement.

Integration with Social Security

While approximately 73 percent of state and local employees are covered by Social Security, only 18 percent are in plans whose benefit provisions are explicity integrated with Social Security (U.S. Department of Labor, 1988). It is apparent that some accommodation has been made in the plans that are not explicitly integrated, however, since, according to Bureau of Labor Statistics computations, the earnings of the employees in these plans are replaced at a lower rate, on average, than the earnings of employees in plans without Social Security coverage. Nevertheless, when Social Security benefits are added to benefits paid by the employer-sponsored plan, the result is replacement rates in excess of those available to non-Social Security covered public employees. These rates are also in excess of those available to almost all private-sector employees, prompting the criticism that they are overly generous and represent an inefficient use of resources (chart 38.1). However, these replacement rates are achieved with substantial employee contributions.

When Congress enacted a new retirement plan for federal employees hired after 1983 (and covered by Social Security), it also chose to avoid explicit integration. The benefit formula was reduced vis-à-vis the one used in the old system in recognition of the fact that benefits would also be paid by Social Security, but it still applied equally at all salary levels. Since normal retirement age occurs prior to the age at which a person becomes eligible for Social Security, an estimated Social Security benefit is payable from the time of retirement to age 62. The new system's combined pension/Social Security benefit exceeds the replacement rate of the old stand alone system at the lower salary levels. (The assumption is that higher-salaried employees would be better able to augment their defined benefits by voluntary contributions to the Thrift Savings Plan.)

The disinclination to integrate pension benefits explicitly with Social Security in the public sector is striking. Integration is complex, difficult to communicate to employees, and apparently at odds with the Civil Service egalitarian tradition. Moreover, salary scales tend to be very compressed in the public sector, with huge numbers of employees bunched in a very narrow pay range. All of these factors probably militate against integration. Since nonintegration yields higher total benefits in many cases, it is often preferred by employee

CHART 38.1

Replacement Rates under Pension Plans Based on Final Yearly Earnings of $25,000, by Years of Service and Social Security Coverage, State and Local Governments, 1987

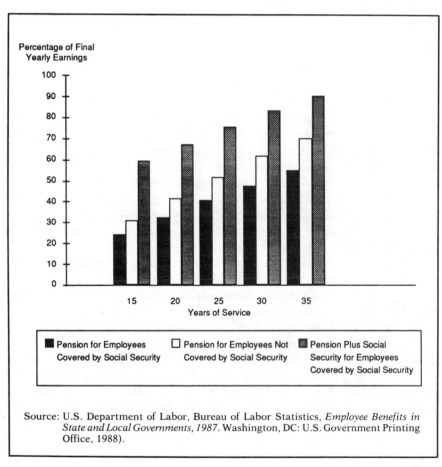

Source: U.S. Department of Labor, Bureau of Labor Statistics, *Employee Benefits in State and Local Governments, 1987.* Washington, DC: U.S. Government Printing Office, 1988).

groups that lobby the legislatures on this issue. The fact that both Social Security and almost all public plans are contributory gives these views weight and reduces the burden on the taxpaying public.

Cost-of-Living Increases

Public employee plans are widely known for their automatic cost-of-living adjustments (COLAs). Both large federal plans have automatic annual adjustments tied to the consumer price index (CPI), although the newer program adjusts by less than the full change in the CPI, and the adjustment applies only to retirees aged 62 or over and to the disabled (retirees and survivors). Among state and local jurisdictions, 51 percent of employees are in plans that have automatic adjustments, with a majority having annual adjustments equal to the change in the CPI but subject to a maximum, usually of from 2 percent to 3 percent (U.S. Department of Labor, 1988). In those states that do not have automatic COLAs, the legislatures may enact periodic adjustments. Table 38.1 shows the distribution of general state retirement systems by types and postretirement adjustments.

The prevalence of automatic COLAs in the public sector contrasts sharply with the lack of such increases in private plans. In sponsoring defined benefit plans, private employers assume a large financial risk, and few are willing to commit to postretirement benefit adjustments, regardless of their firm's profitability. The public sector—which comrises more or less permanent entities that rely on the tax base rather than on operating results for their resources—has historically been more willing to accept this burden. Indexation of benefits can be extremely expensive, however, and full indexation, as provided in the older federal pension system, can account for one-half the cost of the entire plan. COLAs can also be a tempting target for budget cutters. In 1985, Congress decided for budgetary reasons not to pay the 1986 COLA to which federal retirees were otherwise entitled.

Disability Retirement

A final distinguishing characteristic of public-sector defined benefit plans is their treatment of disability. Many public-sector plans originated as disability retirement plans, and in the public sector disability remains primarily a retirement system matter. Approximately 8 out of 10 state and local employees and virtually all federal employees are in plans that allow immediate retirement based on disability. Some state and local employees also have access to long-term disability insurance benefits, and where this is the case, the retirement and disability benefits are usually offset so that the disabled employee does not receive combined benefits greater than his or her predisability salary (U.S. Department of Labor, 1988).

Relationship to Direct Compensation

Defined benefit pension plans are often the most generous part of public-sector compensation, and some view them as "compensating"

TABLE 38.1
Distribution of General State Retirement Systems by Types of Postretirement Adjustment Plans

States with Ad Hoc Adjustments

Alabama	Delaware	Kansas	Montana	North Dakota	Texas
Alaska	Indiana	Kentucky	New Hampshire	Oklahoma	West Virginia
Arizona	Iowa	Massachusetts	New York	Pennsylvania	Wyoming

States with Supplements Based on Favorable Experience

Michigan	Minnesota	Nebraska	Wisconsin

States with Automatic Annual Increases

Arkansas, 3%	Hawaii, 2½%	Illinois, 3%	Rhode Island, 3%

States with Automatic Cost-of-Living Adjustments

State	Maximum Annual Benefit Increase	State	Maximum Annual Benefit Increase
California	2% (also IDDA benefits)[a]	New Jersey	60% of rise in CPI
Colorado	3%	New Mexico	3%
Connecticut	3%	North Carolina	4%
Florida	3%	Ohio	3%
Georgia	3%	Oregon	2%

314

State	Provision	State	Provision
Idaho	1% (additional 5% may be authorized)	South Carolina	4% (if CPI rises 3% or more)
Louisiana	3%	South Dakota	50% of rise in CPI to maximum of 3%
Maine		Tennessee	3%
Maryland	4%	Utah	4%
Mississippi	Old system—unlimited New system—3% 2½%	Vermont	50% of rise in CPI to maximum of 5% (new plan)
Missouri	5% (minimum 4%; maximum 5% based on 80% of rise in CPI;[b] total increases limited to 50%)	Virginia	5% (first 3% rise in CPI plus one-half of each percentage increase from 3% to 7%)
Nevada	2%/3% (2% beginning in 4th year and 3% beginning in 10th year)	Washington	3% (for PERS[c] II)

Source: Martin E. Segal Company, *Retiree Health Care Costs and Post Retirement Supplementation for Retired New York Public Employees, Report to the Permanent Commission on Public Employee Pension and Retirement Systems, State of New York* (New York: Martin E. Segal Company, 1989).

[a]California provides a supplemental COLA through an investment dividend disbursement account (IDDA). Earnings on employee contributions in excess of actuarial interest rates are used to help maintain the purchasing power of the retirement benefit.

[b]Consumer policy index.

[c]Public Employees Retirement System.

Note: Many of the state retirement systems with automatic adjustment plans have also produced ad hoc benefit increases.

315

for restrictions on direct pay. However, deliberate tradeoffs between current and deferred compensation are difficult to document. It is true that public employees' pay is often a controversial political issue (and represents a current expense) and that enhancements to pension plans are less easily understood by the general public (and represent a future expense). For this reason pension enhancements may sometimes be easier to achieve politically. However, to the extent that public employee benefits are legislated over many years by different public officials, it is probably a mistake to attribute too precise an intent to them. They are more likely a reflection of the total environment in which they have evolved than of any sustained design objective.

Bibliography

Martin E. Segal Company. *Retiree Health Care Costs and Post Retirement Supplementation for Retired New York Public Employees, Report to the Permanent Commission on Public Employee Pension and Retirement Systems, State of New York*. New York: Martin E. Segal Company, 1989.

Testin, Blair, and Ronald K. Snell. *Comparative Statistics of Major State Retirement Systems, 1984–1988*. Washington, DC: National Conference of State Legislatures, 1989.

U.S. Department of Labor. Bureau of Labor Statistics. *Employee Benefits in State and Local Governments, 1987*. Washington, DC: U.S. Government Printing Office, 1988.

39. Defined Contribution Pension Plans

Introduction

No federal employees and relatively few state and local employees have defined contribution plans as primary retirement vehicles. The Bureau of Labor Statistics found a total of 9 percent of state and local employees had defined contribution plans, 8 percent had money-purchase plans, and 1 percent had thrift and savings plans in 1987 (U.S. Department of Labor, 1988).

TIAA-CREF Plans

Teachers in public colleges and universities are probably the group of employees most likely to have a defined contribution plan as their primary plan. Many public jurisdictions provide these plans for higher education employees through the Teachers Insurance and Annuity Association and the College Retirement Equities Fund (TIAA-CREF).[1] Since most private colleges and universities sponsor TIAA-CREF plans for their teaching staffs, participation by public jurisdictions provides mobility within the profession across public-private lines without loss of retirement benefits. The immediate vesting that characterizes these plans also facilitates mobility. In some jurisdictions, TIAA-CREF plans are the only option available to higher education employees, while in others the TIAA-CREF plan is offered as an alternative to participation in a plan for other public employees.

TIAA-CREF plans are an example of a unique type of defined contribution plan available to public schools at all educational levels and to certain other public entities, such as hospitals, that may be qualified for tax purposes under Internal Revenue Code section 403(b). For more information about section 403(b) plans, refer to chapter 11.

Bibliography

Employee Benefit Research Institute. *Fundamentals of Employee Benefit Programs for Education Employees*. Washington DC: EBRI, 1987.

U.S. Department of Labor. Bureau of Labor Statistics. *Employee Benefits in State and Local Governments, 1987*. Washington, DC: U.S. Government Printing Office, 1988.

---

[1]For a discussion of TIAA-CREF plans, see Employee Benefit Research Institute, 1987.

40. Supplemental Savings Plans

Introduction

The availability of supplemental, tax-deferred savings plans is fairly widespread in the public sector, but the use of such vehicles by eligible employees is not. According to the Bureau of Labor Statistics, in 1987 only 17 percent of state and local employees participated in savings plans similar to those available in the private sector (U.S. Department of Labor, 1988). While the number may have increased slightly since 1987, more limited, recent surveys continue to show similar participation rates.

There are three different types of tax-deferred savings plans available to state and local employees, and they are defined and controlled by different sections of the Internal Revenue Code (IRC). Some employees are eligible for more than one type. When an employee makes elective salary deferrals under more than one plan, the deferrals are combined for the purpose of determining whether a maximum limitation has been exceeded.

Section 403(b) Plans

As discussed in chapter 39, section 403(b) plans are sometimes used as basic defined contribution retirement plans. They may also be used as supplemental savings plans. In both cases, they are available only to public schools and certain other tax-exempt organizations and agencies.

Section 401(k) Plans

Prior to 1986, section 401(k) arrangements, the popular cash or deferred arrangements for private-sector employees, were also proliferating in state and local governments. The Tax Reform Act of 1986 (TRA '86) prohibited any further increase in the number of these plans in state and local jurisdictions but "grandfathered" those established prior to May 6, 1986. Approximately 16 states currently have such plans. One reason given for eliminating these plans in state and local governments was that a vehicle already existed that was designed specifically for public-sector workers (specifically, section 457 plans).

In the same year that the 401(k) option was removed for state and local jurisdictions, a similar plan—the Federal Thrift Savings Plan—

was authorized for federal employees. This plan is extensively described in the Federal Employees Retirement System Act of 1986, which established the new pension system for federal workers hired after 1983, rather than in the IRC. It is linked to the IRC by the limitation on elective deferrals (10 percent of pay, not to exceed the 401(k) dollar limit). It was also initially subject to the nondiscrimination requirements applicable to 401(k) arrangements, but that provision was later repealed. The plan provides an automatic contribution of 1 percent of pay to all employees under the new retirement system and calls for matching contributions up to a total of 5 percent of pay. Three investment options are available. Old-system employees are allowed to defer up to 5 percent of pay under the plan, but they receive no automatic or matching contributions. In August 1989, the participation rate was 50.5 percent for employees under the new system and 23.5 percent for employees under the old system (Causey, 1989). The Thrift Savings Plan is the only tax-deferred savings plan available to federal employees.

Section 457 Plans

IRC section 457 deals specifically with deferred compensation for state and local employees. Until TRA '86 broadened its coverage to encompass employees of tax-exempt organizations generally, public jurisdictions were the only entities authorized to establish plans under this provision.

Section 457 plans are similar to the previously discussed tax-deferred savings plans in that deferred contributions are not taxed as current income but only when they are ultimately received. They differ, however, in that deferred funds remain the property of the sponsoring employer and subject to the claims of the employer's creditors during the deferral period. As a rule, there are no matching contributions in section 457 plans. A variety of investment vehicles are usually available.

Section 457 plans are subject to the following additional requirements:

- A deferred compensation agreement must be made prior to the beginning of the pay period involved.

- Amounts deferred can only be made available at termination or in the event of an unforeseeable emergency.

- Amounts deferred are limited to no more than 33⅓ percent of includable compensation, or $7,500, if that is less. Includable compensation means

320

compensation for service performed for an employer that is currently includable in compensation and does not include amounts excludable under the deferred compensation plan.

- Any amounts being deferred under a 401(k) arrangement, if applicable, or under a section 403(b) plan must be taken into account in determining whether the overall $7,500 limit has been exceeded. The exclusion allowance of a section 403(b) plan and the includable compensation on which it is figured are affected by amounts deferred under section 457 plans.

Section 457 plans are widely offered by public employers, but participation is relatively low. A 1987 survey of 98 public employers indicated that 70 percent offered section 457 plans but that only 16 percent of eligible employees actually participated in them (Charles D. Spencer & Associates, 1988). Several factors may account for the low participation rate: the relatively modest salaries of public employees, the fact that they make substantial contributions to their defined benefit pension plans, and the lack of employer matching contributions.

In 1987, the Internal Revenue Service (IRS) proposed to broaden the interpretation of deferred compensation under section 457 to include a number of benefits that previously were treated as nonelective and not subject to taxation (IRS Notice 87-13). Under this interpretation, state and local employees could have been required to pay taxes on sick, vacation, severance, and compensatory leave and disability and death benefits at the time they were accrued instead of when they were actually received. After protest from the affected jurisdictions and their employees, IRS withdrew the proposal (National Conference of State Legislatures, 1988). Furthermore, the Technical and Miscellaneous Revenue Act of 1988 specifically prohibited the broader interepretation of section 457 proposed by IRS.

Bibliography

Causey, Mike. "Savings Worth Billions." *The Washington Post*, September 9, 1989, p. B2.

Charles D. Spencer & Associates. "Majority of Government Employers Offer Sec. 457 Plans, Buck Survey Finds Only 16% of Eligibles Are Enrolled." *Spencer's Research Reports*. Chicago: Charles D. Spencer & Associates, 1988.

National Conference of State Legislatures. "NCSL Applauds IRS Decision on State and Local Employee Fringe Benefits." News release, 9 June 1988.

U.S. Department of Labor. Bureau of Labor Statistics. *Employee Benefits in State and Local Governments, 1987*. Washington, DC: U.S. Government Printing Office, 1988.

41. Health Insurance

Introduction

Employer-sponsored health insurance is almost universally available to public employees. Moreover, coverage tends to be very broad, encompassing all of the traditional categories of medical expense, including hospital room and board, physicians' services, and diagnostic x-ray and laboratory services. Mental health care and coverage for treatment of alcoholism and drug abuse—although subject to limitations—are available to nearly all participants in state and local plans and to all federal employees. Coverage of dental care is also available to a majority of public employees.

One salient characteristic of public employee health plans is that employees usually become eligible to participate immediately on being hired. This is true at the local, state, and federal levels. In situations in which waiting periods apply, they tend to be three months or less (U.S. Department of Labor, 1988).

Postemployment Coverage

State and local employers are subject to the continuation of coverage provisions of the Consolidated Omnibus Budget Reconciliation Act of 1985 (COBRA), as amended. While the federal government, as employer, was not originally subject to the act, similar requirements were subsequently imposed on federal agencies by separate legislation. (For details of COBRA's requirements, refer to chapter 19.)

Retiree Coverage

Slightly less than one-half of state and local employees participating in health plans receive wholly or partially employer-provided health benefits during retirement. (Retiree coverage appears to be more common in collectively bargained plans.) Federal workers enrolled in a plan under the Federal Employees Health Benefits Program for the five years immediately preceding retirement may continue coverage during retirement with the same level of employer-paid premiums as active workers. Where postretirement coverage exists in public plans, it almost always continues for the retiree's lifetime. (If a survivor annuity is payable, coverage may continue for the deceased worker's survivor.) In most cases, the level of coverage for retirees is the same as that for active workers, although employer-sponsored benefits are usually coordinated with Medicare for retirees aged 65 or over.

Types of Plans

In the public sector, the law authorizing a health insurance program for employees sometimes sets forth the number and types of plans to be offered and the funding intermediaries that may be used. A majority of public employees are covered by traditional fee-for-service plans. According to the Bureau of Labor Statistics (BLS), among state and local workers participating in medical plans in 1987, 27 percent had policies underwritten by Blue Cross and Blue Shield, 17 percent were insured by commercial carriers, and 17 percent were in self-insured plans (U.S. Department of Labor, 1988). In 1989, slightly more than one-third of federal civilian employees participating in the Federal Employees Health Benefits Program were enrolled with Blue Cross and Blue Shield, and approximately 24 percent were in plans underwritten by commerical carriers. (Technically, the federal government does not insure any plans for its employees, but several employee organizations that participate in the federal program self-insure their plans.)

A relatively high percentage of public employees are enrolled in health maintenance organizations (HMOs). BLS reported that 25 percent of state and local employees were enrolled in HMOs in 1987. A 1989 study of the 50 states found that 32 percent of the employees covered by the 50 state plans were enrolled in HMOs (Mackin, 1989). State and local governments were subject to mandate by HMOs under the original Health Maintenance Organization Act of 1973. In addition, some states legislated their own independent dual-choice laws. The federal government's program for civilian workers has included HMOs and has been continuously open for participation by new HMOs since its enactment in 1959. Approximately 25 percent of federal civilian employees were enrolled in HMOs in 1989 (U.S. Office of Personnel Management, 1989).

The combination of public policy favorable to HMOs and the inherent political difficulty involved in limiting the number that can participate has led to a strong representation of these organizations in public-sector programs. However, the number of HMOs offered by public plan sponsors varies greatly. One survey shows a range among state government employers of from 0 to 28. In 1989, the federal government offered approximately 350 HMOs to its employees nationwide. Reportedly, several states are working to consolidate their HMO offerings and reduce the overall number.[1] Others are still adding plans (table 41.1). (For more about HMOs, see chapter 24.)

Preferred provider organizations (PPOs) are also available under some public employee programs. While the 1987 BLS data reported 7 percent of state and local employees in medical plans were enrolled in PPOs, that number is likely to have increased because the number of PPO plans in the overall health care market has greatly increased in the last several years. (Refer to chapter 25 for more about PPOs.)

Contributions

Among state and local plans, it is common for the employer to pay the entire premium for the employees' coverage but to require a contribution from employees who elect coverage for their dependents. The 1987 BLS survey showed that 35 percent of participants contributed to their own coverage, whereas 71 percent made a contribution for dependents (U.S. Department of Labor, 1988). However, the incidence of noncontributory coverage for the worker may be declining as state and local jurisdictions, like all other employers, seek to manage their health care costs. A survey of state-employer benefit plans found that 24 states paid the entire premium for employee coverage in 1989, whereas 27 did so in 1987 (Workplace Economics, Inc., 1989). At the federal level, substantial contributions (of about 29 percent on average) are required of all participants regardless of the coverage selected.

Cost Management

During the past decade, many employers sponsoring employee health plans have struggled with the problem of how to manage what appear to be ever-escalating costs. In 1982 the massive federal employee program introduced mandatory coinsurance and deductibles in all health plan offerings in an effort to curb utilization and, consequently, costs. Public employers have tried many of the same strategies that private employers have used to eliminate unnecessary service and to control costs. These strategies include second surgical opinions, hospital precertification programs, concurrent review and discharge planning, incentives for outpatient surgery, audit of hospital and doc-

---

[1] *HealthWeek* (14 August 1989) reported that five states had hired contractors to assist with consolidating HMO offerings to public employees.

TABLE 41.1
Participants in State Employee Health Benefit Plans as of January 1989

State	Employees Covered by Plan[a]	Retirees Covered by Plan[b]	Number of HMOs offered	HMO Participation Employees enrolled in HMOs	
				number	percentage
Alabama	33,300	7,000	1	3,400	10%
Alaska	12,500	9,900	0	0	0
Arizona	41,100	1,800	4	23,700	58
Arkansas	18,100	3,500	0	0	0
California[c]	210,800	79,300	28	175,900	83
Colorado	22,700	[d]	2	11,000	48
Connecticut	56,000	17,000	9	11,900	21
Delaware	26,000	9,000	2	7,000	27
Florida	106,500	12,400	19	28,700	27
Georgia	161,000	33,000	4	13,000	8
Hawaii	36,800	20,800	3	11,100	30
Idaho	14,500	2,100	2	1,300	9
Illinois	118,600	45,700	17	58,100	49
Indiana	33,800	0	6	15,400	46
Iowa	28,100	3,100	7	4,500	16
Kansas	35,500	7,200	5	13,200	37
Kentucky	113,000	19,700	8	53,000	47
Louisiana	71,100	25,300	6	30,400	43
Maine	15,800	6,600	0	0	0
Maryland	66,000	18,000	10	24,700	37

(continued)

State				
Massachusetts	95,600	34,800	18	62,100	65
Michigan	59,600	22,400	18	23,000	39
Minnesota	52,900	8,300	8	29,100	55
Mississippi	44,000	3,500	0	0	0
Missouri	36,800	5,300	7	8,500	23
Montana	10,200	1,800	0	0	0
Nebraska	13,000	100	4	4,000	31
Nevada	17,500	2,000	1	4,500	26
New Hampshire	10,000	4,800	3	800	8
New Jersey	249,700	54,100	20	72,500	29
New Mexico	17,000	2,100	1	7,000	41
New York[c]	241,000	79,100	27	66,300	28
North Carolina	214,600	63,000	2	17,200	8
North Dakota	13,000	1,700	3	1,200	9
Ohio	52,800	[d]	28	32,200	61
Oklahoma	43,700	26,500	4	10,400	24
Oregon	26,000	2,500	7	10,000	38
—Bubb Plan	17,000	2,000	5	4,000	24
Pennsylvania	86,600	45,900	22	12,400	14
Rhode Island	18,400	12,900	4	5,000	27
South Carolina	131,400	31,700	2	10,200	8
South Dakota	12,100	1,500	0	0	0
Tennessee	58,800	2,600	9	7,900	13
Texas	119,600	24,500	23	50,500	42
Utah	12,400	3,900	2	2,300	19
Vermont	6,400	1,800	1	800	13

(continued)

TABLE 41.1

Participants in State Employee Health Benefit Plans as of January 1989

(Continued)

State	Employees Covered by Plan[a]	Retirees Covered by Plan[b]	Number of HMOs offered	HMO Participation Employees enrolled in HMOs	
				number	percentage
Virginia	92,600	15,000	4	8,800	10%
Washington	74,000	15,500	10	43,500	59
West Virginia	81,300	20,100	3	2,200	3
Wisconsin	53,600	14,300	28	45,500	85
Wyoming	10,100	2,000	1	300	3

Source: Martin E. Segal Company, *1989 Survey of State Employee Health Benefit Plans* (New York: Martin E. Segal Company, 1989).
[a] Approximate total number of covered employees, including employees enrolled in HMOs.
[b] Approximate total number of covered retirees.
[c] Participants shown are state employees and retirees only (that is, figures exclude local employees and retirees).
[d] Retired state employees are covered by a separate health benefit plan for all retired members of the state public employees' retirement system.

tor bills, individual case management, home health care benefits, hospice benefits, wellness benefits, and mail order drug and preferred pharmacy programs.

Health care costs have continued to rise for both private and public employers despite their efforts to manage them. Recently, some employers in both sectors have attempted to curb utilization and price by using managed care arrangements. A few public jurisdictions have adopted point-of-service health plans under which the method of service delivery (fee for service, HMO, etc.) is selected at the time of treatment, with the expectation that most services will be provided under more cost-effective HMO or PPO arrangements. Other jurisdictions are encouraging employees to opt for HMOs by providing relatively greater financial support to those making this choice. Some smaller jurisdictions have tried negotiating favorable arrangements directly with providers. Finally, at least a few jurisdictions have ceased to offer traditional indemnity coverage altogether, relying instead exclusively on HMOs and PPOs.

While it is clear that some public jurisdictions have worked hard to bring health care expenditures under control, some studies show the public sector lagging behind private employers in this regard. A 1987 survey concluded that public jurisdictions continue to "insulate employees from the cost consequences of their decisions" (William M. Mercer-Meidinger, Inc., 1987). Furthermore, the authors concluded that public jurisdictions "are not as aggressive as the private sector in incorporating medical intervention practices into their plans, or in adopting programs to prevent disease and encourage healthy life styles," nor do they "take advantage of sophisticated data analysis techniques that can identify problems and thus lead to corrective measures." The study also noted that public employers are not active in local coalitions to control costs. A separate survey conducted in 1986 and 1987 of cities with populations of more than 100,000 yielded similar findings, indicating that cities were slower than the private sector to introduce deductibles and that only a small percentage had implemented other cost management measures (Moore, 1989).

One reason that public employers may be slower to implement cost management strategies is that plan administrators may lack authority to change contribution ratios, add or delete benefit categories, change the types of plans offered, or participate with other employers in group purchasing actions. In many cases, it may be necessary to consult legislative bodies and/or amend laws. (Particularly at the local level, collective bargaining agreements may also be involved.) Where this is the case, political forces necessarily come into play.

329

Public employees can hardly be expected to welcome efforts to have them "share in the cost consequences of their decisions" and insurer-provider groups may fight to retain existing practices that benefit them. The politics of health care are extremely complex and intense at every level of government, making it difficult to achieve quick resolution of even apparently minor issues.

Funding

In the public sector, as in the private sector, health care costs, including those for retirees, are treated as a current operating expense. Since public jurisdictions are not taxpaying entities, they could prefund benefits for retired workers without adverse tax consequences in much the same manner as pension benefits are prefunded. Recognizing and prefunding a future liability increases current costs, however, and few jurisdictions are in a position to do so. Currently, only a few states that provide retiree health insurance through their pension systems are partially prefunding postretirement medical benefits (A. Foster Higgins & Co., Inc., 1988).

The total unfunded liability for postretirement health benefits in the public sector is estimated to exceed $158.1 billion.[2] The existence of a similar liability and a proposed requirement to disclose that liability on the financial statements of the sponsoring employer have recently caused concern in the private sector. While there appears to be less concern about calculating or disclosing the liability among public jurisdictions, postretirement health benefits constitute a difficult political issue. Retiree groups are pressing for employer-supported benefits where they are not now available and for greater employer cost sharing where partial support is currently provided. This desire for greater support directly conflicts with many jurisdictions' fiscal problems. Seventy-eight percent of the respondents to a recent survey reported that they planned to pass on future increases in health care costs to retirees (William M. Mercer-Meidinger, Inc., 1987).

Bibliography

A. Foster Higgins & Co., Inc. *Pension Commission Clearinghouse, Report on State Pension Commissions.* New York: A. Foster Higgins & Co., Inc., 1988.

---

[2]Employee Benefit Research Institute estimate was revised in 1989 to reflect repeal of the Medicare Catastrophic Coverage Act of 1988.

Mackin, John P. *Summary of Findings, Martin E. Segal Company's 1989 Survey of State Employee Health Benefit Plans*. New York: Martin E. Segal Company, 1989.

Moore, Perry. "Health Care Cost Containment in Large American Cities." *Public Personnel Management* (Spring 1989).

U.S. Department of Labor. Bureau of Labor Statistics. *Employee Benefits in State and Local Governments, 1987*. Washington, DC: U.S. Government Printing Office, 1988.

U.S. Office of Personnel Management. Retirement and Insurance Group. *March 1989 Headcount Report*. Washington, DC: U.S. Office of Personnel Management, 1989.

William M. Mercer-Meidinger, Inc. *Health Cost Containment in the Public-Sector*. New York: William M. Mercer-Meidinger, Inc., 1987.

Workplace Economics, Inc. *1989 State Employee Benefits Survey*. Washington, DC: Workplace Economics, Inc., 1989.

42. Life Insurance

Introduction

Most public jurisdictions make group life insurance coverage available to their employees, and many pay all or a substantial part of the cost. According to the Bureau of Labor Statistics, in 1987, 85 percent of all state and local employees were covered by group life insurance funded wholly or partly by their employers. Coverage was expressed as flat dollar amounts (53 percent) somewhat more frequently than it was based on earnings formulas (45 percent). A majority of the flat dollar plans provided benefits in the $5,000 to $15,000 range. A more recent survey that related only to state employees indicated that 46 of the 50 states provide life insurance at no cost to the employee (Workplace Economics, Inc., 1989). In a majority of the states the amount of insurance is based either on the employee's salary or on a combination of salary and age. Dollar maximums are sometimes used in combination with a salary-based insurance amount. Fifteen states reported providing insurance in fixed amounts, with the benefit ranging from $2,000 to $18,000.

Coverage

Approximately 90 percent of federal employees participate in a centrally administered group life insurance program. The basic benefit equals the employee's salary rounded to the nearest thousand dollars plus $2,000 (although younger employees receive larger amounts). The employer pays one-third of the level cost (same cost per one-thousand dollars of coverage for all employees regardless of age) and the employee pays two-thirds. Additional coverages with a value of up to five times salary are made available on an employee-pay-all basis. As with many public employee plans, the basic coverage doubles in the case of accidental death and extends into retirement. (Under the federal plan and many state and local plans, coverage is reduced during retirement, however.) Eligibility for life insurance is immediate on being hired for federal employees and for 72 percent of other public workers.

Life insurance benefits are only one form of protection provided to the families of public-sector workers in the event of the wage earner's untimely death. Benefits for active employees' survivors are available to participants in the federal retirement systems and to 85 percent of participants in other public employee retirement plans. Some retirement systems also pay lump-sum benefits to survivors on an employee's death. Virtually all public employee retirement systems provide benefits for survivors of retired workers, at least on an optional basis.

Bibliography

U.S. Department of Labor. Bureau of Labor Statistics. *Employee Benefits in State and Local Governments, 1987*. Washington, DC: U.S. Government Printing Office, 1988.

Workplace Economics, Inc. *1989 State Employee Benefits Survey*. Washington, DC: Workplace Economics, Inc., 1989.

43. Leave Programs

Introduction

Leave, or paid time off from work, is a particularly significant benefit for public-sector workers. These workers are entitled to slightly more paid holidays on average than their private-sector counterparts, and annual and sick leave often play a somewhat different role in their total benefits package.

Sick Leave

The use of short-term disability insurance (accident and sickness plans) in the public sector is relatively rare (U.S. Department of Labor, 1989). Instead, employees rely on accumulations of paid sick leave to provide income during periods of illness and temporary disability. Most public employees accrue sick leave on an annual basis (the rate of accrual may vary by service) and are entitled to carry forward unused sick leave balances indefinitely and without limitation. Thus, long-service employees who have enjoyed reasonably good health can have large sick leave accumulations during the later years of their careers.

In some jurisdictions, employees are compensated for their unused sick leave on termination of employment. However, a more common practice is to compensate them for this unused leave at the time of retirement. This compensation can take several forms. Some states and the federal Civil Service Retirement System credit unused sick leave toward service for purposes of computing retirement benefits. (Under the federal system, this practice adds six months to the average employee's length of service.) Other states pay some percentage of unused sick leave or pay subject to certain dollar maximums. A few states credit the value of some amount of unused sick leave toward insurance premiums (Workplace Economics, Inc., 1989).

Annual Leave

Annual leave (vacation time) is generally accrued according to length of service, with average accruals for state and local employees of 12.0 days at 1 year of service, 17.7 days at 10 years of service, and 21.4 days at 20 years of service (U.S. Department of Labor, 1989). Federal employees accrue 13 days of annual leave during the first three years of employment, 20 days during years 3 through 14, and 26 days thereafter (Chapter 63, Title 5, U.S. Code). Unused annual leave can usually be carried forward to subsequent years, although the amount that can be carried forward is generally subject to a maximum. For most federal employees the maximum carryover is 30 days. (Members of the federal Senior Executive Service have unlimited carryover.) Three states allow leave to be carried over without limit. Among states specifying a maximum, Hawaii allows the greatest accumulation, at 90 days. Accumulated leave is generally cashed out on termination or retirement, although the cashout may be subject to a limit that is different from that imposed on accumulation (Workplace Economics, Inc., 1989).

Leave Sharing/Leave Banks

Since public employees often have leave accumulations in excess of their own needs, some jurisdictions have undertaken programs whereby employees can transfer leave to colleagues in need. Arizona recently passed a law to allow state employees to contribute annual leave to fellow employees in need of additional time off because of a serious illness or the serious illness of a family member. The transferred leave is increased or reduced proportionally by the differences in the salaries of the contributing and receiving employees (Bureau of National Affairs, 1988).

The federal government has also conducted several leave-sharing experiments among its employees. In April 1989, a new five year federal leave-sharing experiment was announced that will operate through a "leave bank" rather than a direct transfer of leave from one employee to another (*Federal Register*, 1989). Other public jurisdictions operate leave banks for their employees, with various rules for contribution and withdrawal.

Parental Leave

Paid leave—apart from annual and sick leave accumulations—that may be used to care for children is extremely rare in the public sector. Unpaid leave for parenting purposes, particularly maternity, is relatively common by comparison. Fifty-seven percent of state and local employees are covered by leave policies allowing unpaid maternity leave and 30 percent are covered by policies allowing unpaid paternity leave (U.S. Department of Labor, 1989). The periods of allowed unpaid leave vary greatly, with 12 months the most common interval.

336

While the leave system covering most federal employees does not recognize any separate category of unpaid leave for parenting, leave without pay may be allowed to fathers or mothers to care for dependent children at the discretion of the employing agency. In all jurisdictions, health and life insurance benefits generally continue during the period of unpaid leave, although the employee may have to pay amounts otherwise contributed by the employer.

An additional benefit not generally regarded as parental leave is the use of an employee's own accrued paid sick leave to care for a family member who is ill. According to a recent survey, all except six states allow paid sick leave to be used for this purpose (Workplace Economics, Inc., 1989). The federal government, however, restricts sick leave usage to the workers' illness or temporary disability.

Bibliography

Bureau of National Affairs. *BNA Pension Reporter* (22 August 1988): 1486.

Federal Register (28 April 1989): 18267.

U.S. Department of Labor. Bureau of Labor Statistics. *Employee Benefits in State and Local Governments, 1987*. Washington, DC: U.S. Government Printing Office, 1988.

U.S. Department of Labor. Bureau of Labor Statistics. *Employment and Earnings* (January 1989).

Workplace Economics, Inc. *1989 State Employee Benefits Survey*. Washington, DC: Workplace Economics, Inc., 1989.

44. Emerging Benefits

Introduction

The pressures on public-sector benefit programs—from employees demanding new benefits, legislatures demanding more cost control, and competition from private employers—are stimulating change and experimentation in many jurisdictions. Change has already occurred and may accelerate in the future in the following areas.

Dependent Care

Like private employers, an increasing number of public jurisdictions have begun to offer dependent care assistance to their employees. The forms of assistance include on-site day care centers, financial assistance, and referral services. Unlike traditional benefit programs for public workers, these benefits tend not to be systemwide but are available on a local basis. Some benefits are the result of collective bargaining agreements. With regard to on-site care, the sponsoring employer often provides facilities and support services, with child care center management handled by an association of parents or an independent contractor.

Long-Term Care

Long-term care insurance for expenses associated with chronic, debilitating illness is offered by few employers in the public or private sectors. Several public jurisdictions are among the early pioneers in this area, however. The State of Alaska was the first public jurisdiction to sponsor a long-term care plan, followed by the State Teachers Retirement System of Ohio. The states of South Carolina and Maryland also offer long-term care plans. Some plans are offered to both active and retired employees, others only to retirees. The plans are commercially underwritten, with premiums based on age and level of coverage. Thus far, long-term care plans have been offered only on an employee-pay-all basis. (For more information, see Friedland, 1990.)

Unmarried Domestic Partners

A benefit issue that to date has surfaced primarily among public, rather than private, employers concerns the extension of the definition of family member to include unmarried domestic partners. The public sector is necessarily responsive to political constituencies, and in several jurisdictions where strong constituencies exist for broadening the definition, benefit programs (bereavement leave and health insurance) have already been changed to include unmarried partners.

Some believe that the coverage of unmarried partners will have a deleterious effect on the claims experience of insurance plans sponsored by the jurisdictions concerned, but experience to date is too limited to support any conclusion. Another outstanding issue is whether the Internal Revenue Service will accord the same favorable tax treatment to employer contributions for benefits covering unmarried domestic partners that it extends to contributions for traditional family members.

Flexible Benefits

Flexible benefit plans have grown rapidly during the last decade in the private sector, and they have also made inroads in the public sector. According to the Bureau of Labor Statistics, 9 percent of state and local employees were eligible for flexible benefit plans and/or reimbursement accounts in 1987 (U.S. Department of Labor, 1988). That number has almost certainly grown, as several states have implemented flexible plans for their employees or passed authorizing legislation for local governments to establish such plans in the last several years. Plans that simply allow salary reduction for the payment of employee contributions to health insurance plans with pretax dollars appear to be growing more rapidly than plans that offer a broader range of choices under a true "cafeteria" arrangement.

Conclusion

Employee benefits constitute an important and distinctive part of public employees' compensation. These benefits have evolved over time and continue to evolve in response to changing economic and political circumstances at the local, state, and national levels. While they parallel and mirror many of the developments in private-sector employee benefit plans and stem largely from the same impulses and imperatives, they are uniquely adapted to the public environment that produced them and in which they operate.

Bibliography

Friedland, Robert B. *Facing the Costs of Long-Term Care*. Washington, DC: Employee Benefit Research Institute, 1990.

U.S. Department of Labor. Bureau of Labor Statistics. *Employee Benefits in State and Local Governments, 1987*. Washington, DC: U.S. Government Printing Office, 1988.

Index

A

Absenteeism, 226, 263
Accidental death and dismember-
    ment insurance, 231–232
Accrual of benefits, 32
    age and, 47
Actual contribution percentage
    (ACP) test, 87
Actual deferral percentage (ADP)
    test, 86–87
Adoption benefits, 268
Alienation *see* Assignment of bene-
    fits
Annuities *see also* Tax-deferred an-
    nuities
    as plan distributions, 44, 123
    ERISA requirements, 31
    tax treatment of, 44, 60–61
Arizona v. Maricopa County Medi-
    cal Society, 221
Assignment of benefits, 29

B

Blue Cross and Blue Shield plans,
    178, 218, 220, 324
Break-in-service rules, 31

C

Cafeteria plans *see* Flexible benefit
    plans
Cash balance pension plans, 119–
    124
    account credits and balances,
        119–120
    administration, 123, 124
    benefit limits, 120
    costs, 122–124
    coverage, 119
    defined benefit plans and, 123–
        124
    defined contribution plans and,
        122–123
    distributions, 121, 123

funding, 121
integration, 121–122
investments and risk, 120
loans, 121
salary reduction and, 123
terminations, 122
vesting, 120–121
Cash or deferred arrangements
    (CODAs), 41, 55, 83–92
    contributions, 85–86, 90
    —limits, 42, 85–86
    coverage, 83–84
    development of, 83–84
    distributions, 87–91
    eligibility, 84
    hardship withdrawals, 88–90,
        91
    investments, 85
    loans, 90
    nondiscrimination rules, 86–87
    public employees and, 319–320
    safe harbor rules, 88–89
    tax treatment, 83, 90–91
    types of, 84–85
    vesting, 84
Capital gains taxes
    lump-sum distributions and,
        45–46
    sale of residence, 170
Career-average formulas, 40, 53–
    54
Child care, 261–270, 339 *see also*
    Parental leave
    arrangements, 261–262
    costs, 262
    employer-sponsored programs,
        263
    —types of, 263–265
    flexible benefits and, 264
    tax treatment, 266–267
Cliff vesting, 30, 59
Closed-panel plans
    dental care and, 189
    legal services and, 257
    prescription drugs and, 194–195

343

vision care and, 199
CMPs *see* Competitive medical plans
COBRA *see* Consolidated Omnibus Budget Reconciliation Act of 1985
CODAs *see* Cash or deferred arrangements
COLAs *see* Cost-of-living adjustments
Collectibles as IRA investments, 133
Communication of benefits, 224, 226
cost management and, 203
Compensation
definition for plan purposes, 40
Competitive medical plans (CMPs), 214
Consolidated Omnibus Budget Reconciliation Act of 1985 (COBRA)
coverage continuation provisions
—dental insurance, 191
—health insurance, 183–184, 323
—vision care, 199
Continuing-care communities *see* Life-care communities
Cost-of-living adjustments (COLAs), 312–313

D

Death benefits *see* Survivor benefits
Deficit Reduction Act of 1984 (DEFRA)
contribution/benefit limits, 42
Defined benefit plans
administration of, 59–60
ancillary benefits, 57
benefit formulas, 40, 53–54
benefit limits, 42, 115
cash balance plans and, 123–124
costs of, 56
coverage, 8, 53
demographic changes and, 8
description of, 53
distributions in, 57, 60
employee acceptance, 58

ERISA funding requirements, 32–34
evaluation of, 282, 283
integration, 135–136, 138–142
investment risk, 53, 57, 282
late-age hires, 59
minimum participation, 151–152
nondiscrimination rules, 149–150
postretirement increases, 58
public employees and, 309–316
tax treatment of, 60–61
vesting in, 30, 59
Defined contribution plans
administration of, 50–60
ancillary benefits, 57
cash balance plans and, 122–123
contribution formulas, 41
contribution limits, 42, 115–116
costs of, 56–57
coverage, 8, 54
demographic changes and, 8–9
description of, 41, 54
distributions in, 57, 60
employee acceptance, 58
evaluation of, 282–283
forfeitures, 54
integration, 135, 137–138
investment risk, 57, 282
late-age hires, 59
minimum participation requirements, 151
nondiscrimination rules, 149–150
portability and, 56
postretirement increases, 58
public employees and, 317
tax treatment of, 60–61
types of, 41, 54–55
vesting in, 30, 58–59
DEFRA *see* Deficit Reduction Act of 1984
Dental care plans, 187–191
benefit limits, 190
claims payment, 190
closed-panel plans, 189
coinsurance, 190
coverage, 187, 289
—continuation of, 191
covered services, 187–188
deductibles, 189–190
dependent coverage, 187

346

past service credits, 148–149
permitted disparity, 149–150
profit-sharing plans and, 72
ratio percentage test, 152–153
safe harbors, 146–147, 149
—tests, 153–154
section 403(b) plans and, 101
SEPs and, 108
uniform allocation formulas,
146, 149–150
unit credit plans, 147
Nonoccupational temporary disability insurance, 245
Nonprofit organization retirement
plans *see* Tax-deferred annuities; Section 403(b) plans *see
also* Public employees' retirement plans

O

OBRA '87 *see* Omnibus Budget
Reconciliation Act of 1987
OBRA '89 *see* Omnibus Budget
Reconciliation Act of 1989
Old-Age, Survivors, and Disability
Insurance (OASDI) *see* Social
Security
Omnibus Budget Reconciliation
Act of 1987 (OBRA '87)
group life insurance and, 233
PBCG premiums and, 34–35
Omnibus Budget Reconciliation
Act of 1989 (OBRA '89)
health insurance coverage and,
183–184
education assistance benefits
and, 251
ESOPs and, 94, 98–99
Open-panel plans, 194, 257

P

Parental leave, 267–268 *see also*
Child care
break-in-service rules, 31
public employees, 336–337
Part-time employees, 280
Payroll-based employee stock
ownership plans, 96

PAYSOPs *see* Payroll-based employee stock ownership plans
PBGC *see* Pension Benefit Guaranty Corporation
PDA *see* Pregnancy Discrimination
Act of 1978
Peer review organizations, 204,
220
Penalty taxes
pension plan distributions and,
47–48, 161–162
IRAs and, 132
Pension Benefit Guaranty Corporation
benefit guarantees, 36
employer liabilities, 36–37
exempt plans, 34
plan termination insurance, 34–
37, 122
premiums, 34–35
Pension commissions, 304–305
Pension plans, 39–51 *see also* specific plan; Public employees'
pension plans
contribution/benefit limits, 41–
42
coverage, 4, 39, 161
coverage determination, 30
demographic changes and, 8–9
development of, 39
distributions, 44–49
—timing of, 49
eligibility requirements, 29–30
employer objectives for, 55–56
evaluation of, 281–283
funding of, 32–34
integration of *see* Integration of
pension plans
legislation affecting, 61 *see also*
specific legislation
minimum coverage requirements, 152–157
minimum participation requirements, 150–152
nondiscrimination rules *see*
Nondiscrimination rules
portability of, 56, 67, 68, 283
postretirement increases, 58
qualification rules, 43–44
tax treatment of, 39–40, 283

350

benefit levels and duration, 230
income plans, 238–240
pension plans and, 47, 240–242
Social Security, 237–238
public employees, 333–334
tax treatment, 240, 242

T

TAMRA *see* Technical and Miscellaneous Revenue Act of 1988
Tax-deferred annuities, 101–105
see also Annuities
cash or deferred arrangements and, 84, 85–86
contributions, 42, 103
eligible organizations, 101
investments, 102
nondiscrimination rules, 101
salary reduction agreements, 102–103
tax treatment, 104–105
withdrawals, 105
Tax Equity and Fiscal Responsibility Act of 1982 (TEFRA)
contribution/benefit limits, 42
Keogh plans and, 114
Medicare HMOs and, 213–214
SEPs and, 108
top-heavy plans, 42–43
Tax Reduction Act stock ownership plan, 96
Tax Reform Act of 1986
CODAs and, 319
contribution/benefit limits, 42
integration and, 136–137
IRAs and, 125
joint and survivor annuities and, 241
lump-sum distributions and, 45–46
minimum coverage requirements and, 152–157
minimum participation requirements and, 150–152
public pension plans and, 306–307
PAYSOPs and, 96
Section 457 and, 320
SEPs and, 107, 109, 110

Tax treatment *see under* specific benefit
Target benefit plans, 41
ERISA funding requirements, 32–33
Teachers, 296, 309
Teachers Insurance and Annuity Association/College Retirement Equities Fund (TIAA/CREF), 317
Technical Amendments Act of 1958, 101
Technical and Miscellaneous Revenue Act of 1988 (TAMRA)
group life insurance and, 233–234
public pension plans and, 307
TEFRA *see* Tax Equity and Fiscal Responsibility Act of 1982
Thrift plans, 41, 54, 77–81
administration, 80–81
contributions, 77–78
—limits of, 78–79
distributions, 79–80
in-service withdrawals, 80
investments, 79
loans, 80
nondiscrimination rules, 77, 78
public employees and, 317
qualification rules, 77
salary reduction and, 78
tax treatment, 79
Top-heavy plans
TEFRA provisions, 42–43
TRA *see* Tax Reform Act of 1986
TRASOPs *see* Tax Reduction Act stock ownership plans
Turnover rates
education assistance and, 249–250

U

Usual, customary, and reasonable charges, 179, 188, 198

V

Vesting *see also* specific plan
break-in-service rules, 31

354